# Social Protection, Capitalist Production

# Social Protection, Capitalist Production

*The Bismarckian Welfare State in the
German Political Economy, 1880–2015*

PHILIP MANOW

# OXFORD
UNIVERSITY PRESS

Great Clarendon Street, Oxford, OX2 6DP,
United Kingdom

Oxford University Press is a department of the University of Oxford.
It furthers the University's objective of excellence in research, scholarship,
and education by publishing worldwide. Oxford is a registered trade mark of
Oxford University Press in the UK and in certain other countries

© Philip Manow 2020

The moral rights of the author have been asserted

First Edition published in 2020

Impression: 1

Published in the United States of America by Oxford University Press
198 Madison Avenue, New York, NY 10016, United States of America

British Library Cataloguing in Publication Data
Data available

Library of Congress Control Number: 2019955953

ISBN 978-0-19-884253-8

Printed and bound in Great Britain by
Clays Ltd, Elcograf S.p.A.

# Acknowledgments

Numerous, far too numerous, debts have been incurred in the long, much too long, process of writing and rewriting this book. First of all, I would like to thank Wolfgang Streeck for his support, his patience, and his steadfast and all in all wholly unfounded optimism that the manuscript *will* finally be published. Gerhard Lehmbruch and Jens Alber provided critical support for the acceptance of an early version of this text as my Habilitationsschrift at the University Konstanz (as did Friedrich Breyer, who provided a review from an economist's perspective). I am also very grateful in particular to the Max-Planck Institute for the Study of Societies in Cologne, where the largest parts of the manuscript were written, and the Centre for European Studies in Harvard, where I spent a year working on the manuscript (and where I also benefited from the incredible collection of the Weiner Library of monographs from 1880 to 1930 analyzing the German economic policies of the time). At the CES, in particular Peter A. Hall provided indispensable inspiration, counsel, and encouragement. He—repeatedly—took pains to comment on a large and often convoluted argument. I would also like to express my special gratitude to David Soskice and Torben Iversen for their continuous support, their exceptional intellectual generosity, and for being such a steady source of inspiration. Long-term cooperation with Kees van Kersbergen and Bruno Palier, and in later years with Hanna Schwander, helped me developing my argument. Stays at the University of Konstanz and at the Center for Advanced Studies, Berlin (Wissenschaftskolleg zu Berlin) provided the necessary time to update the manuscript and to extend its coverage to the period after German unification. At Bremen University, the Collaborative Research Center 'Global Dynamics of Social Policy' (CRC 1342) allowed me to finalize the manuscript. I am grateful to the German Science Foundation (DFG) for its support (grant number 374666841 - SFB 1342).

The Max-Planck Institute supported me in various respects. To highlight only two: I am very grateful for the extremely supportive librarians, Susanne Hilbring and Elke Bürger, and for Cynthia Lehmann's language editing (with the help of Carla Welch, who edited a final version, and Dona Geyer, who had edited previous versions).

Over many years I was so lucky to benefit from the expertise and advice of Martin Höpner, Anke Hassel, Fritz W. Scharpf, Susanne K. Schmidt, Alexander Kuo, Anne Wren, Paul Pierson, Kathy Thelen, Philipp Rehm, Christine Trampusch, Christian Joerges, Josef Hien, Johannes Lindvall, Silja Häusermann and many others.

*Eitorf*
*January 2020*

# Contents

# List of Figures

# List of Tables

# List of Tables

# 1

# The Political Construction of a Coordinated Political Economy

## 1.1 Understanding German Capitalism, Improving Comparative Political Economy

The aim of the present study, in brief, is to improve our understanding of the German political economy and to provide a new and more accurate interpretation of its functioning logic. That, however, is not solely motivated by an interest in this one country case, but by the strong belief that a better understanding of German capitalism would also help improve *Comparative* Political Economy (CPE). The following analysis is therefore cast in strictly comparative terms, and the analytic reconstruction of the German case is at the same time meant as a test as to whether the categories used will also help us to describe and better understand other European political economies.

The key focus of the study is the Bismarckian welfare state and its impact, both past and present, on the German economy, and the reader is already aware of the central claim of the study. Over the following pages, one pivotal point will be emphasized, namely, that in order to acquire an in-depth understanding of the German political economy we must take the interplay between *social protection* and *capitalist production* into account. Again, this turns into a more general proposition—namely that continental political economies' welfare states have been key for the type of long-term economic coordination that historically emerged in them. This argument allows us systematically to distinguish—here borrowing categories from the Varieties of Capitalism (VoC) literature—non-coordinated (liberal) economies (liberal market economies, LMEs) with residual welfare states on the one hand and coordinated economies (coordinated market economies, CMEs) with generous welfare states on the other. And, at the same time, the argument allows us to explain differences in economic coordination *within* the CMEs with reference to the different types of welfare states that they have. It would, thus, provide us both with an explanation for the obvious within-variation among the coordinated market economies, for which the VoC approach itself has not offered much of a systematic explanation, as well as an explanation for the between-variation between liberal and coordinated market economies (see in particular Chapter 6). A central claim of this book is that the welfare state is the "principal institution in the construction of different models of postwar

*Social Protection, Capitalist Production: The Bismarckian Welfare State in the German Political Economy, 1880–2015.*
Philip Manow, Oxford University Press (2020). © Philip Manow.
DOI: 10.1093/oso/9780198842538.001.0001

capitalism" (Esping-Andersen 1990: 5). The present study aims to provide rich empirical evidence—historical, contemporary, and comparative—in support of Esping-Andersen's basic thesis. ⟶ *Welfare st as answer to postwar capital.*

Tracing the genesis and then reconstructing the working logic of the institutional complex that links capitalist production to social protection in the continental countries, with Germany as an exemplary case, means first, explaining in detail what, historically, has led to the close nexus between both spheres in Germany. That is, it means reconstructing the historical processes that created a coordinated political economy and the numerous "strategic complementarities" between work and welfare, which have become so essential for long-term economic coordination within *Modell Deutschland*. Second, it necessitates an analysis of current processes of economic adjustment and contemporary welfare reforms in light of these existing complementarities, and in light of the inextricable link between the economy and the institutional complex that has been politically established to refract, modify, alter, and, in part, suspend the pure functioning of the market mechanism: the welfare state. The central claim here is that neither current political reforms nor adjustments to a changing economic environment can be accurately assessed without a clear understanding of the connection between protection and production in the German political economy.

The German economic model, representative of the conservative welfare state regime as well as of continental Europe's coordinated capitalism, remains, in critical respects, insufficiently understood. Often a dichotomous view dominates the CPE literature, based—explicitly or implicitly—on a comparison of the Anglo-Saxon and Scandinavian models of capitalism as polar cases (see Section 1.2). The continental world in much of the CPE literature was and is frequently depicted as a deviation either from a classical market model and liberal welfare state on the one hand, or from an ideal-typical social democratic regime on the other (Esping-Andersen 1990; Garrett 1989, 1998; Garrett and Way 1999; Huber and Stephens 2001). A similar perspective tends to dominate the Comparative Welfare State literature, even if here—from early on—a distinct continental model *had* been distinguished from either a Scandinavian, social democratic or from an Anglo-Saxon, liberal regime. The conservative model, however, was usually not understood on its own terms, but characterized rather as a "residual" case, as less egalitarian than the one and, at the same time, less market-oriented than the other—as delivering neither social equality nor economic efficiency. In Esping-Andersen's three-world framework it stood for "the ugly," in contrast to the "good" social democratic and the "bad" liberal regime (Manow 2004).

The "intermediate" German case—which, despite the many differences in the detail, could also exemplify Austria, Switzerland, and Benelux as well as some Central and Eastern European countries which acceded to the EU recently—therefore still is often perceived as "anomalous." And whereas Germany has been treated very prominently and with great expertise in the VoC literature as a prototypical case of a coordinated market economy, the binary lead-distinction of that literature—"coordinated vs. liberal" (CMEs vs. LMEs)—has stood in the way of developing a systematic explanation for the varying ways in which different kinds of CMEs coordinate. It has hindered identifying the critical factors causing systematic differences in economic coordination within the broadly defined group of CMEs. My claim is that the welfare state is in fact the most important cause of this variance.

This is why, I argue, a better understanding of the German case, in particular of the welfare state's role in this political economy, will also help us to get a clearer picture of what systematically distinguishes western European political economies from each other. As we will see, the argument developed here suggests differentiating between *four* distinct political economies, with the southern model as an additional regime (cf. Beramendi et al. 2015a; Manow 2015b) (see Chapters 4 and 6)—this, at least, if we restrict our attention to the European cases.[1] And it is against the background of this argument, I claim, that we can then for example also better grasp the crux of the eurozone crisis, an area in which two fundamentally different growth models—a hard-currency, export-led model in the center and a soft-currency, domestic-demand-driven model in the southern periphery (Hall 2014; Iversen et al. 2016; Iversen and Soskice 2018)—have been forced together under one monetary policy regime (see Chapter 6). To avoid misunderstandings: I am of course not claiming to be the first to identify a distinct southern political economy. Quite to the contrary: a relatively rich literature has for some time proposed to treat the southern European welfare state regime as a distinct model (Bonoli 1997; Ferragina and Seeleib-Kaiser 2011; Ferrera 1996, 2010; Gal 2010; Leibfried 1993; Manow 2015b; Matsaganis et al. 2003; Rhodes 1997; Trifiletti 1999). And in the VoC literature these countries are referred to as representing a "hybrid regime" with coordination among business, but much less so among labor. The more recent CPE literature has come to apply this fourfold typology, with the southern European countries representing a distinct model, on a quite regular basis (Beramendi et al. 2015b; Kriesi 2019; Kriesi and Hutter 2019). Without wanting to play down the important contributions of that literature, I simply state that a closer examination of the continental model, as exemplified by the German case, and here especially a closer look at the interconnection between protection and production, promises to provide us with categories for a systematic explanation of the differences between the political economies of Scandinavia, continental Europe, and the South—between them and in comparison to the liberal market economies.

---

[1] For an application of the VoC framework to the Latin American economies see Schneider (2013). See there also the distinction between liberal (Anglo-Saxon countries), coordinated (European political economies), network (Japan and South Korea), and hierarchical market economies (Latin America).

I think that an improved insight into the functioning logic of the German political economy would be valuable for two further reasons. First, the German economy is the most important in the European Union.[2] As such an economic heavyweight, it has a critical impact on the economic fate of the entire region. Understanding German capitalism is paramount, as Wolfgang Streeck emphasized, "if only because of the country's size and the strong external effects it has on others, especially in Europe" (Streeck 2009: 21; cf. Unger 2015). We have seen a substantial increase in the severity of these external effects recently, since within the euro area, member states are now fully exposed to the competitive strength of the German economy without the exchange rate shelter that had previously provided protection (Hall 2014; Höpner and Lutter 2014).

Of course, as the most important economy in the common currency area, Germany has also become one of the key players—perhaps second only to *the* key player, the European Central Bank (ECB)—in managing the euro area's fundamental crisis. In fact, it has recently been accused by many of seriously mismanaging, aggravating, or even causing, rather than solving the crisis (cf. Tooze 2018). Any such judgment is predicated on an understanding of the functioning of the German economy, the country's economic interests, and its pivotal economic actors. As I argue in the following pages, this understanding is still, in many ways, incomplete, which, in turn, also has implications for the debate on Germany's role in the euro area and its crisis (mis-)management. For instance: recent accounts of the euro crisis blame ordoliberalism as a dysfunctional "instruction sheet" not only for "Germany's response to the crisis," but for "the crisis itself" (Blyth 2015: 141). Similar claims abound (Bulmer 2014: 1244; Bulmer and Paterson 2013; Dulien and Guérot 2012; Hillebrand 2015; Nedergaard and Snaith 2015; for a more nuanced account, see Brunnermeier et al. 2016). Yet, few economic doctrines have been less understood than ordoliberalism (only peripherally mentioned in Burgin 2012), and its role in German economic policy, both past and present, is often misinterpreted (but see now Hacke 2018: 335–60; Hien and Joerges 2017), as I will discuss in more detail in Chapter 3.

Besides sheer size and impact, understanding the functioning logic of the German political economy is also, finally, important because many institutional features of the new European market order and of the euro area resemble—by design or by default—core components of *Modell Deutschland*, including:

- a high degree of independence for the ECB, which was deliberately designed along the lines of the Bundesbank model (Dyson 2009; Iversen and Soskice 2018; James 2012), and which, so far, has—despite vocal German criticism of

---

[2] In 2014, Germany accounted for 29 percent of the euro area's GDP and 21 percent of that of the European Union.

its recent monetary policies—delivered price stability as reliably as the Bundesbank had done previously, perhaps even more so;[3]

- an insufficient capacity for macroeconomic intervention combined with limited economic commitment of the central government(s) to provide basic *services publics* (signified by comprehensive privatization of telecommunications, postal services, railways, energy supply, etc., both in and initiated by the European Union); and finally

- an increasing emphasis on balanced budgets and fiscal discipline (signified by the convergence criteria of the European Monetary Union, EMU), in the wake of the euro crisis. This was renewed and reinforced by the European semester and the Commission's various new monitoring responsibilities (Six Pack, Two Pack etc.; see Hancké 2013; Scharpf 2011).

Bob Hancké summarizes this development of the euro area as follows: "In most essential ways, the design of EMU followed the macro-economic policy logic of the previously existing DM-bloc. It involved a conservative (and highly independent) central bank in Germany, fiscal restraint instead of Keynesian countercyclical policies, and wage moderation, all of the key elements of EMU since its inception" (2013: 21). The euro area was designed "on northern European terms" and, so far, has continued to function "on northern European terms" (Iversen and Soskice 2018; cf. Mody 2018). This is precisely why it is so crucial to fully comprehend the operation of Germany's political economy as the prototype of this "northern" (continental northern rather than Scandinavian) model. In this context it is also important to notice that some of the other euro area members lack the redistributive complement) and the corporatist features which, in the German case, have proven to be so essential for the functioning of this institutional arrangement. This deficit has had rather detrimental consequences, as will be discussed in more detail in Chapter 6.

Yet at the same time, the very fact that the ECB in many respects has been modeled after a Bundesbank blueprint means that the established interplay between an autonomous wage-setting regime and an independent and non-accommodating central bank could not work anymore in post-Deutschmark Germany as it had worked before, since now the ECB would not and could not target its monetary signals exclusively to one (national) wage-setting regime only. This then renders the question relevant how German wage setting had functioned outside of the established strategic context, i.e. under the euro (see Chapter 6). And, as we will see, it immediately provokes another question, namely how wage

---

[3] At the same time, membership in the euro area has altered some key elements of the German model, particularly the interplay between the Bundesbank's monetary policy and the system of pattern wage bargaining as established in the late 1950s and early 1960s (Hall 1994; Hall and Franzese 1997, 1998; Iversen 1999, 2000; Scharpf 1991; Soskice 1990b). I will address these changed circumstances and their impact on the German political economy in Chapter 6 (Hancké 2013; Hassel 2007).

bargaining in Germany had actually worked *before* the Bundesbank had been able to discipline the social partners by freely setting interest rates, i.e. before 1972/73, namely under the Bretton Woods system of fixed exchange rates, when interest rates could not be used to influence domestic prices, but "only" to balance current accounts (Holtfrerich 1998; Mundell 1960, 1963); see Chapter 4).

How does such a perspective, emphasizing the importance of the welfare state for the German political economy, relate to the literature? The following section briefly addresses this question.

## 1.2  Worlds of Welfare, Varieties of Capitalism

Analyzing the reciprocal impact of the "protection sphere" and the "production sphere" means taking a perspective that is located at the interface of two larger bodies of literature, the first being the Comparative Welfare State literature and the second being the Comparative Political Economy literature. Esping-Andersen had claimed a potential linkage between these two literatures relatively early on (as noted earlier in this chapter). But his three-world typology never convincingly substantiated his assertion, which may be related to the fact that it lacked a clear account of how and why the three regimes developed historically (Iversen 2006; Manow 2009, 2015a).

Many other contributions to this debate have failed to go beyond stating mere "elective affinities" or a "correspondence" between welfare state regimes and political economies (Ebbinghaus and Manow 2001; Hall and Soskice 2001a: 50; Kitschelt et al. 1999). Spotting affinities, however, is hardly enough if one aims at systematically and analytically reconstructing the production/protection nexus in Europe's emerging postwar political economies. Although CPE scholars have broadened their conventional perspective and begun to look beyond systems of industrial relations, the perspective that dominated the corporatism literature of the 1970s and 1980s, a comparative political economy taking the welfare state as its starting point—presumably the most promising analytical perspective given its sheer size and regulatory and redistributive reach (Esping-Andersen 1990: 12)—remained for a long time underexplored.[4] Peter Hall remarked as early as 1997

---

[4] Today's Comparative Political Economy studies the economic role of broader "ensembles of institutions" in contemporary capitalism beyond industrial relations proper and also looks at differences in legal traditions (LaPorta 1996), the link between vocational training, public education, and production systems (Ansell 2010; Ansell and Gingrich 2013; Busemeyer 2014; Busemeyer and Trampusch 2011; Crouch et al. 1999; Culpepper and Finegold 1999; Iversen and Stephens 2008; Thelen 2004), or the strategic interaction between central banks and wage-setting regimes (Franzese 1999; Hall and Franzese 1998; Iversen 1998a, 1998b, 1999, 2000; Scharpf 1987). The welfare state, however, with only a few recent exceptions (in particular Hall and Gingerich 2009; Hancké et al. 2009; Schröder 2013) has rarely been perceived as an important institutional element in the political economy of postwar capitalism.

that "as yet" we "do not have a clear understanding of how...different kinds of welfare states interact with different models of the economy" (Hall 1997: 196), and this continued to apply many years later (for some of the existing accounts Ebbinghaus and Manow 2001; and, more recently, Schröder 2013 for example). As Esping-Andersen had stated already 30 years ago: "...given the enormous growth of the welfare state, it is understandable that it has become a major test case for contending theories of political economy" (Esping-Andersen 1990: 12). Still, how that relation has to be understood continues to be open to debate. It is to the understanding of that nexus that the present study wants to contribute.

Such a contribution, in my view, would first and foremost have to explain the internal variation among the coordinated economies, since the major problem with linking the CPE literature and the Comparative Welfare State literature was that the latter, as I pointed out above, was often confronted with a rather dichotomous worldview of the former (e.g. Hall and Soskice 2001b). As Hall and Soskice stated, "[v]irtually all liberal market economies are accompanied by 'liberal' welfare states...[but] the social-policy regimes that accompany coordinated market economies are more varied" (Hall and Soskice 2001a: 51). But this then leaves open how exactly, in the case of the CMEs, we should conceive of this "correspondence" between welfare state regimes and different political economies. The welfare state regime literature is not of much help here, since it—most prominently in Esping-Andersen's three-worlds typology—tended to conceive of the continental case mainly in residual terms: not market-liberal, but also not very redistributive either, neither left, nor right, neither egalitarian, nor efficient (Manow 2004). It therefore seems that a closer look especially at the continental political economy might improve explanations for the internal variation among the coordinated economies: it promises to provide us with a better CPE conceptual framework.

Conventional comparisons were often informed by the polar cases of Scandinavia on the one hand and liberal market economies in Anglo-Saxon countries on the other, and such a perspective resonated and continues to resonate well with many approaches in the CPE literature. Take, for instance, the traditional neo-corporatist argument, as endorsed by Garrett and Lange (Garrett 1998; Garrett and Lange 1996). According to it, there are basically two equilibria that are coherent and sustainable from a political institutional perspective: *either* strong labor unions enter into a mutually beneficial relationship with left-wing governments in which the government issues guarantees of full employment in exchange for the unions' commitment to non-inflationary wage bargaining strategies, *or*, alternatively, right-leaning governments pursue strictly market-liberal policies in countries where weak unions are unable to mobilize sufficient resistance against such a neoliberal course. From this perspective, Germany, where, for most of the postwar period, conservative governments confronted encompassing, powerful, and tightly coordinated labor organizations, can only be described negatively as an "incoherent political economy" (Garrett 1998: 15, 35, 48). Yet, the assumption that "institutional incoherence" subsequently results in an economic performance that is systematically poorer than that of either their coherently liberal contenders or of the coherent Keynesian welfare states seems odd in the light of the postwar development of the German economy (see Garrett 1998: 35, 48; Garrett and Lange 1996).

Corporatism's two-equilibria perspective overlaps with the wage-bargaining literature in economics according to which either fully centralized or fully decentralized systems, but not intermediate models, are capable of delivering wage moderation (Calmfors and Driffill 1988). This perspective, however, fails to take German (and Japanese) methods of "coordination without centralization" into account. Again, this view is hard to reconcile with the fact that the German political economy, and the equally "incoherent" Japanese economy, were among the most successful economies in the postwar period—irrespective of the performance indicator used (Streeck and Yamamura 2005), and were in particular able to deliver wage restraint and therefore low inflation in the first postwar decades.

Also the left/right distinction of the "parties matter" literature draws much of its *prima facie* plausibility from an underlying contrast between a conservative Anglo-Saxon and a social democratic Scandinavian world. Yet, how do the continental countries fit into this picture bearing in mind the long-term dominance of their Christian Democratic parties? These parties—given their strong pro-welfare state stance—in no way resembled textbook conservative parties with their support of neoliberal deregulation, but neither were they in favor of social democratic style redistribution and never issued promises of full employment. Here the fact that most of the literature "still assumes a unidimensional conceptualization of partisan competition between Right (capital) and Left (labor)" may have eased the comparison between Anglo-Saxon and Scandinavian countries, but proved to be "not very helpful to understanding current dynamics of coalition formation and policy choice" beyond these cases (Beramendi et al. 2015a: 4). In particular, the multi-dimensionality of the policy space in continental European party systems fitted less easily (Polk and Rovny 2018) and therefore hindered their integration into the CPE framework.

And not only older strands of literature, like the neo-corporatism or the parties matter debate, but also newer contributions continue to apply an analytic frame in which the Scandinavian and Anglo-Saxon countries are the reference cases, polar cases on one single dimension, each of them following a coherent functional logic, whereas the continental in-between cases stand rather for a more cumbersome institutional arrangement. In a recent, influential typology the continental model is equated with "particularism" and "consumption," whereas the Scandinavian and the Anglo-Saxon political economies are associated with "universalism" and "investment" (Beramendi et al. 2015a). A similar view is reflected, for instance, in the recent literature on the expansion of service employment. It highlights the expansion of the low-productivity service sector on the one hand and on the other the increased demand for high-skilled service workers, e.g. in the dynamic information and communication technology (ICT) sectors, in finance, insurance, and similar fields, or in the social services (Ansell 2008, 2010; Ansell and Gingrich 2013; Wren 2013). Again, in both segments the continental model is said to have failed as compared to the other two regime types. Low- as well as high-productivity services, according to the literature, develop in a particularly non-dynamic way in continental Europe due to compressed wages and due to those countries' preference for low levels of public spending, be it in the expansion of public sector employment or in generously financing higher education (Iversen and Wren 1998; Scharpf 1997). Again, two equilibria, one Scandinavian, one Anglo-Saxon, one comprising "mass public, compressed wage, non-dynamic service countries," the other comprising "partially private, dispersed wage, dynamic service countries," are said to "form two self-reinforcing 'high skills equilibria'" (Ansell and Gingrich 2013: 198).

And we also see the "two equilibria" approach of the wage bargaining or corporatism literature prolonging itself in, for instance, the contemporary discussion about the euro crisis. Here more or less the same argument is reappearing: as the benefits of a reflationary response to a recession are obvious, whereas inflationary dangers of an expansionary monetary policy are negligible, in both a centralized corporatist setting as well as in a decentralized market setting, moderate wages and expansionary monetary policy can go together. The German combination of budget- plus wage-restraint apparently can then only be explained by sheer irrationality, German inflation *angst*, or diffuse allusions to ordoliberalism and its purportedly inherent culture of austerity (Biebricher 2013; Blyth 2015). Yet, these attempts at explaining the workings of the German political economy are unsatisfactory both from an analytical and historical perspective (not to speak of their barely camouflaged normativity)—not the least since they seem to systematically ignore the redistributive and thus conflictive dimension which any reflationary measure on a eurozone-wide scale would have had (Mody 2018). Since no European nation was or is "willing to let go of its sovereign right to tax and spend"—the "sovereignty barrier remains alive" (Mody 2018: 7 and 22)—it seems strange to describe this reluctance as somehow ordoliberal and therefore as a German oddity.

Analytically, the reference to "culture" or ideas regularly seems to absolve scholars from the need to identify causal mechanisms that would link ideational dispositions to political-economic outcomes. Closer inspection also reveals many of these allusions to be historically inaccurate (see the account of ordoliberalism in Chapter 3, for instance). That many recent attempts to explain German economic policies take recourse to "culture,"[5] long past historical events (such as the

---

[5] For an explanation of the poor growth in employment in the service sector, see, for instance, the reference to deep "historical ideological roots of Christian democratic opposition to the expansion of

hyperinflation of 1923/24), or to ideas—and that economists are at the forefront of this (Brunnermeier et al. 2016)—possibly says more about the limited explanatory power of their macroeconomic models. In Germany, for instance, low public spending plays a very precise role within a growth model oriented towards exports (see Chapters 5 and 6)—there is not much need to refer to some ninety-year-old "trauma."

If we more narrowly focus on the Comparative Welfare State literature there has of course always been a clearer conception that we are rather confronted with—at least—three and not only two models. Famously, Esping-Andersen's regime typology exactly built upon this distinction among "three worlds of welfare capitalism." But as mentioned already above, it is hard to ignore that his classification is quite asymmetric in its description and explanation of the three regimes—much clearer, and the clustering also much cleaner, when it comes to the Scandinavian and Anglo-Saxon cases, and much more diffuse in the case of the continental regime (Obinger and Wagschal 1998).

It is then all but surprising that when reconstructed, the Esping-Andersen framework again boils down to one dominant dimension plus one major deviation. In their reconstruction of the Esping-Andersen typology Hicks and Kenworthy treat the "social democratic" and "liberal" types as "two poles" of a single dimension. Its positive pole is characterized by extensive, universal and homogeneous benefits, active labour market policy, government employment and gender-egalitarian family policies" (Hicks and Kenworthy 2003: 27). Orthogonal to this is what the authors label "traditional conservatism," and this conservatism is—according to their view—associated with "occupational and status-based differentiations of social insurance programmes and specialized income security programmes for civil servants, but also generous and long-lasting unemployment benefits, reliance on employer-heavy social insurance tax burdens and extensions of union collective bargaining coverage" (Hicks and Kenworthy 2003: 27). What does this second dimension then add? "The principal consequence...appears to be weakened employment performance" (Hicks and Kenworthy 2003: 27). It is not only in the light of the current German employment rate of 76 percent, second in Europe only to the Swedish, that we might want to consider revising these hypotheses, or in fact want to reconsider the conceptual framework underlying such comparisons.

state control over service provision (and in particular education)" (Wren 2013: 40), or for more general references to certain "Catholic values" (which can already be found in early explanations of the conservative political economy model), see Esping-Andersen (1990). For other, rather diffuse allusions to Catholic social doctrine, to tradition, "subsidiarity," a patriarchist social order, or "familialism" and similar, see Esping-Andersen (1999). A favorite commonplace is also to point out that *Schuld* (guilt) and *Schulden* (debts) share the same root in German, but not in English—that is as ridiculous as an "explanation" of German interests in the euro crisis can get.

I think therefore that it is overdue to link institutions back to politics, and to relocate explanations in a framework which includes actors and their interests. However, this presupposes an understanding of these institutions and how they came about (for two of the limited number of accounts on this, see Streeck 2009; Unger 2015).

I sketch the general argument in the following section and briefly provide the reader with an outline of the book.

## 1.3 The Argument and the Outline of the Study

On the most general level, the book argues that political economies are politically constructed. They are the result of relatively stable coalition patterns between political parties. These coalitions, themselves, reflect basic characteristics of the party systems in place. Coalitions vary, since party systems vary. Relevant in this context are: (a) the strong positions of conservative parties in countries with majoritarian rules, i.e. the Anglo-Saxon countries; (b) the long-term coalitions between agrarian parties and social democracy in Scandinavia (under proportional representation; PR)—the so-called red–green coalition; (c) the long-term coalitions between Social and Christian Democrats in continental Europe (under PR as well); and finally (d) the political hegemony of the bourgeois center due to the split of the left in the South, manifest in the strong role that communist parties had initially played in these party systems. When it comes, in turn, to explaining these differences in the party systems, a neo-Rokkian argument gains relevance: the party systems mirror the different cleavage structures that the industrial and the national revolution produced. That is, party systems vary because societal cleavages vary (the most important source of variation: a state/church cleavage in continental and southern Europe, which was either wholly absent in the North, or found no party-political expression in the two-parties systems of the Anglo-Saxon world). At the end of this causal chain—from cleavage structures to party systems to coalition patterns to types of welfare states or political economies more generally—we can distinguish four distinct European political economies: Scandinavian, continental, southern, and Anglo-Saxon, and with them four different ways of coordinating the economy.[6]

How exactly this general explanatory framework applies to the German political economy as a prototypical continental-conservative model is the central theme of this book. The argument starts by describing how the Bismarckian welfare state coevolved with German industrial relations. The welfare state provided the corporate actors of labor and capital with crucial organizational

---

[6] And yes, this indeed implies that "religious cleavages and PR caused particular economic institutions" (Cusack et al. 2007: 373). See the sketch of that argument in Chapter 6.

resources. That also meant that on the labor side, it privileged the two camps that organized or mobilized workers—socialist and Catholic unions and Social Democracy and political Catholicism, which then paved the way for the long-term coalition between Social and Christian Democracy that was going to shape the German welfare state and thereby the German political economy more broadly.

I then claim (in Chapter 3) that the cooperation in the interwar period between, economically, unions, and employers, and politically, between Social and Christian Democracy, estranged the liberal Protestant camp from its former pet project, social reform. An important consequence of this estrangement was the birth of ordoliberalism. Ordoliberalism, however, was much less influential in the postwar period than usually claimed. It legitimized a politics of non-intervention, which rather left a void for the corporate actors to fill, so it involuntarily furthered corporatism, not liberalism. Otherwise it provided the inability of the central state to actively manage the economy with a post hoc ideological justification. Thus, Germany's postwar compromise was "bipolar," combining corporatist cooperation between capital and labor, heavily reliant on the organizational and material resources of the welfare state, with a central government with limited capacity for macroeconomic steering and without the means of credibly issuing promises of full employment (as the main difference in comparison to the Scandinavian cases).

In the three high-growth postwar decades, the welfare state then facilitated corporatist cooperation between labor and capital, specifically in the form of wage coordination, thereby avoiding inflation in periods of (almost) full employment. And the period of high growth and full employment allowed, in turn, welfare state expansion always supported by a grand coalition of Christian and Social Democrats. Once the period of high growth had passed, the welfare state maintained this coordination by providing labor and capital with the resources to alleviate their deepening distributional conflicts—with an increasingly negative impact on the overall functioning of the German variety of capitalism. The fact that the welfare state provided social actors with the possibility of externalizing the growing costs of adjusting to the period of "diminished expectations" led to a pathological pattern of ever higher non-wage labor costs, poor job growth, and high structural unemployment. This proved unsustainable in the medium to long term, and ultimately led to a profound welfare state reform that in many respects broke with the corporatism of *Modell Deutschland*. This has been associated with the spectacular revival of the German economy, before and after the Great Recession, also because its competitive characteristics are significantly strengthened within the euro area. Yet, the success of *Modell Deutschland* of course also contributes to the increasing imbalances and to the divergent economic dynamics within the currency area, which ultimately have the potential to disrupt it.

This line of argument, I claim, sheds light on some puzzling questions that studies on the German political economy have repeatedly raised, but rarely convincingly answered. The argument presented here can, for instance, explain the often noted "anomaly" that "Germany tends to 'cluster' with the corporatist democracies in a variety of outcomes (labor peace, inflation, unemployment, general economic performance, social policy), but—by virtually any theorist's definition or measures – lacks the structural features that are considered precondititions for, or attributes of, corporatism" (Siaroff 1999; quoted in Thelen 1991: 3; Traxler and Kittel 2000). And it provides an answer to the question as to how the Germans, who were apparently so devoted in the postwar years to a specific brand of liberalism (ordoliberalism), nonetheless ended up developing one of the most coordinated forms of capitalism in the OECD world.

In summary, this book examines the impact of Germany's massively expanded late twentieth- and early twenty-first century welfare state on the German economy and the formative influence of the late nineteenth- and early twentieth-century welfare state on industrial relations and the national regimes of production. The argument is presented in five longer excursions into the German political economy. For the most part, these accounts are historical in character, but the last is primarily confined to the contemporary functioning of *Modell Deutschland*. Each of the five chapters examines the German welfare state from a different angle; they cover different time spans and highlight different aspects of a highly complex and "polyvalent" institutional arrangement. However, the five studies all share the conviction that the welfare state has been and continues to be a central factor in the "formation and stratification of modern capitalism"—in the formation of the German political economy as a prototypical coordinated market economy. Hence, the specific analytical focus is not on factors of welfare state growth or on explanations for the specific institutional path that the German welfare state took after 1880 (although this will be touched upon in the following argument), but on the repercussions of market intervention in the name of social welfare for the market itself and for the core political and economic groups in society.

The study has a rough chronological structure. The obvious starting point in historical time is the latter part of the nineteenth century, in particular the 1870s and 1880s. During this period, the German Reich is consolidated, the gold standard is introduced, the economic bubble that inflated after the founding of the Reich burst (*Gründerkrach*), Germany experienced the anti-liberal shift of 1878, the *Kulturkampf*, and the Socialist Law, and, last but not least, Bismarckian social legislation was passed between 1883 and 1889. The obvious theoretical starting point is the impact of social legislation on the emerging system of industrial relations, in particular on the labor movement. Hence, the first empirical chapter (Chapter 2) is confined to outlining in more detail the parallel development of the Bismarckian welfare state and German industrial relations. It takes a closer look at what will be described as the historical coevolution of the German welfare state and German unions. It then focuses on the impact of the

Bismarckian welfare state on the emergence of a system of industrial self-governance or "covert coordination." Chapter 2 argues that the welfare state not only had a significant impact on how German workers organized themselves in modern industrial unions, but that the welfare state also provided the government with an institutional blueprint for the settlement of industrial conflict.

While Chapter 2 focuses on the impact that the welfare state had on the organization of socio-economic interests, particularly on union development and on the emergence of a corporatist system of industrial relations during the first three decades of the twentieth century, Chapter 3 examines the influence of the welfare state on political mobilization. It emphasizes the importance of the welfare state for both the social democratic labor movement and for German political Catholicism. The chapter then describes the increasingly hostile stance that the liberal Protestant bourgeoisie took toward what was previously its favorite political project: social reform (*Sozialreform*). The chapter highlights the religious dimension of the conflict over social policy between 1890 and 1930 and the catalytic role played by the welfare state in the formation of political camps. The impact of these political and religious debates on the post-World War II order is addressed in more detail in the second half of Chapter 3.

Chapter 4 describes the postwar social and economic order. The central theme of this chapter is the functioning of *Modell Deutschland* during the "golden age." Particular emphasis is placed on the contribution of social insurance to the emergence of Germany's coordinated wage-bargaining regime. One of the main claims presented in the subsequent chapter (Chapter 5) is that social insurance was a central element of the "negotiated adjustment" (Thelen 1991), which defined the response of the German economy to the economic crises of the 1970s, 1980s, and 1990s. The second half of Chapter 5 also provides an extensive account of the long-term pathologies of "German capitalism" and the welfare state's contribution to aggravating its crisis. Chapter 6 then analyzes the fate of Germany's coordinated political economy within the fundamentally altered economic circumstances of the euro area. The book concludes with a summary of the argument and a brief outlook (Chapter 7).

I now turn to the early formative period of German state- and welfare state-building.

# 2

# Social Insurance and the Origins of the German Political Economy

This chapter looks at the formative impact that the nascent German welfare state had on German industrial relations. The period covered here stretches from the beginning of the last quarter of the nineteenth century to the end of the first quarter of the twentieth. The following two sections first examine the specific twist that Bismarckian social legislation gave to the development of German unions (Section 2.1) and, second, analyze the impact that the German welfare state exerted on the emerging system of industrial relations—beyond the indirect impact it exerted on industrial relations through its influence on union development (Section 2.2). The chapter distinguishes two formative periods in the relationship between the social insurance system and the German production regime. First, it identifies a period characterized by the organizational coevolution of the social insurance system and the German unions. This period extends roughly from the 1880s to the 1920s. Next, I describe the emergence of a corporatist mode of interest intermediation in industrial conflict as well as in the realm of social policy. My thesis is that the emergence of corporatism was the result of reciprocal influence between both policy domains, principally underpinned by the dual responsibility of the Ministry of Labor for both labor and social policy. This process took place mainly between 1914 and 1933, beginning with World War I and ending with the Weimar Republic. While the Federal Republic (*Bundesrepublik Deutschland*) did not, after 1949, simply re-install the status quo ante of the late Weimar era, many features of the institutional settlement to resolve the conflict between labor and capital in the 1920s were adopted and became central elements of *Modell Deutschland*. In later chapters, I will analyze in more detail the role that the welfare state has played in postwar Germany (see Chapters 4 and 5, in particular).

## 2.1 Social Insurance and the Trade Unions: Organizational Coevolution

It is well known that the rise of the German welfare state was part of a carrot-and-stick strategy. Repression of the working class through the Socialist Law (1878) and the imperial announcement (*Kaiserliche Botschaft*) of 1881, which announced

*Social Protection, Capitalist Production: The Bismarckian Welfare State in the German Political Economy, 1880–2015.*
Philip Manow, Oxford University Press (2020). © Philip Manow.
DOI: 10.1093/oso/9780198842538.001.0001

the imminent social legislation, were indeed closely linked. There is an abundance of evidence proving that many relevant political actors, including workers' representatives from the Social Democratic Party and the unions (Ritter 1983), believed there to be a profound connection between the two. It is also customary to point out in retrospect that the stick failed, while the carrot happened to be quite successful.

The uneven success of political repression, on the one side, and social integration, on the other, can be better explained by focusing on the preliminary end of the period of social legislation than its beginning in the early 1880s. In 1889, old-age and invalidity insurance was enacted. This was the last of the three bills marking the beginning of the German welfare state. In the same year, the Reichstag refused to extend the repressive Socialist Law beyond 1890. Only two years later, however, in 1892, the state enacted several measures that seriously discriminated against the voluntary funds of the workers' movement (*freie Hilfskassen*), which had experienced a significant increase in number and membership under the Socialist Law. To a certain extent, the *Hilfskassen* had acted as substitute and camouflage organizations for the "illegal" unions (Schönhoven 1980a). In the years that followed, this legal discrimination against the voluntary funds, which was clearly aimed at weakening the workers' movement, triggered a massive shift in membership among organized workers from the voluntary to the statutory funds, which had been introduced by the health insurance law of 1883 (Tennstedt 1983).

During the twelve years that the Socialist Law was in force, the workers' organizations had survived mainly as political self-help organizations, at least outwardly (Schönhoven 1980a). It was hoped, but also feared, that the official recognition of state responsibility for the welfare of its citizens, expressed by the Reich's introduction of social insurance, would deprive these organizations of their main purpose: mutual insurance and collective self-help. Yet, the situation turned out rather differently. Rather than weakening organized labor, the distinctive institutional structure of the new insurance schemes covering the risk of sickness (1883), accident (1884), and old age and invalidity (1889) was to become an important organizational backbone of the German labor movement. It was the principle of self-administration in the new social insurance schemes that guaranteed, to different degrees, the prominent involvement of union representatives in the administrative bodies of health insurance funds, employers' liability insurance associations (*Berufsgenossenschaften*), and the new regional insurance offices (*Landesversicherungsanstalten*). Self-administration, which had initially been introduced to ensure that workers would monitor each other to prevent moral hazard, would thus provide an important "organizational stabilizer" for union development. As a result, the rapid development of the organizational structures of the German union movement in the 1890s went hand in hand with the development of the organizational structure of the new social insurance and this coevolution was to shape the paths both would take.

The fact that social insurance schemes had a stabilizing effect on the union movement was precisely the opposite of what government officials had intended—and this can be interpreted as a warning against any analysis that assumes that those who ultimately profited from the introduction of an institution must have also been its supporters in the first place. Even the direct beneficiaries, i.e. union leaders, took some time to realize that the social insurance schemes were less of an attack on workers' voluntary organizations than an unexpected gift. Consequently, it took union leaders until the early 1890s to change their strategy from outward rejection to strategic acceptance of the new social insurance. *labor enjoyed soc. insur. unexpect.*

In part, the positive impact of social insurance on the labor movement was simply an enormous unintended side effect of a series of important modifications of the original concepts made during the legislative process that critically weakened their repressive and paternalistic character. The obstinacy of the civil service elite (Rothfels 1927; Tennstedt 1994; Tennstedt and Winter 1995) who were responsible for drafting the legislation, combined with the necessity of reaching a political compromise in the Imperial Diet and of accommodating the distinctive interests of the states, led to important changes to Bismarck's original plan to establish a centralized social insurance bureaucracy. Originally, the plan was for this bureaucracy exactly *not* to feature any protodemocratic elements of self-governance (*Selbstverwaltung*), to be staffed by civil servants (and not by delegates of the workers' and employers' associations), to be financed solely or primarily by the Reich (and not through employers' and employees' contributions), and to pay out roughly equal benefits (with little or no regard to the extent of contributions made). Instead, the new social security system created between 1883 and 1889 was essentially financed by contributions and payments and benefits were related to workers' incomes. The organizational structure of the new social insurance system built on previously existing forms of collective self-help and self-administration, integrating the "free funds" into the health insurance scheme. The contributions were split equally between employers and employees, which legitimized the prominent involvement of both parties in the administration of the insurance schemes. Because the Federal Chamber (*Bundesrat*) refused to extend the tax collection powers of the Reich, Bismarck's plans to finance social insurance through a centrally collected tax on tobacco had to be abandoned. This restricted the influence of the central state on the administration of the social insurance from the outset.

First and foremost, the necessity to build up an entirely new social insurance bureaucracy provided the unions and the SPD (*Sozialdemokratische Partei Deutschlands*), which rapidly succeeded in dominating the assemblies, with unprecedented opportunities for patronage, first, regarding the health insurance, later also regarding the pension insurance. The SPD and the unions had previously been excluded from any access to real political power in Wilhelmine Germany. The administration of the social insurance agencies was a domain where the equal suffrage by secret ballot resulted in the workers having real responsibility in a specific area of direct interest to them. It was an instance of basic democratic self-determination in a nation where democratic participation was still restricted (given that the federal government was not fully accountable to parliament and that state elections, at least in Germany's largest state of Prussia, were severely distorted due to the plutocratic *system censitaire* that prevailed there). Peter Flora and Jens Alber argue that the early granting of social rights to workers in Germany can be interpreted as compensating for their lack of political rights at the end of the nineteenth century (Flora and Alber 1981: 46–7). However, it is important to note at this juncture that the elections for the social insurance administration provided the workers with their first opportunity to exert democratic influence in an area of immediate interest. The health insurance and also the miners' insurance (*Knappschaftsvereine*) had "an extremely democratic constitution" especially if compared to the "plutocratic franchise in state and communal elections" (Geyer 1992: 1050). Hence, from the beginning, specific political rights of workers were blended with their new social rights.

Thus, elections for the social insurance administration were "as contested as elections to the imperial diet" (Tennstedt 1977: 64 and 65).[1] These elections were dominated by the first major mass party of Wilhelmine Germany, the Social Democrats, and the most important mass organization, the free unions. While, initially, only less than 10 percent of the members of the health insurance fund were also union members, the overwhelming majority of the delegates to the assemblies, and consequently also to the executive boards of the funds, held union membership. This was due to a systematic and disciplined mobilization strategy implemented by the unions, which from around 1892 recognized the extraordinary importance of social insurance for the labor movement. The non-unionized members of the health insurance funds showed only minor interest in the social elections (turnout in the elections was below 10 percent; see Tennstedt 1983: 429–30).[2] A rough estimate of the number of union representatives who played a major role in the administration of the health, accident, and old-age insurances

---

[1] For excellent accounts of the organizational coevolution of the trade unions and the social insurance bureaucracy, see Tennstedt (1977, 1983, 1993). For a highly critical perspective, see Billerbeck (1982). A good account of how the "welfare state and the working class in Imperial Germany shaped one another in complex ways" is also provided by Steinmetz (1991, citation from p. 38). However, in my view Steinmetz overstates the "state's ability to control the effects of worker participation" in the social insurance schemes (Steinmetz 1991: 30 and *passim*). In his 1993 contribution on this topic, Steinmetz presents a slightly different interpretation. Here he juxtaposes the central repression and local representation of the organized workers. Thus, he claims that the "advent of 'proto-corporatist' interventions during the 1890s marked a significant break with the Bismarckian form of social policy" (Steinmetz 1993: 43). As I will emphasize here, working-class integration did not follow a simple, linear, preordained, or planned path. Moreover, integration did not result in a decline in social and political conflict between the milieus (Smith 1995).

[2] In 1892, the Social Democratic MP Paul Singer proclaimed that the "statutory funds have to become the rallying point of the class-conscious workers" (quoted in Tennstedt 1983: 429).

(excluding normal delegates to the funds' assemblies) is around 100,000 to 120,000 executive board members (Tennstedt 1977: 55, fn. 44; 1983: 430). Relative to the total number of trade union members in 1901 (approximately 481,000), every fourth member of the free unions would have been an executive board member of a health insurance fund. Even if we should interpret these figures with some caution, there can be no doubt about the extraordinary import- ance of the social insurance administration as a field of union activity. Since the assemblies of the health insurance funds not only elected the executive boards of the funds but also the delegates to the assemblies of the old-age and accident insurance schemes and the representatives on the numerous arbitration and advisory committees of all three insurance branches, the dominant position of the organized workers in the health insurance quickly spread through the entire system.

The dominance of union delegates in the administrative bodies of the social insurance funds provided them with specific resources particularly regarding the allocation of jobs and the administration of quite impressive budgets.[3] For example, union activists who were put on blacklists by employers could be employed as health insurance employees checking on those claiming to be ill (*Krankengeher*) or took on office work (Tennstedt 1977: 114). Florian Tennstedt estimated that around 1905, roughly 3,000 to 6,000 full-time positions in the social insurance administration were under the control of the unions (Ritter 1983: 51; Tennstedt 1983: 234). Compared to the full-time union positions at the time (around 980 in 1905) the importance of the social insurance as a resource pool for the unions becomes obvious. The union rank and file was particularly able to benefit from this access to positions in the social insurance schemes, and this protected the unions against the ever present danger of syndicalism at the company level.

Given that it was workers' organizations that decided who was eligible for the welfare administration jobs, social insurance had a centralizing effect on unions of which union leaders were keenly aware (Rabenschlag-Kräusslich 1983: 133 and 139–40). Moreover, it is hard to overestimate the symbolic importance of the workers' self-administration in the social insurance system. A career as a "fund's civil servant" or *Kassenbeamte* became the first and most important inroad for workers into a professional sphere, which had previously been occupied exclu- sively by the bourgeoisie and the aristocratic elite of Wilhelmine Germany. The high social status of a civil-servant-like occupation for worker representatives was further elevated through the constant interaction between government offi- cials and *Kassenbeamten*, which was necessary for resolving the multiplicity of

---

[3] In 1913, expenditures of the health insurance scheme alone—roughly half a billion Reichsmark— amounted to one-third of the expenditures of all local governments in Germany (Tennstedt 1993: 84).

practical questions arising in the day-to-day administration of the new system (Martiny 1975).

Needless to say, the state bureaucracy did not simply observe this development from the sidelines. Their countermeasures were either futile or came too late, however. The *Reichsversicherungsordnung* of 1911 (RVO), which was the most important social insurance reform since the social legislation of the 1880s, contained several provisions specifically designed to address the problem of "the dominance of the social democrats" in the administration of the social insurance system (Ritter 1983: 57; Tennstedt 1983: 432–7). Yet, by the time the RVO came into force in 1914, World War I had profoundly changed the general political climate. Anxious to secure peace on the home front, the administrative elite and the high military command sought to appease the labor movement (Feldman 1992 [1966]; Marks 1989: 83 and 107–18). Now the unions were co-opted by important war-planning agencies—against massive resistance from the employers. Instead of rolling back the influence of organized labor and social democracy, the war economy provided a further impetus for the integration of both and created a protocorporatist, tripartite committee structure at the national level in the field of industrial relations (Feldman 1992 [1966]; see further discussion below).

In another respect, social insurance provided an important organizational support structure for the unions. Since the 1870s, the "labor question" had been intertwined with the "housing question," i.e. with the inadequate supply of good and affordable housing for workers in the rapidly growing new industrial centers of the Reich. Thus, the new old-age and invalidity insurance was also designed to address the housing problem. According to Section 129 of the Law on Invalidity and Old Age, the old-age insurance fund was allowed to grant loans to a value of up to 25 percent of its overall assets (from 1899, the figure increased to 50 percent of overall assets) to cooperatives with the status of a public welfare institution like building societies (*gemeinnützige Baugenossenschaften*), if these loans "exclusively or predominantly benefit the insured" (Section 26, RVO). Interest on loans to building societies was allowed to be lower than the minimum interest rate for social insurance investments prescribed by the state. The building societies aimed to ease the shortage of safe, clean, and affordable accommodation for workers and their families. The objective of the building societies was the construction of new housing and the leasing of flats to disadvantaged workers and their families. After the sharp decline in the numbers of cooperatives in the wake of the economic crisis of 1873, the reemergence of this workers' self-help institution coincided with the maturing of old-age and invalidity insurance (see Table 2.1).[4]

---

[4] An important factor contributing to the rapid growth in the numbers of building societies was also the enactment of the *Genossenschaftsgesetz* of 1889 (a law regulating cooperatives), which limited the liability of the cooperatives' members in the event of insolvency. This particularly fostered the growth of workers' building societies, since here the financial assets, and thus the risks involved, were quite substantial.

**Table 2.1** Development of building societies (*Baugenossenschaften*) in Germany, 1869–1919

| Year | Number of building societies | Number of new building societies founded | Number of liquidations | Assets (in Deutschmark) | Reserve funds (in Deutschmark) | External money (in Deutschmark) |
|---|---|---|---|---|---|---|
| 1869 | 2 | –[a] | – | 0.001 | – | – |
| 1875 | 53 | – | – | 0.6 | 0.05 | 1.9 |
| 1880 | 36 | 13 | 30 | 0.03 | 0.03 | 0.3 |
| 1885 | 33 | 3 | 6 | 0.03 | 0.03 | 0.3 |
| 1890 | 50 | 38 | 21 | 0.02 | 0.02 | 0.3 |
| 1895 | 132 | 113 | 31 | 0.7 | 0.14 | 0.2 |
| 1900 | 385 | 294 | 41 | 5.5 | 0.99 | 30.4 |
| 1905 | 641 | 352 | 69 | 25.8 | 2.8 | 124.0 |
| 1910 | 1,056 | 518 | 103 | 41.6 | 7.3 | 362.6 |
| 1915 | 1,534 | 491 | 125 | 45.9 | 10.1 | 544.8 |
| 1919 | 2,266 | 932 | 76 | 55.4 | 13.6 | 584.2 |

[a] No data available.

*Source*: Crüger et al. (1924: 440).

If we compare this data—particularly the figures in the final column showing the extent of external funding—with the figures showing the expenditures of the blue-collar pension insurance program for supplying workers with housing (see Table 2.2), it becomes clear that the building societies were financed almost exclusively by money from the workers' pension insurance scheme.

Estimates show that after 1900, building societies covered 70 percent of their loans through money from the old-age insurance fund for workers (Zimmermann 1991: 207–8). Once the revisionist position of leading Social Democrats and union officials began to gain dominance over the Marxist orthodoxy, which considered any involvement of the workers' movement in running a business to be, at best, a futile enterprise and, at worst, a betrayal of the common cause, worker cooperatives grew rapidly in number and importance. After the turn of the century, the German cooperative movement, which had originally been a project of the lower middle classes, the self-employed, and farmers, became dominated by the working class (Novy and Prinz 1985).

Building societies, which were not only responsible for the construction but also the administration of houses, were relatively large bureaucracies as well. They too offered opportunities for patronage and thus supplied the unions with jobs and resources to allocate. Dense decentralized networks with multiple overlapping memberships emerged, linking the unions, the SPD, health insurance funds and pension agencies, housing cooperatives, and local savings and loan associations. The resources these networks had at their disposal made membership individually

**Table 2.2** Invalidity insurance expenditures on workers' housing, 1910–1917

| Year | Total assets (in millions of Reichsmark) | Expenses for workers' housing (in millions of Reichsmark) | In percent of total assets |
|------|------|------|------|
| 1900 | 845.8   | 78.1  | 9.2  |
| 1901 | 929.2   | 87.5  | 9.4  |
| 1902 | 1,007.5 | 103.4 | 10.3 |
| 1903 | 1,084.3 | 118.4 | 10.9 |
| 1904 | 1,160.4 | 133.2 | 11.5 |
| 1905 | 1,237.5 | 151.0 | 12.2 |
| 1906 | 1,318.5 | 172.6 | 13.1 |
| 1907 | 1,404.1 | 195.7 | 13.9 |
| 1908 | 1,489.6 | 239.4 | 16.4 |
| 1909 | 1,574.1 | 280.5 | 17.8 |
| 1910 | 1,662.2 | 320.1 | 19.3 |
| 1911 | 1,759.4 | 362.2 | 20.6 |
| 1912 | 1,929.1 | 418.3 | 21.7 |
| 1913 | 2,105.4 | 482.6 | 22.9 |
| 1914 | 2,252.4 | 532.4 | 23.6 |
| 1915 | 2,354.5 | 558.9 | 23.7 |
| 1916 | 2,428.3 | 566.6 | 23.3 |
| 1917 | 2,519.4 | 571.9 | 22.7 |

*Sources*: Kolb (1928: 88); Mörschel (1990).

rational. In other words, they offered selective incentives for the unions and the Social Democratic Party. Moreover, social housing provided the unions and the Social Democratic Party with the means to exercise a certain degree of control over their membership. It proved to be easier to collect member fees, mobilize members for demonstrations or strikes, disseminate relevant information, create normative commitment against the temptation to leave the movement or simply go along for a free ride, in short, to create what Lipset et al. (1956) have called an "occupational community," if the membership was concentrated in distinct locations and was not spread across the town.

What was important for the development of German unions and also for German industrial relations, in general, was the fact that these emerging networks were mainly of local character, but that their selective incentives were not exclusively aimed at specific professions or crafts. For example: a worker would be eligible for an apartment constructed by a building society and financed by the old-age insurance scheme of which the given worker was a member. It is important to note that membership of this insurance was mandatory for all (industrial) workers earning an annual wage of up to RM 2,000. Eligibility was thus not linked to membership in any particular union. In the conflict between the different ways of organizing workers of localism versus centralism, craft unionism versus trade unionism, or syndicalism versus revisionism, which dominated the internal debates of the unions soon after the repeal of the Socialist Law (Schönhoven 1980a, 1980b, 1985), this was to become a key factor in tipping the balance toward the proponents of the centralist strategy. Perhaps even more important was that the new social insurance did not generally deprive the workers' movement of one of its most prominent functions, namely to provide the members with insurance against the risks of sickness, disability, or unemployment although it did do so to the small old craft unions, which still stood in the tradition of guilds and "friendly societies." Their exclusive social insurance packages with non-transferable entitlements had a restrictive effect on the mobility of their members. The integration of organized labor into the welfare state offered a "broader basis for union organization" (Heidenheimer 1980: 9) and thus tilted the balance in favor of the new unions. Particularly the shift from craft to industrial unions "coincided closely with the decision [of the unions] to dissociate from the craft-based voluntary funds (*Hilfskassen*) and to utilize the broadly based local funds" instead (Heidenheimer 1980: 9; Tennstedt 1976: 389–90).[5] It is a counterfactual (and to date poorly researched) proposition, but there is, nonetheless, some empirical evidence to support the claim that the rapid process of modernization of the union movement in the second half of the 1890s, which led to the emergence of powerful industrial unions with a centralized bureaucracy, would not have taken place at such speed and would not have progressed so smoothly without the latent support provided by the structure and scope of the new social insurance system.[6] Thus, the specificity of the German development seems to lie, *inter alia*, in the fact that the shift of the important welfare function from the unions as "particularistic class-organization[s] ... to the nation state" has *not* led to a general "decrease in subcultural integration of the workers" (Streeck 1981: 67). This was especially due to the fact that the emerging welfare system in Germany retained a para-public character due to the important elements of self-administration it contained. The shift in welfare responsibility from the unions to the nation state stopped halfway. Thus, the structure of the new social insurance scheme even led to a massive *increase* in subcultural integration in the case of the new unions, which played a major role in the self-governance of the social insurance funds. The new unions were able to use the resources of the social insurance schemes for particularistic purposes, for instance to offer special supplementary packages to the benefits provided by statutory insurance as selective incentives for their members (Trischler 1994). With respect to the older elements of the union movement, still steeped in the tradition of guilds, friendly societies, and organizations of mutual

*modern unions pre-1900 b/c of soc. ins.*

---

[5] If not otherwise noted, translations are by the author.

[6] The pattern of organizational coevolution between the unions and the social insurance system is particularly clear in the case of the "workers' secretariats [which] were set up to parallel the administrative structure of the welfare system" (Marks 1989: 103) and which had primarily advisory functions. On the workers' secretariats, see particularly Martiny (1975). For a more detailed account of the supply of supplementary private insurance through the unions and workers' cooperatives, see Trischler (1994).

assistance (*Unterstützungsvereine*; see Schönhoven 1980b), however, social insurance had a disintegrative effect. The integration of the workers into the new state, which social legislation was supposed to foster (and which it ultimately did bring about), was thus not accomplished by creating a relationship of direct loyalty between individual workers and the state (as Bismarck had hoped), but was largely mediated through the workers' organizations, i.e. through the unions. "The new social policies worked *through* the socialist unions rather than bypassing them" (Steinmetz 1993: 43, original italics).

The importance of mutual organizational support between the unions and the social insurance became most evident when the white-collar movement attempted to imitate the successful model of the organizational coevolution of the free unions and the invalidity insurance (*Invalidenversicherung*). In an almost classical case of "mimetic isomorphism" (Powell and DiMaggio 1991), the internally fragmented white-collar movement identified the promise of unity and organizational stability in a special insurance for the *Angestelltenstand* ("estate" of white-collar workers). The white-collar workers' insurance law of 1911 (*Angestelltenversicherungsgesetz* of December 20, 1911, RGBl. I, p. 989), which even today is often interpreted as an instance of an etatist strategy of *divide and rule* aimed against the—*in abstracto*—unified working class (the Marxian "class in itself"; see for example Esping-Andersen and Korpi 1984: 180), has to be seen rather as the result of a bottom-up process, in which an intensively campaigning white-collar movement tried to achieve both organizational stability and the official recognition of the well-founded rights of its members (Prinz 1991). The white-collar movement ultimately succeeded in gaining its own separate branch of insurance, which, once again, provided jobs, important financial resources, and the means to offer both exclusively to their union members. It is important to note in this context that the cleavage between blue- and white-collar workers, which was institutionally "frozen" through the separate social insurance systems (themselves closely linked to the respective unions of blue- and white-collar workers (Kocka 1981)), can be seen as one of the major impediments for the development of enterprise unionism in Germany.[7]

The above comments on the relationship between the workers' insurance funds and the unions also applied here. The white-collar unions soon came to dominate the self-governance of the white-collar workers' insurance fund and the relationship between the building societies and the white-collar unions developed in much the same way as with the workers' old-age insurance fund. Here, Sections 219–228 of the Employees Insurance Law (*Angestelltenversicherungsgesetz*) regulated the investment of the insurance fund's assets in the same way as the regulations of Section 225 of the IVG (*Invalidenversicherungsgesetz*) did: interests were allowed

---

[7] As Hockerts pointedly remarked, in Germany "the white collar worker ... is the definitory product of social insurance legislation" (Hockerts 1983: 302).

to fall short of the minimal rate of return for investments (set by the state) if loans were extended to enterprises that were "exclusively or predominantly beneficial to the insured."[8] This made it possible to supply the special building societies of the white-collar workers' unions with cheap money.[9] After World War I, when the basic target for investments of the pension funds changed from the investment in state bonds (for war financing) to the investment in the building societies (to secure housing for the homecoming soldiers and to generally ameliorate housing conditions), the links between the unions, the pension insurance schemes, and the building societies strengthened. Thus, in 1918, the *Non-Profit White-Collar Housing Society* (*Gemeinnützige Gesellschaft für Angestelltenheimstätten*; Gagfah) was founded in Berlin as part of the white-collar pension insurance fund.[10]

Between 1924 and 1933, the white-collar workers' insurance fund spent RM 828.7 million on the Gagfah (Herrmann 1936: 57). The purpose of the financial involvement of social insurance in the provision of new housing becomes most evident when we look at the white-collar old-age insurance scheme. Whereas the involvement of the invalidity insurance fund was mainly legitimated by referring to the health risks and the resulting financial burden of pension insurance caused by the poor housing conditions of the workers (the high rates of disability as a result of tuberculosis, for instance), this could not be the primary motivation for the activities of the old-age insurance fund for the significantly better-off white-collar workers. Here it is particularly obvious that the activities were an external inducement for union membership.

To briefly sum up the argument presented in this section: the new social insurance scheme provided the trade unions with Olsonian "selective incentives," which were of crucial importance for the emergence, overall organizational stability, and the specific shape of modern industrial unions in Germany. In this respect, the German case clearly supports Bo Rothstein's analysis in that it also

[8] See the identical Section 164 para. 3, IVG, Section 1356 para. 4, RVO, and later Section 26 para. 12, RVO.
[9] See the guidelines for the white-collar old-age insurance scheme concerning its contribution to the improvement of general housing conditions, February 1914 (*Richtlinien für die Mitwirkung der Reichsversicherungsanstalt für Angestellte an der Verbesserung der allgemeinen Wohnungsverhältnisse; Angestelltenversicherung* 1914: 26–7).
[10] The building societies with strong links to the blue-collar pension insurance scheme were founded at the same time as the administrative domain of the regional insurance offices (*Landesversicherungsanstalten*, LVA), of which there were 31 in 1915. The administrative domains of the LVAs themselves did not match perfectly with the administrative districts and providence of the states. At times this jurisdictional mismatch allowed the LVAs to follow quite autonomous strategies. The financial support to building societies, which was not always welcomed by conservative state governments, is a case in point. In 1924, as a Social Democratic countermeasure to the foundation of the Gagfah, the *Deutsche Wohnungsfürsorge A.-G. für Beamte, Angestellte und Arbeiter* (Dewog) attempted to unify the efforts of the workers' insurance scheme in the construction business (Novy and Prinz 1985). Union activity in the field of workers' cooperatives increased significantly after 1920 since the immediate postwar hope that grand-style socialization would bring German capitalism one step closer to socialism had faded considerably by then.

emphasizes the important influence of "welfare state institutions on working-class strength" (cf. Rothstein 1992).

The pattern of organizational coevolution of the German social insurance system and the unions was generated by a specific sequence of historical events. During the time of repression from 1878 to 1890, the organizational development of the unions was hindered and delayed. While the process of industrialization continued to proceed rapidly, a corresponding development of the unions was suppressed. When the ban on workers' political representation was lifted in 1890, this offered some "latecomer" advantages to the proponents of a modernized, centralized, sector-wide union movement: "It was the state [with its repressive politics towards the unions] ... which had stimulated the rapid conquest of elitist guild traditions and had accelerated the development of modern means of interest articulation which transcended individual trades and involved modern, centralist interindustrial forms of organization" (Tenfelde 1985: 214). The breakthrough of the modern industrial union in the last quarter of the nineteenth century (Ritter and Tenfelde 1996 [1976]) was particularly supported by the simultaneous emergence of a social insurance system—which had originally been intended to weaken the workers' movement. The mutually reinforcing development of the new unions and the new social insurance system led to the kind of dualism between _voluntary organizations_ and _obligatory institutions_ that plays a crucial role in the emergence and stability of corporatist arrangements (Lehmbruch 1977).[11] As will be shown in the following sections and chapters, the "protocorporatism" introduced by the Bismarckian social insurance legislation "laid the groundwork for the full-fledged corporatism of Weimar and adumbrated the main lines of West Germany's 'social partnership'" (Steinmetz 1993: 44).

## 2.2 Social Insurance and the State: The Emergence of a Corporatist Mode of Interest Intermediation in Germany

For a systematic analysis of the relationship between the social insurance system and the distinctive institutional setup of German capitalism, another important starting point would be to take into consideration that social policy and industrial relations in Germany have both always fallen into the regulative remit of one and the same administrative actor: initially, the Office of the Interior (_Reichsamt des Inneren_, RdI), and then, after 1918, the Labor Ministry (_Reichsarbeitsministerium_, RAM), and finally, after 1949, the Federal Labor Ministry (_Bundesarbeitsministerium_, BMA).[12]

---

[11] This dualism thus historically precedes and functionally complements the important dualism between _statutory_ works councils and unions as _voluntary organizations_, which is normally emphasized in the literature on German industrial relations (Thelen 1991).

[12] Furthermore, RdI, RAM, and BMA all showed an extraordinarily high degree of continuity of staff. Despite the high degree of overall political volatility in Weimar Germany, the RAM was led

In a country like Germany, where the bureaucracy has played such an important role in the development of society and where there has always been and continues to be a high degree of factionalism between the ministries, the assumption that important sectoral variances in interest intermediation exist and that these correspond to the boundaries of administrative responsibility, seems to be especially appropriate (Hennis 1961; Lehmbruch 1987, 1991, 1995). Similarly, it is highly plausible to expect multiple spill-over, learning, and mimicking effects between policy sectors if the same ministry has administrative responsibilities for them. Indeed, there is much empirical evidence to support this hypothesis in the case of German social and labor policies. From an early stage, the social legislation of the 1880s had given the RdI a sphere of "natural" competence, which also comprised factory legislation and regulation of occupational health and safety. The RdI, and later the RAM, were relatively strong ministries, which, with respect to social insurance, were neither involved in severe horizontal conflicts over their bureaucratic spheres nor in vertical conflicts with the states, since the social insurance system had been the sole responsibility of the central state from the very beginning. In addition, the RdI/RAM had a relatively high level of autonomy vis-à-vis business interests because these were not always successfully advocated by the Ministry for Economic Affairs, particularly with regard to small- and medium-sized enterprises (Turner 1985: 35). In fact, a special economic committee (*diktatorischer Wirtschaftsausschuß*) was set up at the cabinet level in the early Weimar Republic and the Office for Demobilization (*Demobilmachungsamt*) was established in 1918 as a reaction to the alleged unresponsiveness of the Ministry for Economic Affairs toward business interests and to its—at that time—strong propensity for interventionism and economic planning (Bähr 1989: 16; Biechele 1972: 80–6; Winkler 1985: 196).

The Ministry of Economic Affairs (*Reichswirtschaftsamt*, founded in 1917, renamed *Reichswirtschaftsministerium*, RWM in 1919) also emerged from the RdI. A short time later—in 1918—the RWM created the Labor Ministry in another split of responsibilities (for a detailed account of the founding history of the RAM, see Reichsarbeitsministerium 1929: 12–23; for an equivalent account of the RWM, see Hubatsch 1978). In this respect, it is important to note that the RWM showed little inclination toward a laissez-faire policy or approach. Its experiences of the war economy had resulted in its pronounced interventionist stance and deep skepticism toward the free play of market mechanisms (Anderson 1973: 290–3).

Instead, visions of a social economy (*Gemeinwirtschaft*) and a "controlled" or "bounded" economy (*gebundene Wirtschaft*) ruled supreme (Biechele 1972;

---

without interruption from 1920 to 1929 by Heinrich Brauns (Center Party). This resulted in a relatively coherent political strategy and a systematic promotion policy within the ministry. Indeed, the Center Party and social policy proved to be the two most important foundations for the crisis-ridden first German republic.

Herrigel 1996: 125; Huber 1978: 861–2; Maier 1975: 140–3; Winkler 1985: 191–8). Experience of the war economy "predisposed the men who ran the Economics Ministry to look favorably on big business" (Turner 1985: 35). From the perspective of a "critical experience" theory of the development of sectoral interest systems, it is significant that administrative responsibilities were not divided between the RAM and RWM until after the war. The Economics Ministry, "a product of the war . . . continued to bear the marks of its formative years, during which the imperial government chose, in the name of efficiency, to deal predominantly with large firms and the associational organizations they dominated" (Turner 1985: 35). Heinrich Brauns, Minister of Labor between 1920 and 1928, however, had close links to the coal industry in the Rhineland and later designed his "productivity-oriented wage policy" using the economic situation of the coal industry and the miners' wages as his reference point. The war thus provided both ministries with shared experiences and triggered a similar response to the question as to the best solution to the severe economic and social crisis of post-World War I Germany.[13] In both ministries, an important role was played by concepts that aimed to establish an equilibrium between the large interest organizations of capital and labor at the national level.

Consequently, the Labor Ministry had no reason to fear any substantial level of intragovernmental resistance to its efforts to domesticate the labor/capital conflict through a policy of credentialing the large employers' and employees' associations with public status, centralizing and integrating them into tripartite or bipartite decision-making bodies, and creating broad responsibilities for "associational self-governance" or "social self-determination" (Sinzheimer). On the contrary, to a significant extent, the RAM and the RWM shared ideas about organizing both society and the economy around central corporate (ständische) bodies. When the government planned to give substance to the famous Article 165 of the Weimar Constitution, which explicitly recognized the associations of labor and capital and had promised to supplement the system of political representation with a broad system of "functional representation" (of which the Central Economic Council [Reichswirtschaftsrat] was to be the "institutional apotheosis"), the opinions of the RWM and the RAM on how to best achieve this goal were radically different, but the goal itself remained uncontroversial. On the one hand, the Labor Ministry wanted to complement the existing chambers of industry and trade, artisans and

---

[13] Moreover, the relative weight of both ministries differed: while the Ministry of Economic Affairs still had to align its position with the Prussian Ministry of Trade (Preußische Ministerium für Handel und Gewerbe) and with the respective ministries of the other Länder, the Labor Ministry had more autonomy toward the states and was therefore more influential. While the Länder retained competencies in economic regulation, they possessed only delegated responsibilities in social policy. Through the mandatory arbitration of labor conflicts (in the industrial, agricultural, and public sector), the RAM even resembled a central steering agency in questions of industrial policy. The productivity-orientated social policy of Reichsminister Brauns was a reflection of this broad area of economic responsibility of the Labor Ministry (Bähr 1989: 52–62).

agriculture with "chambers of labor" on the local, district, and central levels, thereby integrating the workers' councils into the chambers of labor and all central chambers into the *Reichswirtschaftsrat*. The Ministry of Economic Affairs, on the other hand, wanted to guarantee workers' equal representation through co-optation into the existing chambers (Maier 1975: 142–4; Ritter 1996 [1994]; Schäffer 1920). Admittedly, the two concepts were based on very different "belief systems" and the practical implications of each would have been fundamentally different. What is of interest here, however, is that the predilection for massive state interference in the structures of the economy in favor of a corporatist mode of organization was more or less equally pronounced in both ministries. Moreover, the liberal opposition within the government against this intervention-ist inclination mainly targeted the more authoritarian and plan-oriented concept of the RWM (Biechele 1972; Ritter 1996 [1994]), and not the "social self-determination" model of the Ministry of Labor.

Although all attempts at establishing an overt and all-encompassing corporatist structure failed, the general orientation toward such a goal clearly prevailed in the Labor Ministry throughout the Weimar Republic. The idea of "economic self-governance," which meant self-governance based on collective contracts between the central interest organizations of capital and labor and based on a rough "balance of class powers" between them, was the leitmotiv inspiring both the Labor Ministry's social and labor policies. This formula proved effective not only in the overall blueprint for policy design, but also in a number of detailed provisions and decrees which were evidence of the RAM's capacity to act as a highly skilled "architect of political order" (Anderson 1973). Here, it is important to emphasize that the implementation of the general formula of social self-determination by the Ministry of Labor *in the realm of industrial conflicts* was heavily influenced by the kind of institutional equilibrium that had evolved earlier *in the realm of social policy*. In this respect, the principle of parity figured most prominently (Lehmbruch 1996a, 1996b, 1997). Parity soon became a peace formula, which proved to be almost universally applicable, transcending the spheres of social policy and industrial conflict proper.[14] However, it was precisely

[14] See the Weimar "school conflict," in which the Center Party fought for parity between confes-sional and secular schools (see Grünthal 1968) or the formula of parity between civil and military defense, which arose in the West German debate about rearmament in the 1950s. Of course, code-termination (*paritätische Mitbestimmung*) has its roots here too. Parity is defined by Lehmbruch (1997: 57) "as an institutionalized system of conflict accommodation among corporate actors with (corporate) equality, as different from a liberal system based on individual autonomy." It is highly plausible, but has not yet been substantiated by in-depth historical studies, that the diffusion of the principle of parity was due (among other factors) to the prominent role which it played in the political program of the Catholic Center Party. The aim of the Center Party's "struggle for parity" was to achieve a proportional share of Catholic civil servants in the Prussian state administration (Baumeister 1987; Hunt 1982; Ross 1988). Due to a policy of "negative patronage" (Eschenburg 1966), Catholics (as well as Jews and Social Democrats) had almost no access to a civil service career. The process of the transfer of the principle of parity out of the Center Party's political program to state policies can be explained by the prominent

in these areas of social policy and industrial conflict where the old interdenominational peace formula was revived. Parity between the organized interests of
capital and labor was to become the dominant mode of "cleavage management" in
German capitalism.

Due to the dual administrative responsibility of the RdI and the RAM for social
and labor policy, for a long time, the history of both policy domains in Germany
comprised a series of spill-over and spill-back effects between the two spheres. An
important factor in this process of reciprocal influence between the two domains
was the fact that the parity between workers' and employers' organizations had
evolved quite early. Accident and old-age and invalidity insurance had made the
principle of parity in the representation of employers and employees a prominent
element in the organizational structure of these associations. Although the executive boards in both insurance branches were dominated either by employers or by
civil servants, the insured and their employers were represented equally in a
multiplicity of auxiliary committees. This is also true for the health insurance
fund, although here the workers dominated the assemblies and the executive
boards at a ratio of 2:1, which corresponded to their share of the contributions.
Another important example of parity representation was the labor or industrial
courts (*Gewerbegerichte*). These had been established in 1890 as a conciliatory
measure in the aftermath of the great miners' strike of 1889, in which the
Christian (Catholic) unions had played a particularly prominent role (Hickey
1985: 243; Tennstedt 1993; see also Chapter 3). The national legislation had
"stipulated that workers were to have equal numbers of representatives on the
courts, to be elected by the direct and secret ballots of all males" (Steinmetz 1991:
27–8). Again, this presented the nascent labor movement with an opportunity to
"overcome the ostracism experienced when demanding collective bargaining over
wages and working hours and to become negotiation partners of the employers"
(Geyer 1992: 1050).

In the emerging social insurance system therefore organized workers and
employers were integrated into a multifaceted system of collaboration long before
the state (and business) had officially recognized the role of the unions as the
legitimate representatives of the workers' interests. As has been described above,
the prominent position of the unions in the administrative bodies of the social
insurance system was originally not the result of deliberate design, but mainly of
unforeseen (and in the view of the state bureaucracy, contra-intentional) organizational adaptation. However, once a protocorporatist system of conflict moderation had been established in the realm of social insurance, it could act as a model

role played by the Catholic ministerial bureaucrats in the Office of the Interior (*Reichsamt des Inneren*)
and the Labor Ministry. One of the reasons for the prominence of the "Zentrums-Patronage" (Max
Weber) in the RdI was that the central ministries had no independent bureaucratic basis (this was part
of the remit of the states) and thus sought political support from within the Imperial Diet (Weber 1988
[1918]: 415–16). Here, the Center Party occupied a pivotal position.

for conflict mediation in the realm of labor/capital antagonism. Further, the involvement of unions and employers' associations in the administration of social insurance provided an important external support structure for corporatist conflict moderation in industrial disputes. What had previously been a chance development now became an intentional one based on deliberate political planning.

The success of the principle of parity as the dominant mode of conflict resolution was a result of a dialectical process, in which the state and the forces of capital and labor alternated in initiating and furthering parity: parity between the insured and the employers was first introduced in the social insurance schemes on certain committees and advisory and arbitration boards. The introduction was relatively uncontroversial in this context, since it did not imply a direct recognition of unions and because parity seemed to be legitimized through the social insurance mode of financing. Once the aforementioned institutional evolution had led to de facto parity between the *organizations* of the insured, (the workers) and the employers in the social insurance fund, barriers were also lowered for the introduction of equal representation of the corporate actors on both sides in other areas. Parity between *unions* and *employers' associations* in relevant agencies was first introduced in the wake of the massive state intervention in the war economy (*Hilfsdienstgesetz* [Auxiliary Service Law] of 1916). Parity was now applied to industrial relations (in particular Feldman 1992 [1966]; see also Sachße and Tennstedt 1988: 46–9). After the war, both parties wanted to free themselves from the interventionist state socialism of the war economy and sought refuge from the early syndicalist and radical socialist factions in the Weimar Republic. Their collaboration was therefore on a voluntary, state-free basis, which, again, followed the bipartite pattern. The establishment of the Central Working Association (*Zentrale Arbeitsgemeinschaft*, ZAG) in 1918 is a particularly striking example of the extent to which the "corporate bargaining channel" had gained dominance over the "numerical democracy channel" (Stein Rokkan) in the German labor movement and, correspondingly, also exemplified the extent to which power had shifted from the party to the unions. Unions were so well integrated into the institutional complex of welfare and labor relations that, in their view, they now no longer needed "paper stones" (Przeworski and Sprague 1986). This hope was soon to be thoroughly dashed. However, the fragmented and paralyzed party politics of the Weimar Republic did not offer favorable prospects for the electoral strategy either. Consequently, once again, a pattern emerged in which the state was supposed to stabilize the corporatist arrangements between capital and labor that the two parties themselves were incapable of sustaining.

The employers in particular were no longer interested in continuing the collaboration with the unions as soon as the danger of massive socialization faded and general economic developments became significantly more favorable to capital. The state, however, now relied heavily on this voluntary arrangement to create its new social and labor policy. In this way, the Labor Ministry essentially stabilized a system of collective governance from outside:

- by declaring bargained solutions as generally binding, even for firms and workers who were not members of the respective associations of capital and labor (*Allgemeinverbindlichkeitserklärungen*; "erga omnes");
- by declaring arbitration in labor/capital conflicts as binding, even if one of the conflicting parties had not consented to the mandatory arbitration (*Zwangsschlichtung*);
- by legally prohibiting private contracts that would undermine minimum standards fixed by collective agreements (*Unabdingbarkeit*);
- and by declaring previous collective agreements to be fallback solutions whenever and wherever new collective agreements failed to come about (*Unmittelbarkeit*).

The legal definition of *tariffähig* (being a partner in a collective bargaining agreement) was stipulated by the state in a number of laws and decrees with the result of excluding employer-friendly "yellow" unions from participation in arbitration committees, from membership in the Central Economic Council, and from access to the administration of social insurance. The law on the elections to the social insurance[15] ascribed a privileged position to unions and employers' associations. They alone held the right to propose delegates to the assemblies of the social insurance fund. Provided that each side only proposed as many delegates as there were positions to fill, the election itself did not take place (known as *Friedenswahlen*, or literally "peace elections"). A small number of additional provisions discriminated in favor of the established unions and against the "free," i.e. non-union-based lists. The parties granted the right to propose delegates for the social insurance administration were defined in the law on the right of representation in the Imperial Economic Council (*Reichswirtschaftsrat*).

With respect to unions and employers' associations, these were the same organizations that signed the Stinnes-Legien Agreement, which created the Central Working Association (Hanow 1927: 370–1; Schäffer 1920). Here, again, we have the distinctive mix of voluntary collective agreements and state-imposed collective governance that is so characteristic of Weimar social policy. The abstract legal term "central" or "peak associations" (*Spitzenverbände*) in the realm of social welfare and with regard to doctors' associations and health insurance funds was defined in much the same way as by the RAM, thus guaranteeing the "managed co-existence of representational monopolies for social groups under the umbrella of the state" (on the health insurance funds and

---

[15] *Gesetz über Wahlen nach der RVO, dem AVG und dem RKG, April 4, 1927* (RGBl. I, p. 95; see Hanow 1927).

physicians see Döhler and Manow 1997: 132; Lehmbruch 1997: 56; on social welfare associations see Sachße and Tennstedt 1988). Thus, the Labor Ministry used the parity between unions and employers in the social insurance system as an instrument to achieve "political closure" on the union side and to establish a stable network of bodies representing workers' interests. The Labor Ministry used subtle techniques of "legal engineering" to help the three leading unions (social democratic, liberal, and Christian) achieve "oligopolistic representation." At the same time, the RAM also sheltered the unions from syndicalist developments through the legal stipulation of the works councils' spheres of responsibility and by preventing the creation of "free lists" in the social insurance administration. The developmental path toward trade and industry unions and away from company unions was the result of the specific historical sequence of state repression and late industrialization combined with the organizational coevolution of unions and social insurance. This path was then institutionalized by political design, in other words, through state legislation.

The hypothesis proposed in this section is that the emerging system of social insurance was not only beneficial to the development of powerful and centralized industrial unions (see Section 2.1), but also provided the model for the integration of unions and employers' associations in an overarching system of interest representation. The reciprocal influence of social policy and industrial relations was essentially mediated by the dual responsibility of the Labor Ministry for both policy sectors. It was particularly the parity between the major central interest organizations of labor and capital on a multiplicity of committees and boards (predominantly the social insurance and arbitration committees) that developed into a routine pattern of conflict accommodation in German industrial relations, whereby the higher degree of legitimate state interventionism in the realm of social insurance could be made instrumental for the stabilization of a collective bargaining regime of a more voluntary character in industrial relations.

While the attempt to impose a system of collective bargaining on unions and business "from above" met with increasing employer resistance, eventually failed, and was succeeded by the extinction of unions and by massive and erratic economic interventionism under the Nazi regime (Bähr 1989; Tooze 2006), nearly all elements of the Weimar system of collective self-governance were made part of  the post-World War II consensus from which "German capitalism" derived its distinctive character. The most important exception, however, was that after 1945, mandatory state arbitration was substituted with the guaranteed "autonomy" of capital and labor in collective bargaining (*Tarifautonomie*). The collective bargaining regime, which during the Weimar years could only be upheld by increasingly authoritarian state intervention, was reestablished and strengthened organizationally after 1945 (Drewes 1958). At the same time, the interests of and power relations between the major actors (state bureaucracy, unions, business associations, and the political parties) had changed profoundly. In postwar

Germany, social insurance lost its tight link with the unions. The significant extension of coverage of social benefits to groups who were not in dependent employment (artisans, self-employed, refugees, artists, students, etc.), on the one hand, and the unification of the unions into unitary unions (*Einheitsgewerkschaften*), on the other, loosened the connection between specific unions and their social insurance funds. To a certain extent, the cleavage between blue- and white-collar workers persisted. This was now primarily because Germany was a divided nation, however. While East Germany followed a social policy rooted in a "productivist" workers tradition, in the West, a contrasting concept of maintaining bourgeois status became the principal social policy objective in the 1950s (Manow 1997b).[16] This had important implications for the overall direction of West German social policy. Policy was now characterized by a specific orientation that comprised, among other things, a strong emphasis on the link between contributions and benefits. This was reflected in a low degree of redistributional capacity of the welfare state, the predominance of status maintenance (in contrast to helping those in need), a tendency toward the sole (male) breadwinner model,[17] an orientation toward a "standard employment relationship," a predominance of transfer payments over services, which, together with other provisions, created disincentives for female labor participation, and the concept of a clear-cut and conclusive exit from work at retirement (in contrast to a system of gradual retirement).[18] These components of social policy, which had previously been specific features of white-collar insurance, now became characteristic of the West German welfare state as a whole (see Chapter 6).

Another important factor was that war had, once again, destroyed nearly all the financial assets of the social insurance program, particularly of the pension insurance fund. As a consequence, the pension reform of 1957 (followed by the *3. Law on the Adjustment of the Old-Age Insurance* [*Rentenversicherungs-Änderungsgesetz*] of 1969) changed the financing system of the pension insurance program gradually from a funded scheme to a pay-as-you-go scheme. Consequently, the long-term capital assets of social insurance declined, despite

---

[16] At the same time, the split between reformist and communist unions, which was to become a significant development for certain West European labor movements in the postwar era, was also a *territorial* split between East and West Germany (Niethammer 1975: 304). The division of Germany totally discredited communism as a political option in the West.

[17] This, in turn, had implications for unions' strategies: "The family's virtually complete dependence on the male earner's income and entitlements meant that unions came to battle for job security (seniority principles, the regulation of hiring and firing practices)" (Esping-Andersen 1996: 75). The regulation of labor market entry and exit now became a central topic in collective bargaining.

[18] In the blue-collar insurance schemes, pensions always had the function of supplementing income in the event of diminishing ability to work in old age. Pensions in the white-collar insurance schemes, however, were designed to allow for a clear-cut transition from working life into a third phase of the life course, the time of retirement, in which previously held standards of living should be maintained. Here the implicit ideal was, of course, the civil servant who, at a certain age, was rewarded for his (usually not her) service.

the fact that transfers skyrocketed. The system accumulated less and less capital, which could have been used to invest in building societies, for instance. The state or private investors now increasingly provided public housing and played the role that had previously been played by building cooperatives (see graph 45 in Alber 1989b: 214; Schulz 1991: 490–1).[19] Moreover, the Nazi regime had removed all union members from the leading positions in the self-governance of the social insurance scheme (and from the entire complex of workers' cooperatives, savings and loans associations, etc.). The long-term effects of this measure on the political character of the self-administration cannot be overestimated. On the whole, it seems safe to say that social insurance lost its function of furthering the "subcultural integration" of the working class in postwar Germany. Again, as in the last quarter of the nineteenth century, the welfare state served the goal of national integration, but the workers were no longer the main target of its integrative efforts. In a divided Germany, national integration had acquired a very different meaning (Manow 1997a).

All this helped to establish a new equilibrium between protection and production, equity and efficiency in postwar Germany, an equilibrium that initially performed extremely well (see Chapter 4). However, before I provide a description and analysis of the postwar equilibrium, its extraordinary economic performance in the 1950s and 1960s, its long-term deficiencies (which became increasingly troublesome from the mid-1970s), and its impressive comeback after 2005, I will first depict the fierce ideological struggles that preceded, accompanied, and influenced the decision-making process regarding its design in the immediate postwar years. In this context, the following chapter will highlight the normative, ethical, and religious foundations of the German social market economy (*soziale Marktwirtschaft*). In Chapter 3, I will argue that, ultimately, the social market economy not only embodied a compromise between economic liberalism and welfare corporatism, but also a compromise between Catholic and Protestant social doctrine.

---

[19] In the 1990s, cost containment measures in the old-age insurance scheme forced the white-collar insurance as well as miners' insurance schemes (*Knappschaft*) to sell the property they still owned.

# 3

# *Modell Deutschland* as an Interdenominational Compromise

As a starting point for this chapter, it is worth highlighting that the plea for a new interdenominational compromise between Protestantism and Catholicism enjoyed considerable prominence in the debates after World War II regarding the design of Germany's postwar economic and social order (Rüstow 1960; cf. Müller-Armack 1950: 559). In this chapter, I argue that the post-1945 allusions to a form of new "Westphalian peace" between the two religious camps were not misplaced or only meant metaphorically to indicate the importance of the claims that were at stake. I assert that Germany's social market economy did indeed come to encapsulate a compromise between Catholic and Protestant social doctrine over the question of how to embed modern capitalism morally and socially (Manow 2000, 2001c), a compromise between (Protestant) economic liberalism on the one hand and (Catholic) welfare interventionism on the other, even if this compromise was largely an unintentional outcome, and not a deliberately struck bargain.

To develop the argument it is first necessary to reconstruct the historical contribution of the Bismarckian welfare state to the formation of the political and confessional camps and milieus in Germany since the 1890s and to depict the conflicts between these camps over social policy. As we saw in the previous chapter, the German welfare state was part of a dual strategy, both repressive and integrative, with which the young German Reich sought to achieve internal unity and national identity after the Franco-Prussian war of 1870/71 had brought territorial consolidation. The two anti-Protestant "enemies from within," Social Democracy and political Catholicism, had been the target of repressive state action in the *Kulturkampf* era of 1873–8 and the period of Socialist Law from 1878–90. In the process of nation-building, these two groups, the "red" and the "black international" as they were polemically referred to, were suspected by the national Protestant camp of lacking sufficient national loyalty and patriotism. Yet, social legislation of the 1880s also provided these two camps with important inroads into Wilhelmine Germany. The welfare state offered social integration, an opportunity which both camps were quick to grasp. While political repression under conditions of universal (male) suffrage furthered the formation of Social Democratic and Catholic camps, the specific institutional structure of the Bismarckian welfare state fostered the social integration of the Catholic and socialist labor movements into the new German nation state and at the same time contributed to their

*Social Protection, Capitalist Production: The Bismarckian Welfare State in the German Political Economy, 1880–2015.*
Philip Manow, Oxford University Press (2020). © Philip Manow.
DOI: 10.1093/oso/9780198842538.001.0001

organizational consolidation. This contradictory process has been fittingly labeled a process of "negative integration" (Dieter Groh).

It comes as no surprise that this unique pattern of social integration *cum* political alienation did not simply spell social harmony. Over time, the Catholic and socialist camps were able to use their organizational resources to dominate Weimar's political landscape as the only two mass-member parties (before the advent of the national-socialist NSDAP), and they benefited from their close ties to the Catholic and socialist labor movements, respectively. Now, in the 1920s, the liberal Protestant bourgeoisie in particular felt increasingly politically and economically excluded from both the game of corporative pluralism between organized labor and capital (Maier 1975), which largely built on the protocorporatism established with the Bismarckian welfare state; and from the political collusion between the Catholic Center Party and the Social Democrats, dubbed the "coalition of Weimar," which played an especially prominent role in all social policy issues (Geyer 1987). The main reason for the growing estrangement between social Protestantism and its former pet project, social reform, was that social Protestantism lacked a genuine connection with the labor movement.

Protestant workers voted overwhelmingly for (and were members of) the Social Democratic Party (SPD), while most Catholic workers voted for the Center Party (Rohe 1992). Social Protestantism failed to mobilize workers and was therefore unable to profit from the Bismarckian welfare state and its social programs which were specifically targeted at the worker elite. Consequently, a social reform project, which had once been of utmost importance to the enlightened German Protestant bourgeoisie, now became one of the main targets of liberal critique against the system of Weimar (see Section 3.2).

As the Protestants were forced to acknowledge, the Bismarckian welfare state apparently now served the specific interests of the two former "enemies of the empire" and anti-Protestants, Social Democracy and political Catholicism. In the 1920s, the welfare state was at the heart of the latent or manifest coalition between the SPD and the Center Party, and it underpinned the tacit cooperation between organized capital and labor at the expense of the middle classes. The liberal Protestant camp increasingly felt that its own brainchild, social reform, had been seized by the socialist and Catholic labor movements and furthered their political and economic dominance. In Section 3.3, I will argue that the new economic doctrine of ordoliberalism, which was later to become influential in the debates over the design of postwar Germany's economic order, was a reaction of Protestant middle-class intellectuals to their perceived political, economic, and religious marginalization.[1] This new economic doctrine developed a vision of an economic order under the control of institutions that would protect the key

---

[1] Given that Tribe's reconstruction of ordoliberalism's doctrinal development does not start until 1937, he is bound to overlook this important early context (Tribe 1995).

characteristics of bourgeois society from the "ill winds" blowing from politics and the corporatist economy. In the second half of the 1920s, the German middle class began searching for institutional safeguards against the political and economic threats to the bourgeois order (Hacke 2018). Ordoliberalism should be understood as a part of this search. Within the scholarly literature on neoliberalism and on the resurrection of markets in the postwar period, however, the specific contribution of this German brand of economic thinking has been largely misunderstood (e.g. Blyth 2015).

Yet, as I will argue in this chapter, the Protestant camp's attack of the welfare state it had once so enthusiastically endorsed should not be interpreted as a general retreat from its support for social reform. On the contrary, the pointed critique of the welfare state only led to a redefinition of the Protestant social reform project. In its new form, it emphasized the need to fundamentally restructure the economy so as to secure social harmony, justice, and national integration *without* having to rely on the redistributive apparatus of the welfare state with its many points of access for interest groups and associations (of predominantly socialist and Catholic leaning). As the Protestant social reformers now repeatedly stressed, a good economic policy is the best social policy. Liberals now called for a fundamental restructuring of the economy, which would make any redistribution of wealth through welfare state programs superfluous. In order to establish an economic order that would "automatically" secure the welfare of all citizens and guarantee an equal distribution of wealth, they were willing to profoundly intervene in the market.

Ordoliberalism's ideas about the extent of state regulation of the economy and about the capacity to design an entire economic order according to abstract principles of justice and equality were anything but liberal. Ordoliberalism's highly skeptical view on pluralist interest intermediation and partisan politics led this group of economists to conceive a social and economic order in which neither interest group pluralism nor party competition would play a decisive role.

In its desperation during the late 1920s, the Protestant bourgeoisie had increasingly opted for an authoritarian regime as a way out of its political and economic marginalization. Ordoliberalism shared this leaning. In 1945, after the catastrophic failure of the authoritarian option, the liberal Protestant camp finally sought a compromise with political Catholicism, while many of the antiliberal traits of ordoliberalism remained influential also for its postwar concepts (Burgin 2012; Tribe 1995). However, *Modell Deutschland* did not represent a compromise deliberately struck between Protestant liberalism and Catholic social doctrine. Instead, it ultimately, albeit unintentionally, combined a reconstructed welfare state and a corporatist economic order with a federal state which lacked the capacity for actively steering the economy. The reconstructed welfare state allowed organized capital and labor to fill the space that the central state had been forced to vacate, particularly since it provided capital and labor with the corporatist infrastructure to successfully do so (see Chapter 4).

## 3.1 The Bismarckian Welfare State and the Antiliberal Shift in German Politics

The German welfare state is often said to have shown an extraordinary institutional stability, surviving—with its basic institutional features almost unchanged—four different political regimes, two world wars, the hyperinflation of 1923/24, the Great Depression of 1928–32, the post-World War II crisis, and German unification in 1990. It is important to note that the basis for this surprisingly stable institutional structure was laid in rather antiliberal times (Stolleis 1979) in the context of the repressive measures against the Social Democratic Party (Socialist Law of 1878), of a pronounced protectionist turn in trade policy (*Schutzzoll*), of the forceful state-led modernization of the German economy, and of the victory of a conservative over liberal orientation in the Prussian bureaucracy after 1880 (Lehmbruch 1997; Nipperdey 1993).

Bismarckian social legislation was paternalistic, centralist, etatist, and interventionist—extremely so in its initial conception, and still significantly so even after the process of political compromise had watered down some of its most radical elements and had combined antiliberal state interventionism with older layers of self-governance and traditions of corporatist self-regulation. The new welfare entitlements, which were supposed to turn German workers into loyal citizens, were based on occupational status and were not universal benefits. The element of choice was almost totally absent from the new social schemes. Workers and firms were forced into the new administrative structure of the accident and health insurance programs. The insurance schemes had the status of bodies of public law (*Körperschaften öffentlichen Rechts*). They subsequently crowded out many forms of workers' collective self-help or employers' welfare schemes. For those voluntary schemes that were integrated into the new welfare state, such as company health insurance or the free, i.e. voluntary funds (*freie Hilfskassen*), character and legal status were profoundly altered. Insurance became mandatory and state regulation was tight. The administration of the welfare scheme was run either by civil servants (old-age insurance), by employers alone (accident insurance), or by both workers/unions and employers (health insurance, where workers held a 2:1 majority).

The element of workers' and employers' self-governance in the social insurance system paved the way toward incorporating the organized interest groups of labor and capital into the (welfare) state's administrative structure. It provided unions and employers' associations with important organizational resources (Heidenheimer 1980; Manow 1997a, 2001a; Steinmetz 1991, 1993; Tennstedt 1983; see Chapter 2) and thereby laid the foundation of Germany's coordinated capitalism. Consequently, the Bismarckian welfare state turned into a central, if not *the* central element in what Werner Abelshauser has described as a "modern system of corporatist interest intermediation" (Abelshauser 1984a: 287). Peculiar to the German response to the "social question" was that the state began to "share public space" (Colin Crouch) with organized societal interests and used "functional organizations as co-opted agents of order" (Crouch 1986: 189; Maier 1975, 1987; Offe 1981). These forms of market regulation and interest intermediation represented a particularly efficient mode of social organization and a particularly flexible way of regulating modern capitalism. Bismarckian social legislation in particular marked the birth of many "historically durable 'modern' elements in German economic policy" (Abelshauser 1984a: 289). In this sense Germany was the first nation to formulate a "post-liberal" response to the social problems caused by modern "unfettered" capitalism.

Being targeted primarily at workers and allowing for the participation of workers' organizations in the administration of the social insurance schemes, the Bismarckian welfare state proved to be especially favorable for the main two political movements that organized the working class: Social Democracy and the Free Unions, on the one hand, and the Center Party and the Catholic worker movement, on the other (Brose 1985; Hiepel 1997; Loth 1997; for the electoral fates of the SPD, the Center, and the liberal parties see Rohe 1992; Schneider 1982). After World War I, the Catholic Center Party and the SPD largely dominated the political agenda of Germany's first republic, albeit soon challenged by radical anti-system parties at either end of the political spectrum. Social and Christian Democrats were the two most prominent and influential members of the Weimar coalition, i.e. the parties that were loyal to the new constitution and republic. And in no other context did we see the two parties, the Center Party and SPD, agree more frequently and easily than on questions of social policy. Heinrich Brauns, a Catholic priest and member of the Center Party, served as minister of the Reich Labor Ministry (*Reichsarbeitsministerium*, RAM) from 1920 to 1928, representing an extraordinary instance of continuity and stability within an environment of extreme political volatility (Sachße and Tennstedt 1988: 84, 169).[2] As a result, the Labor Ministry was able to follow a relatively coherent political strategy, formulated by a ministerial bureaucracy with a strong Catholic leaning. The ministry generally favored a further extension of the welfare state, a position also prevalent in the Center Party. This pro-welfare stance was based on Catholic social doctrine, but also responded to three more pressing and immediate political considerations: first, the wish to support a large number of Catholic charitable organizations, hospitals, asylums, and of course the Christian unions; second, the need to please Catholic workers as voters (or members) of the Center Party; and third, simply the ministry's interest in protecting and possibly expanding its sphere of administrative responsibility. Christian unions in particular had

---

[2] The average length of a cabinet's term of office in the Weimar Republic was slightly less than ten months: interwar Germany experienced seventeen cabinets in the fourteen years between 1919 and 1933.

corresponding interests, since they hoped that their integration into the corporatist, para-public welfare complex would protect them from being "majoritized" by the socialist unions (Rabenschlag-Kräusslich 1983).

With the worsening depression and the growing paralysis of the political system and of industrial relations at the end of the 1920s, the Labor Ministry took an increasingly interventionist position. This is most apparent in the RAM's switch from "voluntary" to "mandatory arbitration" in industrial conflicts in the late 1920s (Bähr 1989). This switch expressed the RAM's growing distrust of and impatience with the organized interests of labor and capital and it revealed that the RAM bureaucrats had lost confidence in the political parties' ability to enact the austerity measures that were—in the bureaucrats' view—urgently needed to overcome Germany's fundamental economic crisis. Finally, the ministry embarked on a strict austerity course facilitated by emergency decrees under the "presidential cabinets" of Brüning and von Papen. Not only was the RAM's strategy of "conservative stabilization" (Geyer 1991) without the consent of the parliamentary majority, it was even pursued against the expressed will of the parliament. The senior civil servants increasingly came to share the view of conservative critics and of German employers who blamed an irresponsible and "unbridled parliamentarism" and the Weimar particracy (*Parteienstaat*) for the grave crisis of the republic and the German economy (Geyer 1991). In these accounts, German industry was portrayed as being overburdened with social costs imposed on it by irresponsible politicians who attempted to outdo each other in handing out excessively generous welfare benefits. The conservative attack on Weimar thus became a dual attack on both the political system of the Weimar Republic and the German welfare state. It is no coincidence that the last cabinet of the Weimar Republic to be legitimized by parliament fell in 1930 over the decision to raise contributions to the unemployment insurance fund.

## 3.2 The Marginalized Protestant Camp

While the social insurance schemes helped to integrate the Catholic and Social Democratic camps into the Reich and then into the Weimar Republic, a reverse development can be observed with respect to the liberal Protestant camp. Among liberals the feeling of being politically marginalized became widespread in the 1920s. In part this was because class cleavage and religious cleavage reinforced one another: workers either voted for the SPD or, if they were Catholics, for the Center Party. Bismarckian social legislation, which was primarily targeted at the (skilled) workers, thus seemed to have both a clear anti-middle class *and* a distinct anti-Protestant bias. This holds especially true with respect to the accessibility and "permeability" of the welfare state for organized interests. The Protestant social reform movement did not benefit from the corporatist structure of the

Bismarckian welfare state since social Protestantism had failed to organize work-ers, the primary target group of the benefit and entitlement structure of the German social insurance system. Due to the lack of workers' political support, the social reform clubs of the Protestant church (*Protestantenvereine*) remained without strong political allies. They were more heterogeneous than the Catholic reform movement, both in regional and in socio-economic terms, and less cen-tralized and more programmatically polarized between Protestant orthodoxy and liberalism (Kaiser 1997; Pollmann 1997). Protestant social doctrine remained abstract and diffuse. Protestants perceived social reform as something that should be proposed by German professors and enacted by an enlightened state bureau-cracy (Nowak 1997). It should certainly not be the object and outcome of pluralist interest politics.

While Protestants could easily identify with the Prussian or German *state*, they were, at the same time, eager to keep *politics* at a distance, as Weimar politics did not have much to offer the Protestant bourgeois milieu, anyway. Protestants emphasized the clear separation between religion and politics, and it is not entirely clear how much this was a "sour grapes" effect: "Any political agitation, even with the best intentions, contradicts the spirit of the *Evangelium*" (quoted in Kaiser 1996: 276). "Those, who think that the church has any social obligation beyond sermons and care for the salvation to the soul (*Seelsorge*) are following a Roman aberration (*römischer Irrweg*)" (quoted in Schneider 1982: 38). As a consequence, German social Protestantism developed a purely practical role and abstained from any social reform activities that went beyond pure charity. Social Protestantism lacked programmatic profile and political influence and exerted no influence on the course of Weimar's social policy (Preller 1978; Reulecke 1996: 63–5; Sachße and Tennstedt 1988). Only in the field of social assistance was social Protestantism able to identify a genuine sphere of responsibility which was compatible with its religious calling. However, social assistance was clearly of marginal importance in the Bismarckian welfare state, which put so much emphasis on social insurance. Moreover, the economic crisis of 1928–32 increasingly shifted the burden onto this "last line" of social support for the poor and needy, resulting in enormous financial pressure on German cities and localities, but also on the charitable organizations such as the Protestant *Innere Mission*, the Socialist *Arbeiterwohlfahrt*, or the Catholic *Caritas*. These denominational organizations were unable to agree on a common political strategy to counter the policy of externalizing welfare costs that the federal state pursued to cope with the crisis (Hong 1998). This only heightened the sense of disaster in the Protestant camp and its longing for an authoritarian way out of Weimar's political and economic morass.

While Protestant social reform had had considerable resonance among con-temporaries before World War I (vom Bruch 1985: 105), the political influence of the Evangelical Social Congress as well of the respected *Verein für Socialpolitik* faded during the Weimar Republic, and the organizational position of the Protestant social reform clubs remained rather weak (Kaufmann 1988: 80; Kersbergen 1995: 255).[3]

Protestant social reform retained a paternalist character. In its liberal variant it was understood to be part of a broader cultural policy (*Kulturpolitik*), which was intended to foster the German *Kulturnation* by educating the workers (Nowak 1997). Religious ambitions, a missionary zeal, and the goal of morally rejuvenating the nation overshadowed the desire to introduce pragmatic improvements in workers' everyday lives. Moreover, as early as 1895, many social reformers believed that the most pressing social problems had already been addressed by the new Bismarckian social insurance system and that the growing national wealth, resulting from Germany's vigorous process of industrialization,

---

[3] Compare this to the Catholic *Volksverein* (literally: association of the people). This association, founded in 1890, became the backbone of political Catholicism and exerted a profound modernizing impact on the Catholic camp. The *Volksverein* experienced a surge in membership and an increase in political influence *after* it had begun to devote all of its efforts to social reform (Loth 1997). Membership increased from about 100,000 members in 1890 to more than 800,000 members in 1914. This was only 20 percent less than the Social Democratic Party's approximately one million members in 1914 (Loth 1997: 151). *Volksverein* members, particularly in the Ruhr area, were predominantly workers, who were mostly also members of the Christian unions. The most important support base of the *Volksverein* was in the industrial centers of Rhineland and Westphalia. In 1914, when membership in the association reached its peak, the provinces of Rhineland and Westphalia alone accounted for more than 50 percent of the members (approximately 410,800 people). The majority of these were workers and two-thirds of the functionaries in these two provinces were also workers (Müller 1996: 103ff.). This indicates that the connection between the *Volksverein* and the Christian unions was indeed very close in the Ruhr area (Müller 1996; Schneider 1982). Because of both the significant overlap in membership and programmatic similarities, it can indeed be said that by 1900 "the *Volksverein* had become de facto part of the Catholic labor movement" (Loth 1997: 152). The *Volksverein* evolved into a counseling body, training workers in questions pertaining to the social insurance schemes. Its main aim was to train the functionaries of the Christian unions (Müller 1996: 85). The elite of the Center Party and politicians such as Stegerwald, Imbusch, and Brauns were all products of the Christian unions and had begun their careers in the *Volksverein*. Moreover, since the majority of Catholic workers were located in the Ruhr area where coal mining was the most important industry, the Catholic unions were able to use the miners' social insurance scheme, the *Knappschaften*, as their organizational support structure. In this respect it is important to note that, as health funds, the miners' social insurance scheme had an "extremely democratic constitution" (Geyer 1992: 1050). As long ago as the early 1890s, workers were allowed to elect their representatives in the self-governance of the miners' insurance funds by secret ballot. The extent to which the former Catholic enemy of the Reich was already politically and socially integrated into German society became clear in 1910 when the German state intervened in Rome to prevent the pope from banning the German mixed denomination Christian unions in the Encyclical *singulari quadam* of 1912 (Schneider 1982: 196, 201). Prior to this, the state had already indicated its support for the Christian unions in the hope that they would act as a counterweight to the influence of the socialist unions and social democracy. Finally, as workers increasingly began to abandon the Center Party and the Christian unions out of disappointment with the party's position on the reform of the Prussian plutocratic electoral system and with the church's continuing support for employer-friendly Catholic unions (what were known as integration-alist unions), World War I came to the rescue of the Catholic labor movement. The auxiliary service law (*Hilfsdienstgesetz*) lent new economic and political importance to the Christian unions by integrating them into the war economy and by effectively excluding what were known as "yellow" unions, as well as the employer-friendly integrationalist Catholic unions, from the emerging corporatist complex (Feldman 1992 [1966]; Patch 1985: 25). Yellow, employer-friendly unions had grown rapidly between 1907 and 1913, increasing their membership from 59,007 (1907) to 121,126 members (1910) to 273,725 in 1913 (Schneider 1982: 267; cf. Patch 1985: 21).

significantly reduced the need for further welfare state growth (Nowak 1997). And because Lutheran Protestantism appeared to be so closely linked to the Wilhelmine authorities, workers remained highly suspicious. This among others prevented social Protestantism from becoming anchored in the labor movement (Blackbourn 1997: 294 and 301).

However, although Protestants might not have been key actors in the development of the German welfare state after 1895, it is inaccurate to assume that they were of no importance for the further institutional trajectory of the Bismarckian welfare state. This becomes clear when we take account of the ever stronger critique of the Protestant camp vis-à-vis the Weimar welfare state. The liberal Protestants became increasingly critical of further welfare reforms and of social policy in general. For them, the key rationale for the state's social intervention had been lost with the abdication of the old regime. They could not pin their hopes on a political system that had apparently escaped the control of the old elite and had fallen into the hands of organized capital and labor and of Social Democracy and political Catholicism, respectively. The Great Inflation of 1921–1923/24, in which unions and big industry fought their inflationary "war of attrition" (Eichengreen 1992: 142) at the expense of German middle-class interests while the state stood idly by, happy to be rid of its massive war loan debts in such a painless way, further infuriated the German middle classes (Childers 1985; Jones 1985) as the "the biggest losers in the inflation" (Widdig 1994: 12).

For liberal thinkers in the late 1920s, the welfare state turned from a lost cause into a prime cause of crisis. It was no longer perceived as being a necessary remedy against capitalism's structural deficiencies and an urgently needed response to the moral problems posed by the "labor question." The liberals believed that social policy had escaped the control of the "scientific, well-educated bureaucracy situated above all class interests and party positions" and had fallen into the hands of "the big economic interest associations ... the political parties and the party- and interest-controlled press" (Herkner 1922, quoted in Janssen 1998: 213–26). Protestant social reformers, who from the outset had felt it was their task to fight a "war on two fronts" (Pollmann 1997) against Social Democracy *and* Catholic ultramontanism, increasingly came to believe that they had lost this war.

The Great Inflation thus also represented a turning point in the liberal assessment of the social and political merits of state intervention in the name of national integration, military strength, and social welfare. Over time, the liberals had shifted from initially being supportive to being covertly critical and ultimately overtly opposed to the Bismarckian welfare state. Most revealing in this respect are the changes in the *Verein für Socialpolitik*: Once the center of the historical school of economics and of intellectual support for social reform (*Kathedersozialismus*), the association became the first source, outside the employers' camp, of vociferous objections to Weimar's course of social policy. Heinrich Herkner's speech on the occasion of the fiftieth anniversary of the *Verein für Socialpolitik* in 1922, which marked the beginning of an intense debate on Weimar's social policy crisis (Janssen 1998; Kaufmann 1999), and Alexander Rüstow's speech in front of the association ten years later, in which he expressed his hope that the state would put an end to Weimar's pluralism, clearly demonstrated the distance the liberals had traveled along the political spectrum within just a short period of time.

Thus for the liberals, the German welfare state appeared to have a clear political and religious bias, and this increasingly estranged the Protestant middle classes from the social reform project they had once so strongly endorsed. Ordoliberalism was a true manifestation of this estrangement.

## 3.3 Ordoliberalism's Antiliberalism

Ordoliberalism is generally understood to "have laid the intellectual foundations for the . . free market economy in mid-1948" and, since then, to have been "the quasi-official credo of West Germany's economic policy" (Giersch et al. 1992: 16) and of its social market economy (cf. Brunnermeier et al. 2016). Yet, ordoliberal doctrine originated from much earlier, as a response to the hyperinflation and the crisis of the late 1920s. Two key papers that to this day are generally viewed as the founding manifestos of this new school of economic thinking were written at the peak of the depression in 1932: Walter Eucken's "Staatliche Strukturwandlungen und die Krisis des Kapitalismus" (structural transformations of the state and the crisis of capitalism) and Alexander Rüstow's short and very pointed statement "Interessenpolitik oder Staatspolitik?" (interest politics or state politics?). A common thread running through both works—and other ordoliberal contributions from the same year (Müller-Armack 1932; Röpke 1962 [1932])—was the fundamental critique of the parliamentary system that resembled in many respects those formulated by thinkers of the radical right. Ordoliberalism was part of a "crisis literature" (Tanner 1987), which mushroomed in the late 1920s and early 1930s (Hacke 2018). The central message of the ordoliberal discourse was that the economic and social crisis that Germany was experiencing at the time resulted from a *political* crisis, from a crisis of the political and constitutional order of Weimar, not from a secular crisis of capitalism. For Eucken and Rüstow, the heart of the crisis was precisely the systematic interpenetration of the political and the economic systems (we would probably call this corporatism today) that had been inherited from the empire and expanded during the Weimar Republic. What might have been bearable, perhaps even desirable, under the old Wilhelmine regime—namely the organization of societal interests into broad and powerful organizations—now, under conditions of full democratization, purportedly became a threat to the economic and political order. What would be perceived as normal democratic practice today, for this milieu in the late 1920s and early 1930s was cause for alarm: "Democratic parties that organize the masses and the interest groups exert an increasing influence on the government and thus on economic policy." Moreover, these parties were to be held responsible for a growing "disorganization of the economy caused by the state" (Eucken 1932: 306, 315; see also Müller-Armack 1932: 113–17). Since political parties were closely linked to clearly delineated camps and socio-economic interests, mass democratization made the state receptive, if not totally enslaved, to these camps and interests. The state, or rather the political parties that run the state, became the instrument of economic interest groups (Eucken 1932: 307). State action then could only take place by way of horse-trading ("Prinzip des Kuhhandels" Rüstow 1959 [1929]: 91) between the parties to the mutual advantage of their clientele but to the detriment of the country's general welfare. In Rüstow's, Eucken's, or Müller-Armack's view, organized interests forced the modern "intervention state" to exclusively serve their particularistic needs. Yet the state, which begins to "feed the interest-group beast," will ultimately be "consumed by it" (Rüstow 1945: 83). The ordoliberal diagnosis—which was as vague as it was polemical— held the effects of pluralist mass politics within a segmented society responsible for the lamentable state in which the German economy and society found themselves. It is therefore erroneous to argue that for ordoliberals the misuse of "private, not public, power was the concern" (Blyth 2015: 135), since for them the former was achieved by seizing the latter.

For ordoliberals, the cure for this ill was obvious: government needed to regain "strength vis-à-vis sectional interests and to preserve its status as the impartial and incorruptible arbiter of the economic process in the face of short-term interventionist temptations by limiting its own scope to a few essential tasks" (Giersch et al. 1992: 29). Only a strong state would be able to acquire this autonomy, to stand "above all groups, above all interests" (Rüstow 1932;1986 [1932]: 69–70), exercising "authority and leadership," "strength and independence" (Rüstow 1932;1986 [1932]: 69–70). The state—as Walter Eucken put it—should "free itself from the influence of the masses" (Eucken 1932: 318). It was supposed to regain "full sovereignty over all particular interests in the economic sphere" (Müller-Armack 1932: 126). It is beyond dispute that the early foundation of German ordoliberalism revealed profound antiliberal inclinations (Abelshauser 1984b; Haselbach 1991; Herbst 1982; Krohn 1981: 173; Manow 2000, 2001c).

Under the moniker of a new or rabid liberalism, Eucken and Rüstow proposed to reestablish a strict boundary between state and society, to make the political system independent from any societal interests again, and to guarantee a new stable economic order through radical "liberal interventionism" (Rüstow 1986 [1932]: 67). This profound reorganization of society and the economy had to be implemented by a strong, in other words, fully independent, state. In his appeal for a strong state, Rüstow explicitly and positively refers to Carl Schmitt's notion of the "total state" (Rüstow 1986 [1932]: 68). Eucken also refers favorably to Schmitt's writings and employs his notion of the "total state" (Eucken 1932: 307

and 319; Hacke 2018). If the "old liberalism" of the nineteenth century essentially pursued a laissez-faire program calling for a clear separation of the *state* and the *economy* and for the state to abstain from any targeted interventions into the market, the "new liberalism," advocated by scholars such as Rüstow and Eucken, was one that wanted to separate the *state* (and its economic policies) from *parliamentarism* and *partisan politics* in order to ensure that state intervention into the economy would be reasonable, appropriate, and independent, and would serve the country's general welfare rather than particular interests. These thinkers did not believe the state should be assigned a residual or minimal role. Quite the contrary: in their view it was the role of modern mass politics that had to be minimized.

Thus, the ordoliberals' plea "to free the economy from the state," to de-state the economy (*Entstaatlichen der Wirtschaft*) was simultaneously a decidedly antidemocratic request. Hermann Heller was right to remark that the call for the state's retreat from economic affairs meant first and foremost that the state should retreat from its historically accumulated obligations in social policy (Heller 1933: 652). Again, it was the corporatist Bismarckian welfare state that was at the center of the attack on the system of Weimar. This was due to the fact that the welfare state was also at the core of the corporatist complex, as the institutional and regulatory framework in which German employers and unions pursued their interests—at the expense of middle-class interests, as we saw above.

To achieve a "healthy economy within a strong state," Rüstow and others tolerated authoritarian means. Eucken's 1932 article was nothing less than a total damnation of the system of Weimar. For Eucken, parliamentarism and particularism had become synonymous. His profound distaste for the "amorphous mass" was shared by Rüstow, Müller-Armack, and Röpke. Instead, Eucken favored a strictly elitist conception of political leadership. In his writings in the 1930s, Böhm repeatedly made his conviction explicit that a free market order could only be reinstalled through "authoritarian state steering" (Krohn 1981: 196; Nicholls 1990: 399; Nörr 1993). Among the ordoliberals, Rüstow was probably the most vociferous critic of the Weimar Republic (cf. Krohn 1981: 172; Haselbach 1991: 205; Meier-Rust 1993: 54–9). In order to fully understand the political implications of his pointed call for a state "above all groups and above all interests," we have to recall that these lines were written at a time when the right-wing von Papen government ruled without parliamentary support, backed only by Reichspräsident Hindenburg and tolerated—at least in the beginning—only by the Nazis and the other parties of the extreme right. It was an open secret that Rüstow sympathized with the von Papen government (cf. Haselbach 1991: 205). He even claimed to have contributed to its economic program (Meier-Rust 1993: 57–9). As early as 1929, Rüstow had contemplated the feasibility of a "dictatorship within the confines of democracy" (Rüstow 1959 [1929]), and the longer Germany's political and economic crisis endured, the less concerned he became about maintaining an overall democratic framework.

Many *mixta composita* (radical or rabid liberalism, new liberalism, liberal interventionism, conservative liberalism) were coined to characterize the strange beast that was clearly no longer liberal. These labels indicate that it had indeed become very difficult to draw a clear line between the camps of former liberal bourgeois and the authoritarian right. Evidently, authoritarianism pervaded the ideas of both conservative and formerly liberal thinkers.[4] It is therefore misguided to assert that the ordoliberal thinkers "were mostly associated with the remnants of left-liberalism in the early 1930s" (Nicholls 1990: 399; 1994). The antiliberalism of the ordoliberals remained strong even when their sympathy for an authoritarian solution to Germany's crisis faded in the late 1930s due to their shattering experience with the Nazi polycracy and its shortsighted economic interventionism. In 1942, Ludwig Erhard expressed a common belief among the ordoliberals when he laconically remarked: "The liberal principle has failed" (Hentschel 1996: 26). These thinkers had nothing but profound contempt for classical liberalism. Rüstow liked to ridicule its laissez-faire principle as "stone-age-" or "paleo-liberalism" (Rüstow 1960).

Perhaps Hermann Heller provided us with the best contemporary account of the character of what had been dubbed "new liberalism," in which he demonstrated that its demand for a strict division between economy and state could only be achieved through antidemocratic means. Heller claimed that what had been termed "radical liberalism" was ultimately synonymous with "authoritarian liberalism" (cf. Heller 1933). In the absence of any powerful political addressee responsive to their call for the construction of a liberal order, the ordoliberals had to seek redress from the state—if necessary, from an authoritarian state. Further, these illiberal leanings of the ordoliberal thinkers did not suddenly vanish after World War II. Closer examination shows that also for postwar ordoliberalism "Ordo [was] necessary and absolute, while Liberalism [was] only contingent and relative" (Nörr 1993: 13).

However, it was not only the severity of the economic, political, and social crisis of Weimar Germany that drove the liberals to the right. In order to acquire a better understanding of the origins of "ordoliberalism's antiliberalism" we need to look at the distinctive influence of Protestant thinking on German Protestant, middle-class *Bildungsbürger* such as the ordoliberals. As the next section will show, the vehement Protestant opposition to the corporatist complex of Weimar, particularly the Bismarckian welfare state, became a trait of ordoliberal discourse. This would regain its political clout in the post-World War II period, when decisions on the institutional design of West Germany's economic and political systems ranked high on the political agenda.

---

[4] See Krohn (1981), Haselbach (1991), Janssen (1998: 184–95). See also the largely hagiographic account by Meier-Rust (1993).

## 3.4 The Bipolar Character of Germany's Postwar Economic Order

In 1950, Alfred Müller-Armack, a leading figure in the translation of ordoliberal dogma into practical politics, proposed a new "social peace" (*soziale Irenik*) and explicitly referred to the Westphalian peace. He expressed his hope that the post-World War II era would become, very much like the second half of the seventeenth century, an "era of reconciliation," confidence, and harmony between opposing worldviews, this time not only between Protestantism and Catholicism, but also between liberalism and socialism (Müller-Armack 1950: 559–60). Particularly if the two Christian denominations could reach agreement on the key question of how modern capitalism should and could be embedded in a wider moral order (in other words, an agreement on how to correct intolerable market outcomes through welfare state intervention and economic policy), this would then ultimately also help socialist critics of the capitalist market economy to make their peace with the principles of the free market and private property. Müller-Armack's concept of social peace thus was essentially a proposal for an ecumenical social policy that would ultimately also reconcile the two major secular political ideologies—socialism and liberalism (cf. Rüstow 1960).[5]

The idea of a "third way" between capitalism and communism was at the heart of Müller-Armack's concept, and the two major Christian denominations were to take the lead in guiding the country along this third path—the idea of a social market economy was thus ultimately cast in theological terms. Accordingly, the reference to the Catholic ordo concept by scholars such as Röpke, Eucken, and Müller-Armack was a very deliberate attempt to build a bridge with Catholic social doctrine. This was clearly expressed in Müller-Armack's hope that the concept would indeed provide the "common fundament of a *Christian* social doctrine" (Müller-Armack 1950: 562; author's emphasis). This description, however, more obfuscated than clarified the concept's character, since ordoliberalism, as we saw earlier, was neither particularly liberal, nor had Catholic social doctrine been an important source of inspiration.[6] Consequently, the ordoliberals suffered massive disappointment when the reconstruction of the Bismarckian welfare state in the 1950s signaled that their vision of a social policy already embodied, already installed in the economic order was not going to be realized. Yet, given that

---

[5] The postwar conclusion that the contemporary crisis signified "our century without God" (Langner 1998: 518–48; Müller-Armack 1948) was of course now primarily directed against the "new" postwar danger of communism.

[6] Partly influenced by the German "historic school" of economic thinking, the concept of order within ordoliberalism was also very similar to the Protestant notion of "orders of creation" (*Schöpfungsordnungen*) particularly as formulated by Paul Althaus in the late 1920s and early 1930s (Althaus 1931, 1934).

Müller-Armack's irenic dream of spiritual unity had remained essentially Protestant in character, its political failure was ultimately no great surprise.

The ordoliberals' efforts to reach an ecumenical agreement on how to embed modern capitalism in society's system of morals, i.e. how to secure social peace within the framework of a liberal market order, was fueled, first and foremost, by their disappointment about the authoritarian solution of the 1930s. Ordoliberals had quite quickly turned away in disgust from the National Socialist regime and its economic policy. Its erratic interventionism, the many failed attempts at coordination within the Third Reich's polycracy, and the "complete fiasco of the National Socialist war economy" (Röpke 1942 quoted in Janssen 1998: 193; cf. Herbst 1982) were clearly not what the ordoliberals had in mind when they had called for a "strong state above all groups and all interests." Further, the new order had rapidly shattered the hopes of the German middle classes (*Mittelstand*), which in late Weimar had sought state protection from big industry, unions, and the agrarian interest lobby (Herrigel 1996: 139–42; Winkler 1991). Böhm, Rüstow, Eucken, and others had advocated small business interests since the 1920s.[7]

In this situation, what Röpke, Müller-Armack, Rüstow, and others were planning—according to their own accounts—was to develop a *Protestant* social doctrine that could confront its better established and dogma-based Catholic counterpart more effectively. Their attempt was not particularly well received, however. Röpke himself complained that Catholic critics regularly mistook him for a liberal. Confronted with unfavorable coverage of his writings in the Catholic press, Röpke lamented in a letter to a friend: "Now these people have found a truly willing Protestant, whose honest efforts are directed toward a 'Christian social doctrine' and they should be happy and grateful to have such a brother-in-arms (*Bundesgenossen*)" (Röpke 1976: 141).

Ultimately, German Catholics remained unconvinced that the ordoliberal market order would secure both growth and social justice and thus represent an acceptable compromise between capitalist efficiency and social equality. And rebuilding a partially modernized welfare state along the old corporatist lines also proved to be the more successful strategy in electoral terms (Hockerts 1980). The ordoliberal vision was anything but appealing to the "(predominantly) Catholic" Christian Democrat electorate (contra Blyth 2015: 139), whereas the reconstruction of the welfare state, in turn, was utterly abhorrent to the ordoliberals. Disappointed, they took an increasingly aggressive stance toward the social legislation of the second Adenauer cabinet (Abelshauser 1997). Since the ordoliberal proposals on how to reconcile modern capitalism with Christian ethics did not meet with as much support as would have been required to become the

---

[7] Yet, it is probably fair to say that for most ordoliberals the decisive factor turning them against the regime had again been religious rather than economic: the anti-Semitic pogroms in November 1938 turned the university professors and members of the Confessional Church (*Bekennende Kirche*), who later became known as the *Freiburger Kreis*, into opponents of the regime.

ecumenical base of Germany's postwar order (as Röpke and others had hoped), ordoliberals became vigorously opposed to the reconstruction of the Bismarckian welfare state in the 1950s. In their view, this step meant that German politics had, once again, plunged onto the slippery slope of pluralist interest politics, which had already resulted in Germany's political, economic, and moral ruin once before (Röpke 1956; Rüstow 1956).

Given their distaste for long-term, corporatist cooperation between economic agents, it is not surprising that the ordoliberals were among the most forceful opponents of the reconstruction and reform of the Bismarckian welfare state that was implemented in the 1950s. For them, such reforms, particularly the pension reform of 1957, meant that Germany was, once again, on the path to serfdom and "collectivism" (Röpke 1956). Very much in line with the distaste for pluralism he had revealed previously, Alexander Rüstow, in the debate over Adenauer's pension reform, now warned that this reform could mark nothing less than the beginning of the end of political and economic freedom since the establishment of the "total welfare state" would inevitably lead straight again into the totalitarian state (Rüstow 1956: 9). Still in 1945, Alexander Rüstow knew who or what was to blame for the catastrophe that had befallen Europe in the form of totalitarianism and fascism: "pluralism" to which "Italy, Germany, and France had fallen prey" (Rüstow 1945: 82–3). Once again, it became clear that, even after World War II and the Nazi regime, "pluralist democracy…remained alien to ordoliberalism" (Nörr 1993: 174).

The fierce opposition to Adenauer's pension plans also reflected the disappointment of the ordoliberals that their proposals for a common Christian foundation of a social market order remained largely without resonance. However, with this opposing stance, Minister of Economics, Ludwig Erhard, and his academic combatants Böhm, Rüstow, and Röpke among others were completely defeated in the battle against the reconstruction of the Bismarckian welfare state. This was due, at least in part, to the inadequacy of their own alternative concept, which mainly held that a flourishing economy is all that was needed in terms of social policy in a modern market economy. For Ludwig Erhard, the word "social" in *soziale Marktwirtschaft* simply meant that "the consumer [is allowed] to benefit from economic progress, from the results of increased efforts and increased productivity" (Erhard 1958, quoted in Djelic 1998: 173). When the naïve hope that the ordoliberals had placed in a "de-proletarization through the diffusion of property" (Röpke 1962 [1932]: 113) failed to materialize, and instead, a significant rise in income inequality and poverty among the elderly occurred as soon as economic growth accelerated, the ordoliberals were left without any convincing economic and political alternative (cf. Abelshauser 1997; Hentschel 1996: 259–71; Hockerts 1980).[8]

---

[8] The sharply increasing income inequality in the second half of the 1950s was, to a considerable degree, itself the consequence of the ordoliberal policy of supporting capital formation through generous tax exemptions in the first half of the 1950s (Adamsen 1981: 45–55, in particular 51).

Given their evident failure in the controversy over the reconstruction of the Bismarckian welfare state, the ordoliberals' influence on the design of Germany's postwar political economy seems to have "been exaggerated" (Glasman 1996: xii). There is not much evidence that justifies qualifying ordoliberalism as the blueprint or even the "instruction sheet" (Blyth 2015: 138) for Germany's postwar economic order. The notion of a social market economy was only an *ex post* label for the rather unintended combination of the Bismarckian welfare state and a central state unable to engage actively with the economy. At the national level ordoliberal doctrine contributed very little to the new institutional setup. It seems much more justified to state that the "ordoliberal political project had failed dramatically" (Wigger 2017: 172)—and that pertains largely both to postwar reconstruction and then a little later to early European integration. But what exactly were the elements of this postwar order?

The Federal Republic's political system was a system with many veto points, the West German state only a "semi-sovereign" state (Katzenstein 1987; Schmidt 1990b), comprising an independent central bank (the Bundesbank), a powerful constitutional court, an influential second chamber through which the *Länder* enjoyed a decisive role in nearly all matters of political importance, the federalist fragmentation of the public purse, and the autonomy of unions and employers' associations in industrial relations. At the same time, however, the restoration of the German welfare state along traditional corporatist lines ensured that the market order would function through the organized interests of capital and labor, offering them multiple opportunities for long-term coordination.

It is no coincidence that the key laws establishing the fundamentals of Germany's postwar economic order (the cartel law and the central bank law, for instance) were enacted in the very same year as the major pension reform of 1957. It was this reform which reinstituted the basic principles of the Bismarckian welfare state such as parity of representation for organized capital and labor in the administration of the insurance scheme, the concentration of benefits on the core workforce, and the reinstatement or even reinforcement of the emphasis on status preservation (Hockerts 1980). Furthermore, important decisions made at an early juncture, in anticipation of the character of the postwar equilibrium, such as the decree on price controls and the currency reform, as well as early social legislation, such as the Social Insurance Schemes Adjustment Law (*Sozialversicherungsanpassungsgesetz*), were also enacted simultaneously in 1948/49 before the German parliament had first assembled (cf. Giersch et al. 1992; Hockerts 1980). The simultaneous establishment of a new economic order and of the corporatist German welfare state reflects the "bipolarity" of the postwar settlement (Nörr 1998: 376). This bipolarity was encapsulated by, on the one hand, the notion of an "economic constitution" (*Wirtschaftsverfassung*) that can be traced back to Franz Böhm's 1933 seminal contribution to ordoliberalism and that depicted the economic order as one imposed and maintained by the state, and on the other hand, by the concept of an economic constitution that was perceived as being primarily contracted between the social partners and referred to older concepts of "economic democracy" (*Wirtschaftsdemokratie*) developed by prominent Weimar Social Democrats such as Sinzheimer or Naphtali. This latter notion was also more akin to Catholic ideas of the semi-autonomous role of intermediate institutions regulating their own affairs (under state supervision) as envisaged in the Catholic principle of subsidiarity. While the Bismarckian welfare state provided the social partners with the organizational framework, the political legitimacy, and the material resources needed to breathe life into the notion of a corporatistically *contracted economic order*, the cartel and central bank laws adhered to the concept of an economic order protected by the state. In this setting, however, the state was understood as being sheltered from politics. Hence, the "twilight of sovereignty" (Maier 1975: 9) that emerged in postwar Germany, was created by the shadows cast by both corporatist industrial self-governance and autonomous bureaucratic rule.

The German postwar settlement therefore essentially embodied a compromise, but not one deliberately struck between the contending camps, but rather one resulting from ordoliberalism's failure to garner enough political support for its "ecumenical" social market economy concept. Chapter 4 examines how capital and labor managed to cooperate within this institutional order and, in particular, how, with the help of the welfare state, they succeeded in establishing an elaborate and dynamic system of wage coordination.

# 4

# Work and Welfare as Strategic Complements in Germany's Postwar Economic Order

How does the analysis outlined in the preceding chapters contribute to our understanding of the functioning of the German model in the postwar period? How exactly did coordinated collective bargaining without state interference (*Tarifautonomie*) and the reconstruction of the Bismarckian corporatist welfare state combine to create a new equilibrium known as *Modell Deutschland*? Why was it that the German political economy appeared to become so much more liberal after World War II?

In order to answer these questions, the following sections will mainly focus on the welfare state's contribution to the stability and efficiency of the postwar equilibrium. With a view to analyzing the pivotal role of the welfare state in the functioning of *Modell Deutschland*, I first provide a brief overview of general arguments linking the welfare state to the emergence and subsequently stability of a coordinated system of wage bargaining (see Section 4.1). Section 4.2 then primarily focuses on the welfare state's crucial contribution to the emergence and stability of Germany's typical system of pattern wage bargaining. I argue that coordinated wage setting was essential to fully exploit Germany's economic growth potential (catch-up) after the war (Eichengreen 1996b, 1996a). Yet wage coordination was not a self-enforcing arrangement. The welfare state provided indispensable support, thus making an essential contribution to the efficiency of the domestic postwar compromise. However, as will become clear in the following sections, the explanation provided in this chapter differs from the traditional, corporatist argument, which assumes that wage moderation by unions is traded against welfare state expansion as a part of a "generalized political exchange" between the labor movement and the (most frequently Social Democratic) government (Cameron 1984; Garrett and Lange 1996; Goldthorpe 1984; Lange 1984). Instead I argue that in the absence of direct state involvement in industrial relations, and in the absence of any capacity for proactive macroeconomic steering, corporatist cooperation was stabilized by indirect means: the welfare state helped to lower the costs of wage coordination (and hence wage moderation) for both unions and employers (Iversen 2000; Swenson 1999, 2002). For the unions the welfare state primarily helped overcome problems of intergenerational fairness

*Social Protection, Capitalist Production: The Bismarckian Welfare State in the German Political Economy, 1880–2015.*
Philip Manow, Oxford University Press (2020). © Philip Manow.
DOI: 10.1093/oso/9780198842538.001.0001

between different cohorts of workers and also ensured that sectoral real wage restraint would benefit the individual worker in the long run even if an economic downturn were to force him or her into unemployment or into early exit from the labor force (given that the German government was neither in a position nor willing to guarantee full employment).[1] For employers the welfare state primarily lowered incentives for leaving the "solidaristic" wage-setting regime and provided a tap on wage drift. Of course, since employers had a strong interest in unions' wage moderation, they were also attracted to anything that would help unions to exert this moderation. Hence, many arguments explaining why the welfare state helped unions to avoid the dangers of wage militancy also explain why employers developed an interest in the welfare state. This rationale can then also clarify why German unions and employers continued to adhere to a social protection system for so long that had become increasingly costly for them (Swenson 1999; Thelen 2000); see Chapter 5).

## 4.1  Business Coordination, Collective Wage Bargaining, and the Welfare State

As is the case with the CPE literature more generally (see Chapter 1), contributions to the more specialized wage-bargaining literature also tend to follow a dualist worldview, juxtaposing a (social democratic Scandinavian) centralized and coordinated equilibrium with a (liberal US American) decentralized and uncoordinated one. Again, the German model, neither centralized nor decentralized, seems inadequately captured by either account.

The functioning logic of these two ideal-typical equilibria can be described in a stylized manner as follows: a decentralized system is the simplest to analyze since it essentially follows standard economic assumptions. Here, the market rules supreme. Each productivity gain will directly translate into wage hikes at the company level. Wages fully reflect productivity, they vary between companies, and wage moderation is imposed via the market, since wage hikes in excess of productivity would quickly price a firm out of the market. The functioning logic of a centralized wage-bargaining system is more complex and not fully self-sustaining, but rather dependent on institutional support. The centralization of wage bargaining leads to wage compression which loosens the link between

---

[1] "Strategic wage restraint may become possible not only when wage bargaining is coordinated, but also when employees are institutionally protected against dismissals and when employers grant codetermination rights to employees. Both features should provide employees with a long-term perspective inside the firm and should therefore encourage forms of strategic cooperation that pay off only in the medium run" (Höpner and Lutter 2014). If, however, employment protection cannot completely rule out the possibility of becoming unemployed, social protection has to secure a high replacement rate.

productivity and remuneration. This then has distinctive redistributive consequences. With compressed wages, the larger and most productive[2] companies pay
below-equilibrium wages and thus enjoy a competitive advantage. For them,
wages are set below the level that would have been established in a decentralized
setting (Moene and Wallerstein 1995). Low-productivity firms, however, are
forced to pay above-equilibrium wages and are consequently often priced out of
the market or forced to invest in order to improve productivity.

If (productive) labor is underpriced, the demand for it increases and it becomes
scarce. At the same time, due to wage compression, the demand for low-skilled or
low-productivity labor decreases. This is something that can be offset by a large
public sector and/or the permanent up-skilling of the workforce (Iversen and
Wren 1998; Wren 2013; Wren et al. 2013). Under conditions of labor scarcity for
productive labor, larger and highly productive firms, able and willing to pay
higher wages, are constantly tempted to surpass centrally set wages, thus producing wage drift (thereby undermining the beneficial effects of wage coordination
and subsequently of wage compression). If this drift comes in the form of fringe
benefits, generous industry-wide welfare programs set up by the state can discipline employers and therefore help stabilize a centralized wage-bargaining system,
which would otherwise be eroded by the evasion strategies of individual employers. This is the reason why employers' associations, which are usually dominated
by the very same (large) companies that profit most from coordinated wage
bargaining, often prove to be, at least tacitly, supportive of welfare state expansion
(for a critical account, see Korpi 2006). This is particularly the case if entitlements
benefit workers, blue- or white-collar, and are introduced during boom periods
when labor scarcity becomes a particularly pressing problem. The employers who
benefit from centralized wage bargaining "acquire interests in policy designed to
protect them against the results of disequilibrium" created by wage centralization
itself (Swenson 1999: 10).

This wage coordination scenario has specific consequences for firms competing
on world markets and thereby also for the link between the exposed and sheltered
sectors of the economy. An economy's export sector is confronted with the risk
that firms in the sheltered sector will give in too easily to workers' aggressive wage
demands since these sheltered firms more easily can pass wage costs on to
consumers through high prices. Exposed firms then would face both the negative
impact of high prices for input factors on the prices of their products and the
adverse effects on the national wage level exerted by aggressive unions in the
sheltered sector. Once again, wage centralization (or, as we will see, also "pattern
wage bargaining," where the exposed industries take the lead in wage setting),

---

[2] Given that big firms within a decentralized setting would be forced to engage in "rent sharing" by
their workforce (Katz and Summers 1989), in particular if union membership is positively correlated
with firm size. See on the "local pushfulness" of decentralized wage bargaining also Soskice (1990b).

provides solutions for this potential conflict. And welfare state expansion and/or accommodating monetary policies may help to solve the problems which successful wage coordination then produces.[3]

In a decentralized system, employers develop quite different interests in terms of the welfare state. In a decentralized, non-coordinated setting, companies with production technology demanding a high level of skills and thus low labor turnover pay "above-equilibrium" (efficiency) wages. In their bid to stabilize a core workforce, employers offer better pay, more job security, and more generous company-based social benefits than the average firm. In this way, they create dualistic wage dispersion and contribute to the emergence of a segmented industrial structure with a small number of (large) "high-commitment" firms and a large number of (small) "low-commitment" firms. Efficiency wages and welfare capitalist benefit schemes, however, are placed under pressure during a recession, when low-wage, low-benefit firms with no commitment to their workforce start to challenge larger firms with cut-throat price competition. In this situation, it is often far too costly for big industry to revoke past commitments and risk destroying the trust and loyalty that has gradually been built up over time and is so critical for the production technologies they use. Instead, employers often support extending high social protection standards and generous social benefit entitlements to the entire economy, thus forcing their less committed competitors to comply with the same costly social protection standards. This may explain why the "corporate liberals" of large US companies were advocates of Roosevelt's New Deal legislation during the depression of the 1930s (Gordon 1994; Jacoby 1999; Swenson 1997) whereas Swedish employers backed the Social Democrats' agenda for social policy reform during the high growth period of the 1950s and 1960s rather than during times of economic slump. According to Swenson (1999), Swedish employer *solidarism* and US employer *segmentalism* reveal the different business cycle responsiveness of centralized and decentralized wage-setting regimes, which can account for the distinctive asynchronous development of welfare policies in these two countries. Once the long postwar growth period

---

[3] Iversen (2000) offers a variation on this argument. He does not emphasize the necessity of coordinating wages between the sheltered and exposed sectors of the economy, but rather the distributive problems between low-wage and high-wage groups. Since the centralization of wage bargaining leads to egalitarian wage policies, unions have an incentive to "use inflationary wage demands as a 'hedge' against inequalizing, market-generated wage-drift... Because wage-drift tends to primarily benefit high-wage groups (whose wages are held back in the collective-bargaining process), it undermines the distributive terms of the centralized wage bargain. Confederal leaders are therefore prone to demand nominal-wage increases that lead to 'excessive' total wage increases during periods of low to moderate growth. This kind of nominal-wage rigidity produces sticky prices that can be combined with real-wage flexibility only if some of the nominal increases are accommodated through growth in the money supply." Moreover, in "centralized systems an expansion of solidaristic—that is de-commodifying and egalitarian—welfare benefits can help to contain wage demands from especially low-wage groups. In this fashion, the government can potentially ameliorate the inflationary pressures from solidaristic wage policies, while at the same time contributing to wage leveling" (Iversen 2000: 207–8, 209; see Iversen 1999: 31).

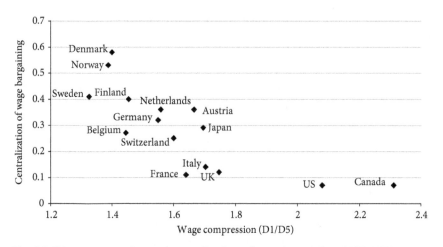

**Fig. 4.1** Wage compression and centralization of wage bargaining, 1979–1995

*Note:* Wage compression is defined as the ratio between the lowest and the median income decile, D5/D1. For centralization of wage bargaining, I follow Iversen's definition (1998a: 59). He defines centralization as $\Sigma\, w_j p^2_{ij}$ where $w_j$ is the weight accorded to each bargaining level j ($\Sigma\, w_j = 1$), and $p_{ij}$ is the share of workers covered by union (or federation) i at level j.

*Sources:* Iversen (1998a, 1999), OECD Employment Outlook (various years).

had eased the competitive pressures on US big industry, the welfare capitalist trajectory became attractive for the major industrial enterprises again.

Neither of these accounts seems to apply to the German case, however. Germany is a country that combines a relatively high degree of wage coordination and wage compression (see Fig. 4.1) with a welfare state that is quite unlike the Swedish model—and a wage-bargaining system that is completely different, too. It lacks almost all of the features that are said to underpin the solidaristic wage policy between the Swedish Trade Union Confederation (LO) and Swedish Employers' Association (SAF). These comprise the government's strong political commitment to full employment demonstrated by the importance attached to active labor market policies, the willingness and capacity of the government to engage in proactive macroeconomic steering, a "dependent" central bank, being much more accommodating than the German Bundesbank ever was, Social Democratic hegemony, etc.

This would then motivate the search for a different explanation for the interplay between wage coordination and the welfare state in the German case. One such explanation has been developed by Barry Eichengreen. He develops a more general argument for the importance of economic (particularly wage) coordination for Europe's postwar period of high economic growth, and his explanation claims relevance also for the German case. His principal thesis is that there are primarily two interrelated explanations for Europe's exceptional economic performance after World War II. First, to an important extent Europe's impressive economic growth was simply due to "catch-up," i.e. the narrowing of the productivity gap between the European countries (and Japan) and the US. This gap had been quite significant in the late 1940s after almost three decades of economic crisis, protectionism, "economic autarchy" policies, and thirty years of "European civil war" from 1914 to 1945. Yet catch-up does not provide a full explanation for Europe's postwar economic success, since some countries showed above-average performance in terms of productivity growth and low inflation, among them, most prominently: Germany.

To solve this conundrum, Eichengreen argues that it was the mixture of substantial investment by employers and wage moderation by unions which explains that part of Europe's exceptional growth after 1945 not explained by simple catch-up. Yet how could this combination be sustained? Eichengreen claims that the

> elements of Europe's growth miracle—wage moderation, high investment levels, and rapid export growth—were delivered by a tailor-made set of domestic and international arrangements: on the domestic side, the social market economy and on the external side, international agreements and supranational institutions. These arrangements solved problems of commitment and cooperation that would otherwise have hindered the resumption of growth,   (Eichengreen 1996a: 65)

For our purposes, it is primarily the domestic side of these "tailor-made arrangements" that is of interest—and we need to ask whether it was really as effective as Eichengreen suggests. Why did high growth not result in high wage demands by the unions, subsequently giving momentum to an inflationary process that would have prevented world market success and above-average growth to the extent that they occurred? According to Eichengreen, it was primarily economic coordination between labor and capital that averted the inflationary risks of the high-growth, full-employment trajectory. He stresses the importance of the institutions that allowed capital and labor to enter into an enduring coordination game.

To depict the basic strategic logic of this game Eichengreen refers to formal models in which "welfare is maximized when capitalists and workers both agree to defer current compensation in return for future gains" (Eichengreen 1996a: 43):

> Workers moderate their wage claims in order to make profits available to enterprises and to make their investment in capacity modernization and expansion profitable. Capitalists limit dividend payouts in order to reinvest. Investment stimulates growth, increasing the future incomes of both capitalists and workers. In the cooperative equilibrium in which both workers and capitalists exercise restraint, the costs of forgoing current consumption are outweighed by the benefits of the future increases in income accruing to both.
>
> (Eichengreen 1996a: 43; see also Eichengreen 2007)

A distinctive set of domestic and international institutions is required to overcome the numerous problems of "dynamic inconsistency" and the danger of post-contractual opportunism inherent in this capital/labor coordination game. If workers moderate their wage demands, what prevents capitalists from consuming instead of reinvesting the higher profits that result from wage moderation? If capitalists reinvest profits, what will hinder workers to capture all of the product-ivity gains generated in the next wage round? Yet, anticipating the incentives for each player to renege on past promises in future rounds of the game, both would opt for the non-cooperative strategy in the first round, were it not for the fact that institutions render cooperation possible by allowing compliance to be monitored and defection to be sanctioned.

Eichengreen argues that "social and economic institutions developed in Europe after World War II" helped capital and labor avoid the myopic equilibrium and succeed in forgoing consumption in favor of high long-term growth (Eichengreen 1996a: 44).[4] Yet how exactly did these institutions help surmount problems of credible commitment and dynamic inconsistency? When analyzing the German case, Eichengreen refers to various mechanisms that enabled unions and employ-ers to monitor each other's behavior, to create bonds "that would be lost in the event that either side were to renege" (Eichengreen 1996a: 48), and that rendered commitments credible. One such mechanism, according to Eichengreen, was the extensive German codetermination law introduced in 1951. He argues (and Wolfgang Streeck concurs with his position) that "granting labour institutional-ized influence on the management of the enterprise was one way of reassuring them that wage restraint would actually translate into investment" (Eichengreen 1996a: 47). Eichengreen also claims that in Germany state subsidies—to the steel industry, for instance—were made conditional on employers' compliance, i.e. on their willingness to reinvest profits into the firm (Eichengreen 1996a: 48) and thus helped to stabilize economic coordination between capital and labor.

These mechanisms assured unions that employers would indeed reinvest profits and thus honor earlier workers' wage moderation. But what would con-strain unions, and how would wage moderation during a time of high growth and labor shortage be in accordance with the interests of individual *workers*? In this respect, Eichengreen's account is far less convincing (Paqué 1995) and does not

---

[4] "Insofar as the earnings of one company could pass through the capital market and finance another company's investment, the benefits of wage moderation for one group of workers also accrued to other workers. Since wage levels affected economy-wide determinants of investments, such as the interest rate, there was a need to coordinate wage demands across sectors...Any one company contemplating investment had reason to be concerned that its decision to invest would encourage its workers to raise their wage demands in order to appropriate the profits generated in the process. However, if wages were determined economy-wide rather than within enterprise level negotiations, an individual company's investment decision no longer affected the wages it had to pay. In these circumstances, centralized [or coordinated] wage negotiations led to a higher level of investment and, insofar as labor productivity was increased, to higher wages in equilibrium" (Eichengreen 1996a: 44).

seem to fit the German case particularly well. Neither "the concertation of negotiations between labour and management by government" (Eichengreen 1996a: 50), nor the centralization of bargaining "under state control" (Eichengreen 1996a: 50), nor the "powerful voice [of labor] in postwar coalition governments" (Eichengreen 1996a: 48), nor the government's marked "commitment to policies of full employment" (Eichengreen 1996a: 52) have been main features of Germany's postwar political economy.[5] Here, Eichengreen closely follows the arguments traditionally made in the corporatism literature regarding the central political exchange between a Social Democratic government and a national union confederation (Cameron 1984; Goldthorpe 1984) in which "commitments on social or economic policy [are exchanged] for a wage agreement" (Hall 1994: 4). Yet, it is generally agreed that exactly this scenario does *not* apply to the German case, but only to "fully corporatist" countries such as Austria, Norway, and Sweden (Allen 1989; Thelen 1991). What Garrett and Lange call the "Keynesian Welfare State" (Garrett and Lange 1996: 55–6) comprising

- heavy reliance on Keynesian demand management (to smooth domestic business cycles)
- the imposition of capital controls (to increase the effectiveness of domestic demand management)
- industrial policies (to bolster output and employment in designated sectors), [and]
- substantial public provision of welfare and other social services (to redistribute wealth to poorer segments of society)

has never been a fitting characterization of the German political economy (Hall 1994: 15). There is no historical evidence of an explicit or implicit political exchange between the German government and the labor movement—as comprising wage moderation in exchange for welfare state expansion or a guarantee of full employment (Paqué 1995: 19). Already the lack of centralization and the organizational fragmentation among the German unions would have prevented such a traditional corporatist exchange from taking place (Lehmbruch and Schmitter 1982; Schmitter and Lehmbruch 1979). In his critique of Eichengreen's explanation, Paqué is therefore right to conclude that "other reasons than a 'tripartite corporatist effort' must be sought to explain the apparent

---

[5] This is also true for his account of a "social market economy, in which the state played a role in regulating and even running industry, became deeply involved in wage negotiations and investment decisions, and extended a generous social safety net" (Eichengreen 2007: 68). Only the final point seems relevant for Germany—yet, how exactly the "generous social safety net," in the absence of neo-corporatist exchanges with Social Democracy in government, could have contributed to wage moderation remains unclear in Eichengreen's account.

wage moderation and the concomitant persistently high profit margins of the private sector of the German economy" (Paqué 1995: 20).

An equally unconvincing argument is that "the institutions of the welfare state... served as bonds that would be jeopardized if labor reneged" (Eichengreen 1996a: 44). It remains completely unclear how the government could have made welfare state provisions conditional on unions' wage moderation and particularly how it could have credibly threatened to revoke previous extensions of the welfare state in the event of labor's non-compliance. It is well known that the significant expansion of the welfare state in the 1950s and 1960s was not, by any means, something which could have been easily revoked (Pierson 1994, 1996).

So, we must look for a different explanation. The following sections provide an analysis of the early development of collective wage bargaining in Germany between 1956 and 1963 and, in particular, highlight the parallel establishment of collective bargaining in the industrial sector and the reconstruction of the Bismarckian welfare state. My focus is on how social policies helped to stabilize wage coordination and lower the costs of collective action for employers in times of economic upswing, in particular by keeping wage drift under control. And the welfare state also helped the unions to moderate their wage demands in Germany in the 1950s and 1960s, but not as part of a "generalized political exchange" between the government and the unions, but as an institution that solved distributional problems between different cohorts of workers and different sectors of the economy, which—in other words—provided economic coordination with a micro-foundation.

## 4.2  Why at That Particular Moment? Full Employment, Domestic Demand, and Wage Moderation

In Germany, coordinated wage bargaining and the leading role of the metalworkers' union (*IG Metall*) in the annual wage rounds is said to have first been established in 1956 with what was known as the "Bremen agreement." Coordinated wage bargaining was then ultimately fully established in the wake of the 1963 conflict in the Baden-Württemberg metal industry (Noé 1970). The first question that then arises with respect to the establishment of pattern wage bargaining in Germany is: why did coordination happen at that particular moment?

In 1955, the German economic miracle or *Wirtschaftswunder* recorded its first postwar peak. GDP growth reached an impressive 11.9 percent. For the first time since 1945, the labor market was almost swept clean with unemployment fluctuating around 3 percent during the summer and fall. In absolute terms, Germany had fewer than 500,000 unemployed in September 1955 as compared to more than

17 million in gainful employment. It is therefore inaccurate to state that "unemployment remained in the high single digits" (Eichengreen 2007: 87) until the influx of migrants from the East was absorbed. The border was not closed until 1961, but full employment was almost achieved already in the mid-1950s. Since Germany's current account remained relatively stable (but positive), the boom in the second half of the 1950s was now driven at least as much by domestic as by external demand (Giersch et al. 1992: 63–5). In the second half of the 1950s, Germany witnessed the onset of consumerism. Germans began to spend their money on consumer goods. They started to buy cars, television sets, washing machines, etc. While the Korea boom during the first half of the 1950s enabled heavy manufacturing to prosper, the second half of the 1950s saw the rise of the German consumer goods industry.

However, notwithstanding de facto full employment and the union's official announcement of its plans to implement an expansionary wage policy (Victor Agartz's *expansive Lohnpolitik*), designed to redistribute wealth through wage demands above the level set by productivity growth plus inflation, real unit labor costs consistently fell throughout the 1950s, though the decline was slightly less pronounced during the second half of the decade (see Table 4.1; Eichengreen 1996a: 45–6).

Giersch et al. examine four different explanations for the decline of real unit labor costs throughout the 1950s: "organizational weakness," "political

**Table 4.1** Determinants of labor costs in Germany, 1950–1960 (annual average rates of change in percent)

|         | Earnings | Labor productivity | Inflation | Real unit labor costs |
|---------|----------|--------------------|-----------|-----------------------|
| 1950–51 | 15.8     | 7.0                | 11.8      | −3.2                  |
| 1951–52 | 8.3      | 6.9                | 4.7       | −3.3                  |
| 1952–53 | 5.9      | 6.0                | −1.3      | 1.2                   |
| 1953–54 | 5.0      | 4.7                | −0.3      | 0.6                   |
| 1954–55 | 8.1      | 7.8                | 2.1       | −1.8                  |
| 1955–56 | 8.0      | 4.6                | 2.7       | 0.6                   |
| 1956–57 | 6.6      | 3.6                | 2.8       | 0                     |
| 1957–58 | 6.9      | 3.5                | 2.9       | 0.4                   |
| 1958–59 | 5.6      | 6.6                | 1.6       | −2.5                  |
| 1959–60 | 9.0      | 6.8                | 3.2       | −1                    |
| 1950–55 | 8.6      | 6.5                | 3.3       | −1.3                  |
| 1955–60 | 7.2      | 5.0                | 2.6       | −0.5                  |
| 1950–60 | 7.9      | 5.7                | 3.0       | −0.9                  |

*Note*: Earnings = gross annual income of employees (including social insurance contributions of employers). Labor productivity is defined as GDP at constant prices divided by active labor force. Inflation = deflator of value added (i.e. GDP). Real unit labor costs are defined as income/(labor productivity × inflation).

*Source*: Giersch et al. (1992: 72).

distraction," "economic surprise," and "social responsibility" (Giersch et al. 1992: 73–9; see also Flanagan et al. 1983: 216–75). They present robust reasons for dismissing the organizational weakness (of unions, that is) argument, but their rejection of the political distraction argument has a less convincing justification. This latter argument holds that the political struggle, particularly for codetermination in the early 1950s, meant that unions "temporarily [stood] still at the wage front so as not to endanger the far more daring prospect of a thoroughly syndicalist 'industrial democracy'" (Giersch et al. 1992: 75). While it is true that the conflict over codetermination (*Mitbestimmung*) and works councils (*Betriebsverfassungsgesetz* 1952) had ended by 1953 and thus cannot be an explanation for the unions' continuous wage moderation in the years that followed, Giersch et al. fail to acknowledge that the conflicts over weekly working time (1956), over sick pay (1956–7), and more generally over social reform and the reconstruction of the German welfare state (pensions in 1957 and health reform in 1959–61) had become the key issues in union campaigns during the second half of the 1950s. These social policy issues replaced the emphasis on redistribution through generous wage hikes (Pirker 1979). And they were not only of general political relevance in the unions' manifestos, but, in contrast to the conflict over codetermination, the pension reform and the sick pay law in 1957 in particular had a direct impact on workers' (social) wages.

In this context, it is also frequently overlooked that the Bremen agreement on reducing weekly working time from 48 to 45 hours was "only one part of a more encompassing social policy concept" advocated by *IG Metall* (Kalbitz 1978: 183). The fierce battle for sick pay reform in Schleswig Holstein's metal industry in November 1956 fits into the picture. At the same time, the emphasis on social issues in *IG Metall*'s campaigns helped to establish its leadership role within the unions' national confederation, the *Deutsche Gewerkschaftsbund* (DGB). A closer look at Table 4.1 reveals that the years between the struggle for codetermination and the battle for pension reform and sick pay (1953–7) were the ones in which real unit labor costs showed an upward tendency.[6]

What was the historical background of the 1956–7 conflict over working time reduction and sick pay? *IG Metall* had entered the 1955 annual wage round by canceling all collective contracts in the North Rhine-Westphalia district, by far the largest of all districts with 900,000 *IG Metall* members. Interestingly, the union sought to reach a different settlement for the iron and steel industry than it did for

---

[6] The other two explanations for the persistent gap between wages and productivity in the 1950s proposed by Giersch et al. (1992) will not be discussed at any great length here, however. "Economic surprise," which they believe played a role, is largely incompatible with rational expectations, particularly if we try to explain persistent differences over a time period of ten years. "Social responsibility" presumably played a role, yet this explanation clearly overlaps with the one endorsed here, which holds that the *IG Metall* leadership attempted to keep wages internationally competitive, but at the same time sought to improve workers' welfare and to avoid an increase in unemployment.

metalworking. The union wanted a moderate settlement in the more export-oriented metalworking industry, which had a preponderance of small companies, and was quick to accept a moderate arbitration proposal. At the same time, the metalworkers' union hoped to achieve a stronger wage hike in the iron and steel industry, where demand was more domestic in nature and where firms were much larger. This strategy backfired dramatically (Pirker 1979: 174–6). Its failure was largely due to the fact that the leading union representatives in the large iron and steel companies considered *IG Metall*'s wage demands to be disproportionate and therefore refused to support them. The *Arbeitsdirektoren* in particular (union members belonging to the board of directors in the coal, iron, and steel industry thanks to the codetermination law (*Montanmitbestimmung*)) opposed IG Metall's aggressive wage policy. The union was thus faced with a dilemma: it could not champion the cause for higher wages in sectors where companies were under intense competitive pressure from world markets. However, the union also faced considerable resistance in those sectors where demand was more domestic in nature, but where codetermination had fueled among union representatives an interest in company-level syndicalism or social partnership. All this coincided with workers' raised expectations of wage increases given the metalworker union's radical rhetoric—in times of very tight labor markets.

While companies' union representatives were often reluctant to implement *IG Metall*'s aggressive wage policy, union members were frequently more radical than they had been, as is shown by the wildcat strikes of 1955 which even involved occasional violent clashes between works councils and (communist) workers (e.g. during the strike at the *Howaldt* shipyard in Hamburg in August 1955; see Pirker 1979: 177). *IG Metall*'s first response to this situation was to declare that bargaining should take place at the company level. However, this was an even riskier strategy given the radical tendencies of the workforce in many firms (Pirker 1979: 176, 179). Further, *IG Metall*'s claim that it should take a leadership position within the unions' umbrella organization, the DGB, was hardly made more credible by it stepping back from its former responsibility for wage bargaining. This created a danger that either radical forces (the much-feared communists) or accommodative forces (believers in company-level social partnership) could undermine the union's position.

*IG Metall*, under the leadership of Otto Brenner (a member of the "progressive wing" in the DGB), "was [finally] forced to act" (Kalbitz 1978: 184) if it did not want to lose out against the more moderate faction within the DGB. Over the following years, aggressive mobilization in support of significant welfare state expansion became the solution to *IG Metall*'s dilemma, as the Bremen agreement and particularly the Schleswig-Holstein metalworker strike over sick-pay reform in 1956–7 demonstrated. It was soon to become clear that employers in the exposed sectors of the economy also favored welfare state expansion because they hoped that this would weaken the upward pressure on wages in times of full employment. Insofar as the welfare state was becoming essential for the stability of coordinated collective bargaining and the ensuing intra-industry wage compression, welfare state programs were increasingly perceived as being in the general interest of all employers, be they in exposed or sheltered sectors of the economy (discussed further below).

So what was the primary economic rationale behind pattern wage bargaining? The large companies in the Ruhr region knew that the unions had selected them as their prime targets in the struggle for higher wages during the 1955 wage round, even though *IG Metall*'s "dual track" strategy had been a complete failure. While the large enterprises in the West could clearly afford to pay higher wages, they were not particularly eager to do so. Hence, the "autocratic" firms in the Ruhr region (Herrigel 1996) had most to gain from collective bargaining for the entire industrial sector with the export industries setting the pace, since this would lead to wages being significantly lower than if unions negotiated company contracts (Swenson 1999, 2002). If, in turn, wage moderation in export-oriented firms were to be achieved by an increase in workers' social wages (through welfare state expansion), those exposed firms and workers most vulnerable to external shocks would profit disproportionately should the welfare state provide employers with instruments to flexibly and painlessly adjust employment to sudden shifts in demand. Such instruments would include social programs such as short-time pay (*Kurzarbeitergeld*), early retirement programs, and disability pensions. This was exactly what Adenauer's 1957 pension reform delivered.[7] "Wage redistribution" in favor of the large companies in the coal, iron, and steel industries would be offset by "welfare redistribution" in favor of those firms that used (contribution-financed) welfare state programs to adjust their workforce to sudden shifts in demand or changes in market conditions.[8]

Insofar as industry sector wage bargaining with a compressed wage structure was thus externally stabilized by welfare programs, the welfare state became an indispensable part of Germany's postwar economic order. This was true both in the sense that the political mobilization supporting the reconstruction of the Bismarckian welfare state temporarily helped moderate unions' wage demands, and in the sense that the welfare state, once in place, helped compensate workers

[7] Apart from the significant increase in benefits, the Adenauer reform also contained two elements of particular importance for unions and workers: first, by strictly linking benefits to contributions, the reform put high premiums on stable career paths, high incomes, and the early acquisition of skills. It thus particularly benefited the core union clientele, the highly qualified core workforce (*Facharbeiter*). Second, by also entitling blue-collar workers to a pension at the age of 60 (after being in unemployment for more than 12 months) the Adenauer reform provided workers with the assurance that they would not, under any circumstances have to endure a longer period of unemployment in the final years of their career.

[8] Further, given that large companies usually have to bear a disproportionately large share of the burden of organizing business interests, we can interpret the beneficial effects of collective wage bargaining for big business as a "payback" for the higher expenses they incurred in organizing collective action.

from those companies that either were no longer productive enough to afford the higher social wage or had to cope with adverse external demand shocks. Compensation worked as follows: high wage costs exerted constant pressure on companies to increase productivity. Uniform wages within the sector resulted in redistribution from the less productive to the more productive firms. However, this redistribution was offset by a flow of welfare income in the reverse direction, which was spent on supporting those workers who had lost their jobs as a result of company bankruptcies or external demand shocks. Unlike social spending programs in Sweden, however, those implemented in Germany were passive, not active, in nature.[9] The status-protecting, insider-oriented welfare state thus provided essentially a functional equivalent to the Scandinavian full-employment promise that a fiscally federalized, politically conservative, and in terms of monetary policy restrained German state could not issue.

The next two sections reconstruct how this within-sector coordination came about.

### 4.3  Why There?

### 4.3.1  Shipbuilding, World Markets, and the Intra-Industry Compromise

Both the Bremen agreement and the Schleswig-Holstein metalworkers' strike of 1956–7 were meant to lend credibility to IG Metall's claim to be the pace-setting union among the sixteen DGB unions and that they should be fully autonomous from the directives of the unions' umbrella organization. In Bremen and Schleswig-Holstein, the metal sector was dominated by shipbuilding. In the Schleswig-Holstein metal industry, 38.9 percent of all workers were shipyard workers, making it by far the largest occupational group, but many more metalworkers were employed in the supply industry. A closer look at the economic conditions in the shipbuilding sector can explain why so much union activity occurred in this industry in the mid-1950s.

A considerable share of the demand for ships up to 1955 was domestic. The rebuilding of the German trade fleet, made possible by generous tax subsidies and Marshall Plan funds (Wend 2001), maintained high employment and production

---

[9] Cushioning the effects of economic downturns and/or compensating for job loss if a firm at the low productivity end of the market was no longer able to pay the "above equilibrium" wages was a functional strategy provided that the industry sector itself (here, particularly the manufacturing sector) was still growing or provided that employment continued to shift from agriculture to manufacturing (Paqué 1996, 1998). However, once the employment shares of manufacturing had begun to shrink, while employment in the services sector remained moderate due to high non-wage labor costs, particularly social insurance contributions, the whole arrangement mainly led to an increase in labor market hysteresis and ever-increasing levels of structural unemployment; see Chapter 5).

levels during the first half of the decade. Recovery had been slow for many reasons: the destruction caused by war (which was far worse in shipbuilding than in other industries), the "deconstruction" after the war, an inadequate supply of steel for the shipyards, and the military restrictions placed on production that were only gradually lifted in the wake of the Korea boom. If the year 1936 is used as a yardstick, shipbuilding had only reached 72 percent of its prewar production capacity by 1951, while at that point coal mining was at 103 percent, the automobile industry at 166 percent, and the textile industry at 132 percent of their prewar levels. Industry as a whole had reached 136 percent of its 1936 capacity level (Albert 1998).

Over time, external demand became increasingly important for German shipyards. As much as 48 percent of all ships built between 1952 and 1955 were exported, and this figure increased to 65 percent between 1956 and 1961 (Albert 1998: 85). As early as 1955, German shipyards were the world's second most important producers of ships (Kuckuk 1998: 20), and shipbuilding accounted for the highest export share of all German industries (Kuckuk 1998: 22), having reached 77.7 percent by 1960 (Kuckuk 1998: 22). This sector was therefore especially sensitive to changes in the international terms of trade and in domestic wage costs, particularly since wage costs were comparatively high in shipbuilding (between 20 and 35 percent of total production costs; Albert 1998: 107) and opportunities to substitute labor with capital limited.

At the same time, shipbuilding was also exceptionally important from a broader macroeconomic perspective: it was the seventh most important export sector measured in terms of its contribution to the German trade surplus (DM 1.368 billion in 1957, in absolute terms). However, terms of trade had steadily declined since the mid-1950s and suddenly deteriorated rapidly in 1957. While the closing of the Suez Canal had led to a sharp increase in the demand for ships and in freight rates, in early 1957, freight rates plummeted and literally overnight shipyards stopped receiving new ship orders and all existing orders were cancelled. International competition became extremely fierce, a development that had been anticipated for some time due to the advent of a new and competitive challenger: Japan. Japanese shipbuilders had increased their world market share significantly within only a short period of time, from 11 percent (1951–5) to 32 percent (1956–60; see Albert 1998: 85). The rise of this new international competitor was partly a result of the comparative wage cost advantages of the Japanese shipyards. However, Japan's shipyards were also more productive and enjoyed more generous government subsidies. The impact of Japanese competition on the profit rates of German shipyards had been evident for some time, but became particularly acute during the second half of the 1950s. In 1958, German shipyards started to lay off workers.

Another important factor to take into consideration is that by the 1950s, all the major German shipyards had become vertically integrated into the Ruhr region's "autocratic" iron and steel industrial complex (Leckebusch 1963). From 1916, *Thyssen* held the majority of the stocks of Bremen's *Vulcan* shipyard. *Krupp* had holdings in the *Deutsche Schiff- und Maschinenbau AG*, a merger of *Vulcan Werke Hamburg* and *AG Weser*, and the latter was acquired entirely in 1941 (Chandler 1990: 511). The *Germania* shipyard had been part of the *Krupp* concern since 1896. *Thyssen* bought *Blohm & Voss* in 1955. *Gutehoffnungs-Hütte* had acquired *Deutsche Werft* back in 1918 (Bankverein 1954). *Stinnes* owned *Nordseewerke Emden* and the *Stumm* conglomerate owned the *Frerichs* shipyards (Leckebusch 1963). The purpose of vertical integration was to help balance business cycles since these were rarely synchronous in the shipbuilding and steel industries (see Albert 1998: 124). Another rationale was to diversify and thereby to facilitate the "rapid shift to production areas other than new ship construction" (Strath 1994: 75). What had applied following World War I became relevant again after World War II: steel producers foresaw the necessity of finding new areas of activity given the significant expansion of their production capacities during wartime. However, another important motive, rarely mentioned in the literature, is that most of the vertical integration had taken place back in the 1920s (Chandler 1990) since shipyards had been allowed to import the steel they needed to build ships without having to pay duty and were thus able to circumvent the high protectionist import tariffs for iron and steel. In a market that was almost completely cartelized, that was territorially split among the three major centers in Silesia, the Ruhr, and the Saar, and that was protected from foreign competition by high tariffs, this remained the only crack in the iron and steel cartel, and the big firms in the Ruhr region were very eager to close it (Feldman 1977; Leckebusch 1963; Preiss 1933; Weisbrod 1978). However, the vertical integration between the iron and steel industry and the ship construction industry, which was barely affected by the Allied deconcentration policy after World War II (Diegmann 1993; Wend 2001), also meant that managers and unions had to take into account the different economic positions of these two industries if wages were to be set uniformly for the entire metal sector. Further, it is important to note that the more extensive version of German codetermination was practiced in the iron and steel industry (*Montanmitbestimmung*), but not in the shipyards.

Shipyards were highly unionized even by the standards at the time. In many shipyards, 80–90 percent of the workforce were union members. Across all of Schleswig-Holstein, union density was 71.9 percent in 1956 (Metall 1978: 51), but in the shipyards, one of the best organized industries, second only to the electrical industry, union density was even higher.[10] Workers were also highly politicized, as was underlined by the fact that many shipyards had been occupied by workers

---

[10] In 1961, across Germany as a whole, *IG Metall*'s membership in the ship construction industry was second highest among all metal sectors with 53.7 percent and in 1963, it was highest with 56.9 percent (Noé 1970: 340).

immediately after the war, resembling the Japanese postwar experience of unions' "production control" (Gordon 1985: 329–66). The communist movement enjoyed a relatively strong foothold in the shipbuilding industry. In the 1956 works council elections at the Kiel *Howaldswerft*, the communist candidate won 50 percent of the votes (Metall 1978: 208). Evidence of the radicalism of many shipyard workers is provided by the exceptionally long duration of the Schleswig-Holstein strike, where, even after fourteen weeks of strike action, union members still rejected the results of negotiations with 76.2 percent of the vote despite the fact they were endorsed by their own union leadership. In the end, it took four strike ballots before union members finally accepted the settlement agreed between their union and the employers (Kalbitz 1978).[11] Works councils, on the contrary, had mostly pursued a policy of *Burgfrieden*, named after the domestic "armistice" between the state, the military, and the workers' movement during World War I. Given that *external factors*, namely the capital shortage and the Allied restrictions on pro- duction, were seen as the main obstacles to the postwar recovery of the German shipbuilding industry, management, works councils, and local politicians formed broad coalitions and considered it to be in their common interest to put their internal conflicts to one side for the time being (Wend 2001). These were the economic conditions within the shipbuilding industry during the second half of the 1950s, when major wage increases, triggered by a growing domestic demand, were expected to further endanger the industry's precarious international com- petitiveness, while a highly mobilized union membership was impatient to profit from Germany's economic miracle.

### 4.3.2 Cartels, Coordinated Capitalism, and Collective Wage Bargaining: The Metal-Producing versus Metalworking Industries

Whereas the Bremen agreement and the metalworkers' strike of 1956–7 repre- sented the first steps toward introducing pattern wage bargaining, coordinated wage setting finally became fully established in the south, in the industrial region of Baden-Württemberg where mechanical engineering, automobile manufactur- ers, and the electro-technical industry dominated. Again, in order to explain the rationale of wage coordination for the metal industries we have to step back in time a little.

---

[11] In this context, it is also not surprising that the first sector-wide lockouts in postwar Germany in the Bremen ship construction industry in 1953 ended in an almost complete fiasco for business (Kalbitz 1979: 151). This is one of the reasons why employers in the metalworking industry ultimately chose the district in northern Baden-Württemberg as the battleground for their struggle with *IG Metall* since this was the only district where employers appeared capable of carrying out district-wide lockouts (Noé 1970: 254).

A fundamental problem of Germany's dual industrial structure, namely the conflict of interests between large domestic-oriented iron and steel producers and medium-sized export-oriented steel consumers (Herrigel 1996) was solved through vertical integration in the shipbuilding sector in the 1920s. Historically, the other metalworking industries, particularly the machine tool, automobile, and electrical industries had identified different solutions for this issue. While rapidly gaining in economic importance, the metalworking industry had been unable to acquire the corresponding political influence until the end of 1924 because of seemingly insurmountable collective action problems (Feldman and Nocken 1975).[12] The lack of lobbying power was due to the profound heterogeneity of interests within the metalworking sector. First, metalworking firms were smaller and more numerous which meant that economic concentration was far less pronounced than in the German heavy industries of coal, steel, and iron (Chandler 1990: 550–61; Weisbrod 1978: 93–119). Second, the wide spectrum of products ranging from automobiles and machine tools to cutlery and the corresponding heterogeneity of product markets hindered effective interest aggregation and organizational unity. Since the metalworking industries had become more and more export oriented, however (see Table 4.2), they were increasingly concerned about the price policy of the highly cartelized and politically very influential heavy industry.

When the metalworking firms finally managed to organize themselves into the *Arbeitsgemeinschaft Metallverarbeitende Industrie* (AVI) in 1924–5, the path was clear for settling the serious conflict with heavy industry through a complex contractual arrangement between the AVI and the Association of German Iron and Steel Producers (*Reichsverband Eisen und Stahl*): what was known as the AVI

**Table 4.2** Export shares of the iron industry and mechanical engineering industry, 1926–1931, in percent

|      | Iron industry | Mechanical engineering industry |
|------|-----------|---------------------|
| 1926 | 32        |                     |
| 1927 | 20        | 28                  |
| 1928 | 24        | 29                  |
| 1929 | 28        | 34                  |
| 1930 | 29        | 42                  |
| 1931 | –         | 48                  |

*Source*: Preiss (1933: 76, 94).

[12] In 1930, employment in the metalworking sector was around 1.8 million and in the metalproducing industries around 300,000 (Wrede 1933: 137).

agreement (Feldman 1977; Hoffmann 1928; Nocken 1977; Weisbrod 1978). The essence of the compromise between heavy industry and the metalworking firms was that, on the one hand, the latter would support heavy industry's campaign for protectionist tariffs on iron and steel once the Versailles Treaty provision granting the victorious nations access to the German market on a most-favored-nation basis expired in 1925; while, on the other hand, the former agreed to compensate the metalworking firms for the difference between the high German cartel prices and the world market iron and steel prices for exported products (and also supported efforts to acquire privileged access for these products particularly to the French and Belgian markets). It would obviously go beyond the scope of this chapter to describe in any detail the workings of this sophisticated inter-sectoral arrangement (Blödner 1934; Hoffmann 1928; Preiss 1933; Schmid 1930; Tübben 1930), but the domestic price for iron stabilized from 1929 on (see Wrede 1933: 124).

But obviously, this form of conflict settlement through cartel price control and inter-sectoral price compensation could clearly not be restored after 1945, when the Allied deconcentration decree (*Entflechtungsverordnung*) was issued, nor later, in 1957, when the passage of the Cartel Law (*Gesetz gegen Wettbewerbsbeschränkungen*) forestalled the further use of these extreme practices of Germany's "organized," "guaranteed," "risk-free" capitalism so prominent in the interwar years (Liefmann 1938; Michels 1928; Winkler 1974). Yet the AVI agreement continued to be important after World War II as business leaders recalled this successful example of inter-industry coordination. In addition, the complex but highly effective cartel agreement between the two metal sectors preserved and even reinforced the dual structure of the German metal industry, since the agreement not only halted the trend toward further vertical integration, particularly the integration of the metalworking industry into the huge industrial complexes of *Stinnes*, *Thyssen*, and *Krupp*, but even reversed that trend (Chandler 1990; Feldman 1977; Weisbrod 1978).[13] The Nazis, who had extended all cartel agreements and had given the Ministry of Economic Affairs the power to "federate enterprises into syndicates, cartels, conventions, or similar agreements" shortly after their advent to power,[14] thereby left the metal sector's dual industrial structure to the young Federal Republic in an almost unaltered form (Fear 1997).

---

[13] Part of the AVI agreement was that United Steelworks (*Vereinigte Stahlwerke*) had to sell its mechanical engineering enterprise, Thyssen Maschinenbau, in 1926 and that heavy industry promised not to move any further into metal finishing, since the metalworking industry justifiably feared that an effective price cartel for steel and iron would increase incentives for the steel magnates to further integrate vertically. Metal finishing subsidiaries of the large iron and steel producers could then acquire an unfair advantage over their independent competitors by being sold raw materials at below the cartel price. In 1926, the Thyssen Machine Company was sold to an independent competitor, *Deutsche Machinenbau-Aktiengesellschaft* (DEMAG), "which immediately shut it down and sold its electro dynamo production to Siemens-Schuckert" (Fear 1997: 213).

[14] *Gesetz zur Errichtung von Zwangskartellen*, July 15, 1933 (RGBl. I 1933: 488).

After 1945, cartelization was no longer available as an instrument of economic coordination. "Business coordination" of the kind embodied by the AVI agreement was clearly ruled out by the cartel law, despite the fact that the law was only a heavily watered-down version of what Minister of Economics, Ludwig Erhard and his ordoliberal combatants had initially sought to achieve (Hentschel 1996; Nörr 1993; Wigger 2017). Moreover, the far-reaching deconcentration measures imposed by the occupation forces on heavy industry (Herrigel 2000: 363–9) rendered the agreement on and enforcement of cartels a highly unlikely enterprise. In addition, the European Coal and Steel Community, as established in the wake of the Schuman Plan in 1952 (Gillingham 1991), had marked a clear break with cartelist traditions in this industry (Kipping 1996).

However, the fact that the 1950s marked a sharp break with both the massive vertical integration of the early 1920s and with the cartel practices of the late 1920s is rarely emphasized enough in the literature.[15] In particular, scholars hardly ever discuss how the "autocratic" firms in the West and the export industry in the South once again found a *modus vivendi* after the war. It is rarely asked what replaced the cartel agreements and compensatory side payments in postwar Germany (Herrigel 1996 is the exception here). The move away from the cartels in the 1950s did mark a substantial change in the practices governing the "regulation of competition among business" (Swenson 1999: 8).[16] A central claim of this chapter is that coordinated wage bargaining, first established in the metal industry, proved, at least in part, to be a functional equivalent for intersectoral coordination through cartel agreements. Yet, as Peter Swenson has convincingly argued, wage coordination, as a non-self-enforcing arrangement, then needed reinforcement from an outside source, and it was the welfare state that came to its aid when the costs of coordination threatened to undermine the solidarity among employers that was so essential for the functioning of the entire system.

It was the employers who took the initiative and urged the unions to centralize wage bargaining in the early 1960s. The goal of the employers' association in the

[15] It might be important to note here that the vertical integration of the early 1920s was of course eased by galloping inflation. The "kings of inflation" such as Wolff, Flick, Herzfeld, Hugenberg, or Stinnes were able to build large industrial conglomerates within just a few years (Feldman 1993, 1998). After the stabilization of the Deutschmark, cartelization replaced vertical integration.

[16] Despite the lack of detailed information on coverage and efficiency, we have relatively robust evidence that the iron and steel cartels of the interwar years were highly effective and now, in contrast to prewar and wartimes, also covered most of the markets for semi-processed metal products. For instance, the rolled steel (*Walzeisen*) prewar cartel agreements had covered between 37 and 43 percent of total production, on average. The corresponding figure for April 1925 was 7 percent, for June 1925, 36 percent, and for January 1926, 90 percent (Preiss 1933: 22–3). A similar picture emerges for other iron and steel products (see, for example, Hoffmann 1928; Weisbrod 1978: 101–2). The establishment and enforcement of cartel agreements became much easier in the second half of the 1920s, because of "the increased concentration within industry and the resulting economic power of the merged enterprises" (Chandler 1990: 512), itself a result of the huge industrial mergers that had taken place in the wake of hyperinflation.

metal sector, *Gesamtmetall*, was to fully centralize wage bargaining on the national level. *Gesamtmetall* had already been granted full authority from its regional members' associations to bargain on their behalf. In 1961, employers nationwide simultaneously cancelled all collective agreements with *IG Metall* in order to synchronize wage bargaining in the various districts (*Tarifdistrikte*). Once this had been achieved, employers entered the 1963 wage round with the offer of a general wage stop in the metalworking industries, and later proposed to increase wages by 3.5 percent, the expected rate of average productivity growth for all industrial sectors. Only in the district of Baden-Württemberg had the union prepared for a strike, and it was here that both parties finally decided to flex their muscles in 1963. Taken by surprise by massive lockouts and unable to play large and small employers off against each other, the union soon had to cave in to most of *Gesamtmetall*'s demands. The agreement reached between the two parties brought about a wage hike of 5 percent, which was roughly equal to the product-ivity growth in the metal industries (Flanagan et al. 1983: 242) or to the rate of economy-wide productivity growth plus the "natural" rate of inflation of around 1.5 to 2 percent (Noé 1970: 316). This settlement was then rapidly extended to all other metal districts. While it already represented a compromise between the medium-sized and large employers within the Baden-Württemberg metal indus-try that particularly benefited the larger enterprises, the extension of the settle-ment to other districts once again benefited those (especially larger) companies that would otherwise have been forced to "share their rents" with workers to a far greater extent.

Although, strictly speaking, this bargaining practice did not quite equate to top-level negotiations between the national headquarters of *Gesamtmetall* and *IG Metall*, nonetheless, centralized wage bargaining did establish itself, since employ-ers were then represented in each and every regional negotiation by the same national *Gesamtmetall* delegation. Only later did *IG Metall* centralize decision-making in a similar manner by establishing obligatory consultation between union representatives from the districts and the central *IG Metall* wage committee before the districts could present specific wage demands.[17] However, wage coordination was not only important for the metalworking sector. Although the iron, steel, and coal industry was not represented by *Gesamtmetall*, given that the specific form of codetermination in this sector granted unions a seat on the executive board of these companies so that unions could be represented on both sides of the bargaining table, there is ample evidence that employers of *Montan* industry and of metalworking made a concerted effort in the Baden-Württemberg conflict.

---

[17] The history of the establishment of German pattern bargaining highlights the importance of the *employer's* ability to act collectively for the functioning of corporatist labor and capital coordination (Soskice 1990a) as compared to the factors usually emphasized in the corporatism literature, such as union centralization and employer associations' and union umbrella organizations' monopoly of representation (Schmitter 1979).

They agreed on a common strategy in the "wage bargaining committee" (*Tarifpolitischer Ausschuß*) as well as in the "contact committee" (*Kontaktausschuß*), where the Federation of German Industry (*Bundesverband der Deutschen Industrie*, BDI) and the Federation of Employers' Associations (*Bundesvereinigung der Deutschen Arbeitgeberverbände*, BDA) convened and where heavy industry was represented by the employers' association of the iron and steel industry (*Arbeitgeberverband Eisen- und Stahlindustrie*) (Noé 1970: 120–1, 258–60).[18] Employer coordination between metal-producing and metal-consuming industries was secured in the form of a "'core commission' of representatives of large enterprises in the heavy . . . industry sector [and joint] management teams in the various regional negotiations with the multi-industrial union *IG Metall*" (Flanagan et al. 1983: 238). Although pattern bargaining, once established, did not simply put wages in the iron and steel industry on a par with those set by *IG Metall* and *Gesamtmetall* in the metalworking sector, we can safely assume that the signaling function of wage agreements in metalworking effectively set the corridor for wage demands in the iron and steel sector *below* what would have been the case without "the pattern." The dual track strategy pursued by *IG Metall* in the mid-1950s in particular would have been far more economically unfavorable for the large Ruhr companies.

As became obvious with the Baden-Württemberg conflict of 1961–3, the leadership role of the metalworker union tended to be exploited by employers. Once *IG Metall* had successfully established its pace-setting role within the DGB, particularly by championing social policy issues in the late 1950s, the union could be "tamed" by employers with the help of coordinated, sector-wide lockouts. Yet the resulting wage restraint would not only be in the interest of big business, but would ultimately also benefit the union itself, since wage and price stability under the Bretton Woods regime of fixed exchange rates would, in the medium term, lead to an undervaluation of the Deutschmark. This would, in turn, fuel exports and bring about employment growth, which could (and did) ultimately result in union membership growth (Flanagan et al. 1983: 298; Holtfrerich 1998; Kreile 1978).[19]

The extent to which employers used the main disciplining device to pressure IG Metall into wage coordination, namely sector-wide lockouts, can be seen in Tables 4.3 and 4.4 showing the types of lockout, number of lockouts, number of workers affected, and number of workers affected by industrial sector.

---

[18] Whereas there were no major metalworking companies in Baden-Württemberg owned by Ruhr industrialists, some of them owned important holdings. For instance, the Flick company had major holdings in Daimler Benz AG and Hanns Martin Schleyer, a member of Flick's managerial board, was the president of the regional branch of *Gesamtmetall*, VMI, and at the same time deputy president of *Gesamtmetall*.

[19] In Germany in the 1960s this was called the "quantity boom" (*Mengenkonjunktur*). To the extent that wage coordination also triggered an interest among employers in wage compression (Swenson 1999, 2002), wage coordination also met the traditional union call for "wage solidarity."

**Table 4.3** Lockouts in Germany, 1949–1969

|           | Number of lockouts | Workers affected | Company lockouts (in percent) | Sector lockouts (in percent) |
| --------- | ------------------ | ---------------- | ----------------------------- | ---------------------------- |
| 1949–1958 | 7                  | 5,543            | 57.7                          | 42.3                         |
| 1959–1968 | 15                 | 302,371          | 4.2                           | 95.8                         |

*Source*: Kalbitz (1979: 26, 42).

**Table 4.4** Sector unions affected by lockouts, 1949–1976

| Union             | Number of lockouts | Workers affected | (in percent) | Days lost | (in percent) |
| ----------------- | ------------------ | ---------------- | ------------ | --------- | ------------ |
| Metal industry    | 39                 | 640,973          | (87.9)       | 4,953,825 | (85.5)       |
| Textiles          | 12                 | 8,317            | (1.1)        | 161,129   | (2.8)        |
| Public services   | 7                  | 17,166           | (2.4)        | 469,887   | (8.2)        |
| Construction      | 5                  | 1,650            | (0.2)        | 39,276    | (0.6)        |
| Chemical industry | 5                  | 1,413            | (0.2)        | 18,914    | (0.3)        |

*Source*: Kalbitz (1979: 86).

Once confronted with sweeping union success in the fierce conflict over working time reduction and sick pay in the late 1950s, German metal employers "moved over to the counter-offensive" (Flanagan et al. 1983: 241), but now also discovered the advantages of national wage coordination. These were obvious. Big industry benefited from wages that represented a middle road between the different "abilities to pay" of small- and medium-sized enterprises, on the one hand, and larger firms, on the other (Flanagan et al. 1983: 237). Moreover, "if wages were determined in economy-wide rather than at enterprise-level negoti-ations, an individual firm's investment decision no longer affected the wages it had to pay. In these circumstances, centralized wage negotiations led to a higher level of investment and, in so far as this raises labour productivity, also to higher wages in equilibrium" (Eichengreen 1996a: 44). Both employers and workers benefited from the new settlement.

With the establishment of pattern wage bargaining, company-based welfare schemes lost their role as a fundamental alternative to the collective, corporatist social policy as represented by the Bismarckian social insurance schemes. In particular, the Ruhr industrialists lost their interest in the old-style welfare capitalism so dominant in the *Krupp*, *Stinnes*, and *Thyssen* conglomerates before the 1930s. Once heavy industry had lost its control over the market via cartel agreements, it developed an interest in better wage control. For this it required coordination with the metalworking sector. But wage coordination and thus wage moderation in times of almost full employment create strong incentives for firms to overbid the collectively negotiated wages, undermining the effects of collective agreements. In Germany's dual system of industrial relations in which works councils are prohibited from bargaining over wages, but are allowed to negotiate on fringe benefits and other supplement pay to the union wage, this wage drift often was "welfare drift."[20] Exactly this was increasingly contained by the dynamic growth of public social programs.

The central conflict of the 1920s over the relative importance of public versus private provision of social protection was over by the 1960s. Welfare corporatism and wage coordination became "strategic complements" for each other (Cooper 1999; Milgrom and Roberts 1990, 1994), complements in the sense that wage coordination reinforced employers' interests in corporatist social policy, while, at the same time, welfare state growth increased industry's interest in the coordination of wages, especially in heavy industry. Having been the fiercest opponents of the Bismarckian welfare state in the interwar years (Weisbrod 1978), employers in heavy industry slowly made their peace with the postwar compromise and even learnt to appreciate its specific advantages.

In the following section, I briefly discuss the extent to which the parallel reconstruction of the Bismarckian welfare state had an impact on the political and economic equilibrium in industrial relations that developed in the late 1950s/ early 1960s.

## 4.4  The Reconstruction of the Bismarckian Welfare State in the Late 1950s

The Adenauer pension reform of 1957 boosted welfare state spending. Social spending as a share of total public spending jumped from 55 percent in 1955 to 59 percent in 1958 and the contribution rate to old-age insurance increased from 11 percent of gross wages in 1956 to 14 percent in 1957. Total pension expenditures doubled in just three years, from DM 6 billion in 1955 to DM 12 billion in 1958 (at current prices, but during a time of low inflation). With regard to social spending as a share of GDP, Germany ranked highest of all West European countries throughout the 1950s and up until 1965 (see Table 4.5).

What is particularly noteworthy is how little criticism was heard within the contemporary reform debates about the sharp increase in social spending triggered by Adenauer's pension reform (Hockerts 1980). The main concern was that the new "dynamic" pension would endanger price stability and that it would set in

---

[20] Another aspect of this nexus which cannot be pursued in greater detail here is that company pensions, which in Germany are mainly held in the form of book reserves and represent one of the most important sources of investment capital, then allow companies to honor the promises of long employment that they have given their workforce; see Manow (2001d).

**Table 4.5**  Germany's rank among OECD countries in terms of social spending, 1950–1980, in percent of GDP

|      | Germany | Rank | OECD average | OECD maximum | OECD minimum |
|------|---------|------|--------------|--------------|--------------|
| 1950 | 14.8    | 1    | 9.3          | 14.8 (Germany)     | 5.7 (Norway)       |
| 1955 | 14.2    | 1    | 10.2         | 14.2 (Germany)     | 6.8 (Switzerland)  |
| 1960 | 15.4    | 1    | 11.4         | 15.4 (Germany)     | 7.5 (Switzerland)  |
| 1965 | 16.6    | 2    | 13.4         | 17.8 (Austria)     | 8.5 (Switzerland)  |
| 1970 | 17.0    | 5    | 15.8         | 20.0 (Netherlands) | 10.1 (Switzerland) |
| 1975 | 23.5    | 5    | 21.2         | 26.8 (Netherlands) | 15.1 (Switzerland) |
| 1980 | 23.8    | 6    | 22.8         | 32.0 (Sweden)      | 13.8 (Switzerland) |

*Source*: Alber (1989b: 40, Table 4).

motion a *scala mobile* between prices, wages, and the "dynamic" pensions. Inflation, not the immediate steep increase in social spending seems to have been the most troubling issue (Arbeitgeberverbände 1956; BDA 1956a, 1956b; Hockerts 1980). In response to the pension reform plans of the Adenauer government, the BDA recommended that firms begin to use "reservation" when deciding on new voluntary company-based social programs, given the significant expansion of the public commitments. Further, employers called for a binding upper limit on the replacement level of private and public pensions combined and for the option of adjusting past private commitments (downward) to the new situation (Arbeitgeberverbände 1956; BDA 1956a, 1956b). This clearly indicates the extent to which the growth of public social programs in the late 1950s had begun to crowd out the private schemes.

With the onset of the social reform debate in the second half of the 1950s, German unions shifted their emphasis from wage demands to demands for general "social policy" issues such as working time reduction, sick pay, or early retirement (Pirker 1979). The 1956 Hamburg DGB conference was entirely devoted to the discussion of social policy issues. The new DGB chairman, Willi Richter, elected at the Hamburg conference, was a Social Democrat MP and an expert on social policy. With the 1956–7 Schleswig-Holstein strike, unions had visibly added "social concerns to the predominantly economic issues considered 'strike-worthy' by the labor movement" (Markovits 1986: 193). Apparently, the idea of substituting political demands involving the extension of welfare entitlements for wage demands pointed to a solution for the dilemma *IG Metall* found itself in after 1955. Both the intense conflict over sick pay (in which, in 1956–7, the Schleswig-Holstein metalworkers' union staged the longest strike—sixteen weeks—in the Federal Republic's history up to that point and ever since; cf. Markovits 1986: 190–5) and the significant extension of workers' pension benefits through the pension reform of 1957 have to be seen in this light.

Workers could expect to benefit from the "industrial achievement performance model" as established with the Bismarckian regime. Initially, the welfare state helped balance unions' wage demands and the necessity of remaining competitive in world markets. In giving social policy issues top priority, *IG Metall* had almost automatically established itself as a pacesetter, since no other union could afford not to fight for the extension of "social achievements" such as the 45-hour week, sick pay, or increased employment protection. Employers, in turn, struggled to justify treating workers differently across industries with respect to social standards. These social policy issues focused primarily on issues of justice, fairness, workers' dignity, and status, and not on the more mundane issues of productivity, business cycles, and income distribution. It was then in 1963, after the metal employers had learnt of the strength of the metalworkers' union, that a concerted and organized lockout in the Baden-Württemberg region established pattern wage bargaining (Kalbitz 1979; Noé 1970).

From the employers' standpoint, welfare expansion was viewed less critically provided it helped moderate unions' wage demands. Employers, particularly those in charge of the shipbuilding companies confronted with "severe market fluctuations" within a "rapidly changing industry" (Strath 1994: 74 and 73), valued the flexibility that the various welfare state programs offered them when dealing with market volatility. Also, by coupling the interests of the large companies in the Ruhr region with the economic interests of the small and medium-sized enterprises and the exposed firms, companies like *Thyssen*, *Krupp*, and other representatives of German heavy industry were then integrated into the new equilibrium comprising industry sector bargaining and the occupational but corporatist welfare state. The Ruhr magnates gave up their old paternalist attitude of "ruling the roost" and slowly reduced their elaborate "welfare capitalist" systems. Part of these company-specific voluntary benefit packages had comprised continued wage payments in the event of sickness much like those for which *IG Metall* had called the Schleswig-Holstein strike. Again, it was evident that the strike's outcome had only had a slightly negative impact on big companies.

In the concluding section, I will summarize this chapter's main argument and will make some connections with the literature on German corporatism and the new Comparative Political Economy literature.

## 4.5 The Strategic Complements between Monetary Politics, Wage Bargaining, and the Welfare State: Swedish versus German Capitalism

The chapter started by asking which institutions underpinned the labor/capital coordination game in postwar Germany. How could the problem of "dynamic inconsistency" in the implicit bargain between employers and workers be overcome (Eichengreen 1996a)? How could workers be motivated to moderate their wage demands, which would guarantee they would profit from this bargain in the future?

Unions and employers need alternative methods of responding to external shocks if macroeconomic demand management to smooth the business cycle is not an option, as was the case in Germany in the 1950s and 1960s. As has been argued in this chapter, wage coordination as a non-self-sustaining equilibrium was reliant on the support of the welfare state. Thus, we may get a fuller picture if the traditional central bank/wage bargaining arguments (Hall 1994; Hall and Franzese 1998; Iversen 1999, 2000; Scharpf 1991; Soskice 1990a, 1990b) are complemented by arguments about the role of the welfare state in the Scandinavian or German variants of capitalism (Iversen and Pontusson 2000). This might then provide us with a more complete picture of the German political economy by putting the interplay of wage bargaining, monetary policy, and the welfare state at the center of our explanatory model.

The nexus between these three elements can be formulated in roughly the following way: whereas the Scandinavian model of capitalism is based on a combination of "centralized and solidaristic wage bargaining, flexible monetary policies, and expansion of a labor-intensive and redistributive welfare state" (Iversen and Pontusson 2000: 205), German-style capitalism up to the introduction of the euro (see Chapter 6) was based on coordinated and semi-solidaristic wage bargaining (industry bargaining), non-accommodating monetary policies (monetarism), and a transfer-heavy ("capital intensive"), non-redistributive welfare state (Iversen and Pontusson 2000: 206). The egalitarian Scandinavian welfare state was able to use decommodifying social policies and a full employment guarantee (particularly by extending public—most often: social service—employment, i.e. by the welfare state) to encourage wage restraint in nationally centralized wage bargaining—and to provide the unemployed with extensive training and active labor market policies. This is the traditional corporatist argument regarding the "Scandinavian" political exchange between wage restraint and welfare expansion which today, however, with the retreat from the full employment promise, is increasingly resembling the German equilibrium. The Bismarckian welfare state, in contrast, used social transfers strictly linked to previous wage levels and mainly passive labor market policies to reassure individual workers that their wage restraint was likely to pay off, even in the event that a downturn in the business cycle were to force workers into unemployment or into an early exit from the labor market. Countercyclical fiscal spending plays no role in this model, unlike both the Anglo-American and Scandinavian economies (cf. Carlin et al. 2015: 80). An expansion of the public sector was also not an option. In a federalist setting, with diverging political majorities at the federal and the state level, there was simply no single public sector and no single unified political will to expand it (Burkhart 2005; Lehmbruch 2000 [1976]).

A key precondition for wage moderation *à la continentale* is that the independent central bank is unwilling or unable to accommodate inflationary wage setting with an increase in the money supply, and that similarly, the government is unable or unwilling to accommodate external shocks with a loose monetary and fiscal policy. It thus becomes important for the welfare state to be in a position to provide unions with protection against recession risks, particularly unemployment. Without these welfare provisions, workers who are laid off during an economic downturn would be penalized for the wage moderation they exercised in the past, since they would not be able to benefit from future returns from previous wage restraint—in the form of higher productivity and increasing real wages. They would then not engage in wage moderation in the first place. In other words: even without being able to guarantee full employment, the German postwar welfare state had to "socialize the risk of unemployment" by other means— through a formal guarantee that unemployment would not lead to a significant drop in the standard of living for the individual worker. Moreover, the welfare state ensures the worker's participation in future income growth by way of wage-linked pensions and wage-indexed unemployment benefits.[21]

However, unions and employers first still had to learn about the "beneficial constraints" of the coordination model (Streeck 1997). Who pushed them into this beneficial equilibrium? It could not have been a non-accommodating monetary policy of the central bank (Carlin and Soskice 1990; Hall 1994; Hall and Franzese 1998; Iversen 1998b, 1999, 2000; Soskice 1990a), since the monetary policy of the German central bank was not exactly autonomous or sovereign within the Bretton Woods system (and since the introduction of the euro definitely is not nowadays).[22] On the contrary, within the Bretton Woods regime of fixed but adjustable exchange rates, an increase in the interest rate would have fueled inflation, since higher interest rates within a fixed exchange rate regime would have triggered an inflow of foreign money (Flanagan et al. 1983: 276; Holtfrerich 1998: 348; Giersch et al. 1992: 140; the problem of "imported inflation").[23] In

---

[21] Within his theoretical framework, Iversen provides a convincing explanation as to why a strongly redistributive egalitarian welfare state would have inflationary effects in semi-centralized wage-bargaining systems (Iversen and Pontusson 2000: 209). Yet he is less able to provide us with a "positive" explanation for the Bismarckian welfare state's role in "Germanic capitalism." In particular, his account is unclear on why the Bismarckian welfare state would have helped instill wage moderation in the semi-centralized German wage-bargaining regime.

[22] "If there is a miracle to be found in West Germany's postwar performance it must thus be searched for in the second stage, the continued expansion of productive capabilities after the reattainment of capacity output. It has been argued that this second wave, between 1953 and 1961, in which production was twice the 1938 level, was due to the democratic organization of industrial relations, the preservation and integration of craft and mechanical skills within the economic system, and an active state policy of promoting industrial and trades production. Germany had a productive rather than a financial economy and the strength of its currency was based on its high value-added superiority in the production of consumer goods" (Glasman 1996: 83).

[23] At the same time a decrease in the interest rate would have triggered an outflow of capital, but would not really have dampened domestic growth.

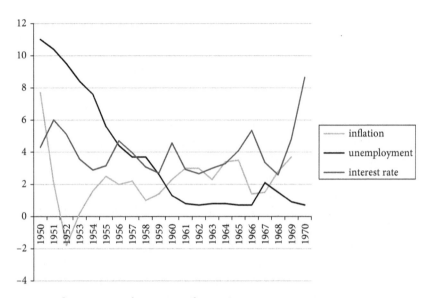

**Fig. 4.2** Inflation, unemployment, and interest rates 1950–1970
*Source*: Holtfrerich (1998).

fact, unemployment fell dramatically, inflation remained fairly stable, and the Bundesbank interest rates for the money market *decreased* in the second half of the 1950s (see Fig. 4.2).

The only efficient disciplinary instrument against wage-induced inflation would have been a revaluation of the Deutschmark, an instrument for which the government, and not the central bank, held sole responsibility and which it used only sporadically (twice between 1948 and 1971)[24] and—as critics repeatedly pointed out—each time too late and too little (Kaufmann 1969; Höpner and Lutter 2019; see section 4.4).[25] But 1961 was the year of the first revaluation of the Deutschmark which left its mark on Germany's foreign account—in 1962 it went into the red for the first time since 1950. This also motivated unions to pursue a less aggressive wage campaign.[26] So, with the central bank lacking the

---

[24] The initial rate of the Deutschmark to the US dollar was set at DM/USD 3.33 on June 20, 1948, devalued to DM/USD 4.20 on September 19, 1949. There were only two revaluations, in 1961 and 1969: on June 3, 1961 from DM/USD 4.20 to DM/USD 4.00 and then on October 26, 1969 to DM/USD 3.66 (Bordo 1993: 23–4).

[25] I therefore consider it problematic that Hall (1994) and Hall and Franzese (1998) use data from 1955 to 1990 to discuss their central bank/wage-bargaining hypothesis. Iversen (1999) correctly only uses data from the period between 1973 and 1993, i.e. post-Bretton Wood and pre-EMU data.

[26] One important factor was that the fierce Schleswig-Holstein conflict over sick-pay reform had legal consequences for *IG Metall*. It was ruled that the metalworker union should compensate companies for the economic damage caused by the strike because the union had started it despite the fact that ongoing negotiations with the employer side would have compelled the union to remain "peaceful." The compensation was set so high that *IG Metall* would have gone bankrupt or at least would have been unable to wage a strike for the foreseeable future. Consequently, the union was very

monetary instrument to instill wage discipline (Alecke 1999; Höpner and Lutter 2019; Scharpf 2018) the answer has to be found on the trade union or labor side.

This chapter presented several possible solutions to the conundrum of wage moderation in times of high growth and full employment: I argued that first the struggle for broader welfare protection pushed unions to become rather moderate on the wage front ("political distraction," Giersch et al. 1992: 75). However, I also claim that the political distraction argument does not only apply to the first half of the 1950s, with its fierce conflicts over codetermination and the Work Council Act (Giersch et al. 1992: 75), but also to the second half of the decade with the unions' struggle for sick-pay reform, reduced working time, and pension reform (and against retrenchment in healthcare). In other words, political distraction was not only due to industrial relations issues, but also to social protection issues, and not only in the early, but also in the late 1950s. In 1961 and 1963, massive lockouts in the metal industry then forced unions onto the defensive. Employers recognized the advantages of wage coordination with *IG Metall* in a pace-setting role—a pattern that became established in the late 1950s with *IG Metall*'s struggle for welfare improvements. Moreover, the coupling of welfare benefits to wages ensured that the beneficial effects of wage moderation would be fairly distributed across the different cohorts of workers and the expansion of welfare state programs helped to keep wage drift in form of firm-specific welfare programs under control.

Hence, institutional features such as autonomy in collective bargaining (*Tarifautonomie*), central bank independence, but also the fiscal autonomy of the German welfare state, its employment-based entitlement structure, the high degree of "juridification" of these welfare entitlements, and the central role played by the social partners in the administration of the welfare state, largely predetermined the course of public economic policy. These features also offered organized capital and labor a high degree of autonomy in wage and welfare issues and have therefore increased the willingness of economic agents to enter into long-term cooperation with each other (Hall and Soskice 2001a: 40).

Germany is the most open of Europe's large economies.[27] Nonetheless, the country has been able to cope with unforeseen contingencies such as unfavorable exchange rate fluctuations or a slump in international demand for German manufacturing goods without resorting to the strategies of social corporatism so prominent in the small open European nations (see Katzenstein 1984, 1985). These strategies comprise tripartite central concertation, macroeconomic demand

---

keen to settle this issue with the employers and behaved much less aggressively in the late 1950s and early 1960s.

[27] "Openness" before unification, in 1990: Germany 51 percent of GDP, France 40 percent, Italy 36 percent, UK 44.3 percent (Japan 19.6 percent; US 19.9 percent). Openness is defined here as (Imports + Exports)/GDP.

management including a flexible money supply to respond to external demand shocks, and welfare state compensation for the risks of economic openness (Frieden and Rogowski 1996; Rieger and Leibfried 1998; Rodrik 1997; Ruggie 1982, 1997). To explain this more "liberal" character of the German political economy, its lesser dependence on state intervention, and active economic policy, cannot be explained without taking the specific incentive and support structure provided by the Bismarckian welfare state into account.

In Chapter 5, I discuss how the equilibrium described above became pathological after 1973, with the onset of the first oil shock.

# 5

# Pathological Adjustment, Structural Change, and the Welfare State

## *Modell Deutschland* after the Golden Age

How did the German economy fare after the golden age, once the "days of plenty" were over? What role did the welfare state play in this period?

In this chapter,[1] I will argue that the economic slumps experienced from the early 1970s, including the post-1992 unification crisis, have regularly triggered a pathological economic response from the German political economy, producing ever higher levels of unemployment, a low level of total employment, and steadily increasing labor costs. High labor costs, particularly caused by continuously rising social insurance contributions, had adverse effects on job growth in the low wage/ low productivity service sector. Thus, the structural change from manufacturing to services—a secular trend across all developed countries (Wren 2013)—was delayed and partially forestalled in Germany, and long-term structural unemployment became more firmly rooted. The divide between labor market insiders and outsiders became increasingly entrenched. As a consequence, the German political economy was stuck in a low employment equilibrium (Esping-Andersen 1996).

What exactly is meant by the notion of a "pathological response pattern" of the German economic and political system? The response of the German production-and-protection-regime to economic downturns followed a fairly regular pattern: both the independence of the German central bank and the federalist fragmentation of the "public purse" prevented the use of strategic devaluation or expansionary fiscal or monetary policies as an immediate response to economic shocks in order to maintain high levels of employment (Scharpf 1987). At the same time, real wage flexibility within Germany's semi-centralized wage-setting system provided for wage moderation. However, this was regularly insufficient to prevent large-scale job losses in sudden economic downturns. Consequently, the welfare state became the main instrument of economic adjustment. The welfare state cushioned economic crises with the help of various social insurance schemes— most of them designed to bring relief to the labor market by reducing the labor supply. German labor market policy was primarily a passive policy of "negative

---

[1] Parts of this chapter (Sections 5.1 and 5.2) were jointly written with Eric Seils and published as Manow and Seils (2000a, 2000b).

*Social Protection, Capitalist Production: The Bismarckian Welfare State in the German Political Economy, 1880–2015.*
Philip Manow, Oxford University Press (2020). © Philip Manow.
DOI: 10.1093/oso/9780198842538.001.0001

supply," and welfare state programs were the most prominent of the many instruments that channeled people into various forms of non-employment. This strategy was costly and led to rising social insurance contributions. Given the (short-term) rigidities of Germany's wage-bargaining system, an increase in labor taxation was usually not fully offset by a corresponding drop in wages, but translated into higher wage costs, at least in the short term. As a consequence, unemployment and non-employment increased even further, because high (non-wage) labor costs rendered certain jobs unproductive or internationally uncompetitive or dampened the job growth that otherwise would have taken place.

Yet, since all features of the German production-*cum*-protection system were geared toward stable employment relations, toward long-term economic coordination between workers and managers, and a high level of status protection for workers, reemploying dismissed workers was difficult. Companies were hesitant to employ new workers once economic growth had picked up again. While companies "hoarded" labor during economic downturns and tried to avoid layoffs as long as possible (for instance through short-time work), they used overtime work and capital investments to cope with increased demand during economic upturns. If layoffs became unavoidable, numerous social insurance provisions offered workers a relatively "soft landing" (most often with early retirement). Thus, highly stable employment relations, once terminated, translated into long-term stable unemployment or into various forms of generously compensated non-employment. The welfare state institutions designed to make employment economically "shock-proof" simultaneously produced pronounced labor market hysteresis.

While the vicious cycle of negative labor supply policies, rising welfare and therefore labor costs, low employment and high unemployment, further increases in social spending, and a constant wage pressure to improve productivity already put both the system of social protection and the labor market under stress, the response pattern of the German political economy to economic crises revealed yet another pathology. Given that the Bundesbank's tight monetary stance forced the government to exercise strict fiscal discipline during economic downturns, not only could the government not engage in countercyclical spending, it even had to cut public spending in order to reduce the budget deficit (since tax revenue decreased and government outlays—particularly social spending—increased during a recession). This led to the specific adjustment dynamic of the German political economy: the German welfare state cushioned the immediate effects of an economic downturn. Increased social spending regularly translated into contribution rate hikes—usually in a quasi-automatic fashion, since contributions to health and pension insurance have to be raised automatically if expenses systematically exceed revenue. Only for unemployment insurance do contribution rate hikes have to be legislated by parliament. However, since the federal government is obliged to cover deficits in this insurance branch, it has an incentive to raise contribution rates. Later, once the trough of the recession has been passed, the government has strong incentives to use the increased revenue from higher contributions to bring financial relief to the public budget at the expense of the social insurance budgets. Cost shifting took place in many ways. For instance, the primarily contribution-financed German welfare state was burdened with new tasks previously financed from taxes, or financial transfers from the public budgets to the special budgets of the social insurance schemes were cut, or purely contribution-financed schemes (e.g. health insurance) assumed responsibilities from schemes where the public budget was financially involved (e.g. pension and unemployment insurance), etc. Rarely have German governments, of whatever political composition, managed to withstand the temptation to reduce budgetary strain at the expense of the welfare state once the worst of an economic crisis was over. My proposal is to term this pathological adjustment pattern typical of the German political economy *asymmetrical welfare Keynesianism*—asymmetrical because contribution rates rise in a crisis, but do not fall in a recession.

Thus, in Germany, recessions regularly triggered a dual process of cost externalization: firms sought to shift their adjustment costs onto the welfare state through early retirement, short-time work, unemployment insurance, etc., and the government attempted to ease budgetary pressures by reducing its share of social spending. This response pattern is largely procyclical, but more so during a crisis and less so during an upturn, since, in the latter case, labor is not relieved of costs as much as it had previously been burdened. As a consequence, social spending, contribution rates to the social insurance schemes, and structural unemployment displayed ratchet effects: with each new crisis they all reached a higher plateau.

The steady increase in non-wage labor costs due to rising social insurance contributions impeded employment growth in the domestic (low wage/low productivity) service sector. This led to an unfavorable employment ratio, especially when industry could not anymore generate the employment growth it had generated in the 1950s and 1960s. Declining employment, in turn, was problematic within a social policy model that relied primarily on revenue from dependent employment. The resulting financial crisis of the welfare state and the labor market distortions caused by the exaggerated cost burdens imposed on labor were salient characteristics of the unification crisis in 1992. However, the aforementioned pathological response pattern of the German political economy had already become established with the first and second oil crises of the early 1970s and 1980s (for more details see Hemerijck et al. 2000; Manow and Seils 2000a, 2000b). *Modell Deutschland* continued to be characterized by it until the early 2000s, when, at least to some extent, the *Agenda 2010* reforms broke with this adjustment pattern (see Chapter 6).

It is evident that my explanation for Germany's sluggish economic performance from the mid-1970s to the late 1990s uses elements outlined in the preceding chapters. To reiterate, these components are:

- the importance of a high degree of central bank independence;
- limited (short-term) wage flexibility in an autonomous wage-setting system;
- the federal government's limited capacity for macroeconomic intervention within Germany's "multi-veto-point" polity;
- a production regime based on long-term employment relations and stable economic coordination between managers and workers, employers and unions;
- a government forced by the Bundesbank to exert strict fiscal discipline;
- a welfare state designed to buffer economic shocks and to absorb redundant labor either with generous early retirement programs or with unemployment insurance, which allows for long drawing periods at relatively generous replacement levels (Nickell and Layard 1999); and, finally,
- the vulnerability of the German political economy with respect to external shocks given the high degree of "openness" and the high level of export dependence of the German economy.

The independence of the German central bank plays a role in this explanatory model, not only because its strict monetarist strategy forestalled an active, Keynesian macroeconomic management, but also because the bank forced the government to follow strict fiscal discipline in an almost procyclical fashion (Hall 1994: 18).

The adverse employment effects of increased non-wage labor costs were neither offset by an active labor market policy combined with an expansionary public employment policy, as in Scandinavia, nor were the moderately centralized German unions able to fully factor the rising non-wage labor costs into their wage demands. In this respect, we can plausibly claim that Germany's "latent corporatism" primarily burdened the increasing number of labor market outsiders with the costs of economic adjustment. Unions, employers, and the state colluded (with the help of the Bismarckian welfare state) at the expense of women, the long-term unemployed, the low-skilled, and frustrated job-seekers in the "hidden reserve"—the swelling ranks of those excluded from the regular labor market (Esping-Andersen 1996; Scharpf 1997). The tendency both of firms and of the central government to externalize their costs at the expense of the German welfare state has certainly become particularly salient in the wake of German unification, but, as will be shown below, it was already a well-established adjustment pattern in the mid-1970s (Jochem and Siegel 1999).

Thus, in contrast to the conventional globalization argument about the detrimental effects of a generous welfare state on international competitiveness, in the following sections I will argue that, in the German case, it is more important to analyze the adverse impact of an expensive (payroll-tax financed) welfare state on job growth in the sheltered sectors (Iversen and Soskice 2015), particularly in the service sector. I claim that the poor job growth record of the service sector was the prime reason why Germany's coordinated political economy has come under such stress since the second half of the 1970s. Further, in contrast to the conventional arguments about the unfavorable impact of German unification on an otherwise highly successful economic model, I will stress the long-term pathologies of *Modell Deutschland* dating back to "the end of the golden age" as signified by the first oil shock in 1974.

The following sections will describe how three consecutive crises have fundamentally altered the "terms of trade" for the German political economy, in general, and the German welfare state, in particular: the two oil shocks of the early 1970s and 1980s and German unification (see Section 5.1). In Section 5.2, I describe the political responses, particularly the cost-shifting strategies used by the federal government to move social spending obligations increasingly onto employers and employees. Section 5.3 discusses the impact of both the "negative labor market supply policy" and of the cost externalization strategy of firms and the government on the German employment structure and the economy in general. In this respect, I emphasize the poor job growth in the service sector and its unfavorable effect on welfare state finance. In the last section, I summarize the argument.

## 5.1 "Shocks to the System": The First and Second Oil Crisis and German Unification

It has often been said that 1973 marked a watershed in the postwar economic history of the OECD countries. This is certainly true for Germany, which was severely affected by the eventual collapse of the Bretton Woods system and the steep rise in the price of oil.

In May 1971, the Deutschmark was allowed to float against the US dollar. This event had a dual impact on the German economy. First, it freed the Bundesbank from the obligation to support the dollar (Buchheim 1989: 192) and for the first time provided the central bank with the tools to effectively fight domestic inflation. The German central bank switched almost immediately to a tight monetary policy which it pursued until the economy was in the midst of a recession. As early as 1973, the Bundesbank had begun to use instruments targeting the volume of central bank money rather than bank reserves (OECD 1983: 30). In 1974, the Bundesbank officially shifted to monetarism announcing that growth in the volume of money had become the new guideline for its monetary policy. With its harsh response to the inflationary wage settlements in the 1974 wage round, the central bank lent

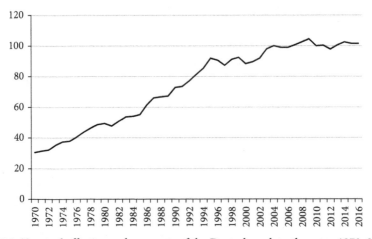

**Fig. 5.1** Nominal effective exchange rate of the Deutschmark to the euro, 1970–2015
*Source:* OECD, Economic Outlook.

credibility to its anti-inflationary stance and established itself as a powerful actor whose signals neither governments nor unions dared to ignore (Hall and Franzese 1998; Scharpf 1991). Second, floating the Deutschmark led to a substantial appreciation of the currency over the next two decades, creating additional risks and cost pressures for Germany's export-oriented industries (see Fig. 5.1).

The first oil shock was the most obvious sign that the period in which Germany had miraculously been able to combine high growth, low unemployment, and low inflation, had come to an end. With the central bank turning monetarist, a Keynesian response to the crisis—like the one in 1966/67—was no longer an option. Admittedly, the government's initial reaction signaled that it had switched from a restrictive course to a policy approach that fostered investment (Finanzen 1974: 9–10; 1975: 7–8). However, its expansionary measures were increasingly counteracted by a central bank committed more than ever to monetary rigor. The Bundesbank continued to stick to a tight monetary policy until its battle against inflation had pushed Germany into a deep recession (Scharpf 1991: 132). Within the Social Democratic/Liberal coalition, faith in Keynesian macroeconomic steering gradually waned, until the government ultimately made a U-turn and embarked on a restrictive fiscal policy in the mid-1970s. In 1976, fiscal policy was tightened considerably as a result of the government's new political priority: the consolidation of the budget. Public investment was severely curtailed. Retrenchment in pensions and health insurance combined with major contribution rate hikes accompanied this policy shift.

Germany was hit hard by the recession. Economic activity had already decelerated in 1974, not least because of the Bundesbank's restrictive monetary policy.

**Fig. 5.2** Employment rate (total labor force in percent of population aged 15–64)
*Source*: OECD Annual Labour Force Statistics, various years.

However, in 1975 the situation deteriorated further. With growth turning nega-tive, unemployment climbed to over a million and industrial employment declined dramatically. The country was unable to make up for this loss when the economy finally recovered. The permanent decline in industrial employment contrasted with developments in the service sector, where the only impact of the recession was to hamper, but not stop, job growth. However, growth in service employment still proved insufficient to absorb job losses in manufacturing. The overall result was therefore a drop in the employment rate below the international average, despite a shrinking working-age population (see Fig. 5.2). It goes without saying that the decline in employment created a problem for a welfare state largely financed from social insurance contributions levied on labor.

Toward the end of the 1970s, public spending rose again and this was accom-panied by measures promoting housing construction, lower taxes, and providing additional incentives for investment. This brief Keynesian revival was, to a large extent, due to growing international pressure. At the G7 Summit in Bonn in the summer of 1978, the Schmidt government was urged to pursue a more expan-sionary fiscal policy. Germany, together with Japan, was expected to act as the locomotive pulling the western world out of its recession and into a new period of growth and prosperity. Tax cuts and additional measures implemented as a result of the summit amounted to about 1 percent of GNP (Finanzen 1978: 7). Thus by the time Germany entered another recession in the early 1980s, fiscal policy was clearly on an expansionary course again.

When another oil price hike depressed demand and fueled inflation in the industrialized countries at the start of the 1980s, history seemed to repeat itself. Once again, there was a precipitous decline in manufacturing employment, while growth in service employment was not sufficient to absorb all the redundant labor. This time, however, the job losses were accompanied by strong growth in the working-age population. The result was another million unemployed and another drop in the employment-to-population ratio (see Fig. 5.2). A subsequent upturn was too weak to reduce unemployment significantly until 1986. Thereafter the country's economic recovery gained momentum and developed into a boom that peaked around 1990.

How did the central bank and the federal government respond to the second economic downturn in the early 1980s? Again, the Bundesbank continued with its hard currency policy and urged the federal government to consolidate its budget. In 1980, the fiscal stimulus that resulted from the G7 Summit in Bonn two years earlier combined with the growing energy bill from the second oil crisis to produce Germany's first current account deficit in fourteen years. The central bank soon came to regard the "locomotive experiment" as a failure and resolved to maintain a strong external value for the Deutschmark. In order to achieve this goal and to fight inflation, the bank had already adopted a tight monetary policy back in 1980 (Sachverständigenrat 1980: 97–102). The central bank continued with its restrictive policy until the trough of the recession had been passed in 1983. The fiscal expansion prior to the recession also left its mark on the federal budget. It went into deficit. The central bank made it clear that it was not willing to accept persistent budget deficits, since these would strengthen inflationary pressures and undermine confidence in the Deutschmark (Franz 1990: 25). Given that the Bundesbank's restrictive policy contributed to high real interest rates, this monetary stringency compelled the Schmidt government to initiate a shift toward a more restrictive fiscal policy (Schmidt 1990a: 53–5, 60).

When the Kohl government came to power in 1982, it shelved expansive policies altogether and embarked on a policy of budgetary consolidation with the aim of subsequently reducing taxes. It intended to do this primarily by curbing public spending, particularly social welfare. The Kohl government further announced that it would reduce public ownership in industry and deregulate labor markets. This moderate supply-side policy was finally in line with the Bundesbank's monetarism and with the views of the independent Council of Economic Experts (*Sachverständigenrat*). In the 1980s, the Kohl government achieved unequivocal success when it turned a deficit of −3.3 percent of GDP in 1982 into a slight surplus of 0.1 percent of GDP in 1989.

How was this achieved? First and foremost, economic recovery after 1983 reduced budgetary pressures. Second, the government increased revenue by raising the VAT in June 1983. Third, the Bundesbank's profits, which had been negligible in the 1970s, were quite substantial after 1982. From 1986 onward, privatization also proved to be a rich source of revenue (cf. Finanzen 1997: 200–3, Table 6). While this additional revenue clearly helped the government achieve its goals, the CDU/CSU/FDP coalition also undertook efforts to curb expenditures, particularly welfare state transfer payments and public investment. Toward the end of the government's first term, a two-stage tax reform became a political priority, for which it was even prepared to accept somewhat higher deficits (Sturm 1998: 186). In 1985, the Bundestag approved the tax reform, which provided taxpayers with aggregate tax relief of DM 19.4 billion in two stages (1986 and 1988). A third stage, to be implemented in 1990, involved the biggest cuts. All in all, the tax cuts amounted to around 2.25 percent of GDP. Unfortunately, the revenue losses from the final stage coincided with additional costs for incorporating the former GDR into a united Germany (Sachverständigenrat 1990: 136–7). It was during the drive for unification that the Kohl government finally departed from the consolidation policy it had embarked on in the 1980s.

Unification led to a major economic crisis in Germany since a crumbling industrial structure had to be integrated into one of the world's most modern industrial countries under conditions of a one-to-one exchange rate between the East German mark and the Deutschmark. This conversion rate was based primarily on a political calculus dictated by the first free election in the GDR in March 1990, by the upcoming national election in December of that year, and another seventeen elections at the regional or state level in 1990 (Streit 1998: 698–9). As had been predicted by the major economic research institutes, the politically determined conversion rate between the East German and West German mark "largely wiped out whatever competitiveness eastern firms retained, sealing the collapse of the eastern economy" (Carlin et al. 2015: 51. The disastrous economic consequences, namely a massive surge in unemployment, had to be offset first and foremost by the welfare state. The Kohl government had simply ignored the forecasts of the major economic research institutes and the warnings of the Bundesbank. The president of the Bundesbank, Pöhl, resigned in protest. Yet the central bank still possessed a "second-strike capacity" and soon made use of it.

The adverse effects of an exchange rate largely out of sync with the economic fundamentals were aggravated by the failure of the wage-setting regime to at least partially cushion the enormous cost pressures generated by the sudden introduction of the Deutschmark into East Germany. Instead (West German) employers and unions and the government opted for a high-tech/high-wage strategy for rebuilding the East German economy. The aim was for East Germany to quickly catch up with western standards. The shock therapy that characterized the monetary union was now repeated with respect to wages. As early as a month prior to unification, demands for rapid improvements in living standards had already resulted in wage increases of around 17 percent (Sinn and Sinn 1991: 145). In March 1991, when a steep rise in unemployment had already been recorded, the metalworkers' union and the metal employers negotiated an agreement that would have closed the gap between eastern and western German wages by 1994. In contrast to wage negotiations in the "old" Federal Republic, collective bargaining in East Germany was not linked to productivity plus expected "natural" inflation, but to the existing wage differences between the East and West. There was little to prevent the unions from getting their way. In the West, neither organized labor nor capital was keen to see competition from cheap labor in the eastern parts of their domestic market. In addition, employers in the East were much weaker than their counterparts in the West. Since there was no way for productivity to be increased in line with wages, unit labor costs skyrocketed above western levels (Sachverständigenrat 1997: 92, Table 36; 1998: 80, Table 28).

As a result of this major maladjustment, continued labor shedding in the eastern part of the German economy was unavoidable. Overall employment in the GDR had always been much higher than in the West, even if this was at the cost of massive overstaffing. In the second half of 1990, employment in the East began to decline sharply, however. Between 1991 and 1993, total employment shrank by 15 percent and manufacturing employment fell by some 45 percent. Employment in manufacturing even continued to decline into the late 1990s (Sachverständigenrat 1998: 90–7).

The regions of the former Federal Republic initially benefited from unification. Massive financial transfers to the East stimulated demand for western consumer goods. The tax cuts carried out during the third step of the tax reform further fueled the boom. In the wake of unification, the federal government believed that the additional budget outlays would be covered by a new economic miracle in the East and by the privatization of the former state-owned companies (Czada 1995: 5). The German chancellor firmly promised not to raise any additional taxes. Facing the first all-German elections in December 1990, few politicians were prepared to publicly dampen these optimistic expectations. The Christian Democrats easily won this landmark election.

Yet instead of experiencing a renewed German economic miracle, eastern Germany was devastated by depression. The privatization of the former East German state-owned companies placed a serious burden on the federal budget (Deutsche Bundesbank 1994a: 22–31). In 1991, it was still possible to cover a large proportion of expenses with additional tax revenues resulting from the ongoing boom in western Germany. The remaining costs were financed with rising deficits. In view of the steeply rising profits in the wake of the unification boom, the unions were unwilling to pursue a policy of wage moderation. Starting in 1990, they pushed for wage increases that outstripped growth in labor productivity (Sachverständigenrat 1991: 200–1). Along with budget deficits resulting partly from the Kohl government's tax reform, this wage push was one of the factors fueling inflation.

Even in the face of a challenge as huge as unification, the Bundesbank maintained its hard monetary policy. It made clear from the very beginning that it would not accept deficit financing of the unification process beyond a level that could be justified by initial "unexpected burdens" (Deutsche Bundesbank 1991b: 21). The bank also had no patience with the high wage increases and signaled to both the federal government and the unions that it was unwilling to accommodate their inflationary policies (Deutsche Bundesbank 1991a: 17). In the months following unification, it raised the bank rate to record postwar levels (Deutsche Bundesbank 1992). With the Deutschmark as an anchor currency within the European Monetary System (EMS), this necessarily had a wider European impact (Höpner and Spielau 2016). Other EMS member countries had to follow the Bundesbank's high interest rate policy if they wanted to stay within the monetary system. This caused turmoil in the EMS. Eventually, Britain and Italy were forced to leave the system in 1993, at least temporarily. Hence, the Deutschmark appreciated even further. High wage increases aggravated the German industry's competitiveness problem. Because the Bundesbank waited until September 1992 to begin lowering interest rates, the western German economy slumped into a deep recession in 1993. With the onset of the recession, a decline in employment ensued that did not really come to an end until 1997 (see Figs. 5.2 and 5.3).

The unification crisis revealed largely the same pattern as the earlier recessions. Employment in industry (i.e. mainly manufacturing) declined significantly, and employment growth in the service sector was unable to offset the major drop in employment. Although the economy recovered quickly in 1994, overall employment continued to fall. By and large, the economic situation had improved considerably by 1995. Wage negotiations that year were, however, unusually

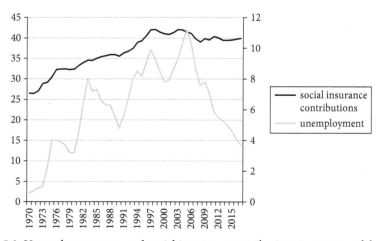

**Fig. 5.3** Unemployment rate and social insurance contributions in percent of the gross wage in Germany, 1970–2017

*Sources*: OECD Annual Labour Force Statistics and German Federal Ministry of Labor and Social Affairs (BMAS), *Statistisches Taschenbuch. Arbeits- und Sozialstatistik* (Bonn: Bundesministerium für Arbeit- und Sozialordnung 2000).

confrontational despite soaring unemployment. The metalworkers called a strike limited to a prosperous district in Bavaria and ultimately managed to push through a wage increase of 5 percent (Thelen 2000). At the same time, another surge in the exchange rate aggravated exporters' cost competitiveness problems (Lindlar and Scheremet 1998). Labor shedding continued, despite the return to wage moderation in 1996 and 1997 and the Deutschmark's simultaneous depreciation.

In all three crises, Germany's economic and political response pattern looked strikingly similar: a massive employment loss, partially due to the lack of (short-term) flexibility of the wage-setting system,[2] triggers rising welfare spending. Firms use the many instruments of the welfare state to make "painless" adjustments. This leads to rising social insurance contributions, which, in turn, contribute to the increase in wage costs, which, again, are not fully offset by moderate growth of wages. The consequences are an increase in the number of long-term unemployed and in the percentage of the population that is "economically inactive." In the attempt to get welfare costs and the public deficit under control again, governments of different political persuasions have applied basically the same strategies: various cost-cutting measures combined with a rise in contribution rates to balance the social insurance budgets. Once the worst of an economic downturn is over, governments have repeatedly used the surplus revenue generated by increased contributions to bring financial relief to the public budget. Hence, recovery from the previous economic shock has always been slow, particularly because the government uses favorable economic circumstances to reduce public debt and to shift financial burdens from the official budget to the special budgets of the social insurance schemes. This further contributes to making labor more expensive. As a consequence, employers increasingly substitute labor with capital within the rigid German labor market and wage-setting regime. Hence, domestic job growth is too poor to reduce unemployment and non-employment, while German industry retains its high level of productivity and international competitiveness.

Every time, the external shocks hit Germany during a period of expansionary fiscal policy and at a point when welfare provisions had been extended again in order to assist those left unemployed from the last crisis and/or to bring financial relief for the public budget. In each crisis, the same sequence could be observed in which the welfare bill increased, and attempts were made to cut back government and welfare spending, thereby aggravating the crisis. With each crisis, Germany

---

[2] To make the point clear: the lack of flexibility is mainly short term—which is not at all surprising given that the advantage of wage coordination lies precisely in making wage costs more predictable in the short to medium term. In the longer run, German unions remain moderate. This at least is true for the 1980s. From 1983 onward, the share of national income accounted for by income from dependent work fell (Sachverständigenrat 1998: 289). This was accompanied by a rise in the rate of return on capital and investment (Sachverständigenrat 1996: 62). Some observers have concluded that this was the reason for strong job growth in the 1980s (Lapp and Lehment 1997).

reached a higher level of mass unemployment and a lower level of total employment.

In the following section, I will analyze in more detail the use and misuse of the welfare state as part of a strategy to cope with external shocks. In this respect we can observe first, the use of the social insurance schemes to handle the *labor market consequences* of the crisis, then second, and with a certain time lag, the use of the social insurance schemes to manage the crisis's *fiscal implications*. In respect of the latter, cost shifting at the expense of the contribution-financed social programs was the most distinctive trait of the political reaction to the three consecutive economic shocks.

## 5.2  The Welfare State as a Buffer during Economic Downturns: The Labor Market

The practice of using the welfare state as a policy instrument for labor market adjustments and for economic restructuring started with the first recession that hit postwar Germany in 1966/67. At the same time as (and, in part, as a consequence of) the first postwar recession, the Grand Coalition government formed by the Christian Democrats and the Social Democrats came into power in 1966. The Social Democrats, in particular, planned to combat Germany's first recession with "active policy" and "integrated planning." At this point, the welfare state was already a prominent means of "active" economic adjustment. Politicians and experts not only contemplated the role that social insurance could play in a Keynesian policy of countercyclical spending (especially due to the time lag in pension adjustments), but also debated the beneficial labor market effects of a generous pension policy, particularly of generous early retirement provisions. This linkage between labor policy and social (pension) policy was a result of the integrated administrative responsibility of the Federal Ministry of Labor and Social Affairs (BMAS) for both domains and of the bipartite/corporatist structure of the German social insurance system (see Chapter 2). This helps explain why the government was not proactively pursuing a policy of massive deficit spending and low interest rates when the first oil crisis hit the German economy. Neither did it encourage or support central wage coordination. Rather it used the welfare state as an absorber for an economic shock that was considered to be only temporary. To be more specific, the German version of a full employment policy was designed to achieve full employment not through the state generating an increase in the demand for labor (the traditional *Keynesian* response), but by decreasing the supply of labor through the welfare state (the traditional *conservative continental* response; Esping-Andersen 1996).

In Germany, *social policy*, rather than income policy, appears "to constitute a core domain of liberal corporatism" (Lehmbruch 1977: 96). Given the fact that the postwar economic miracle of the 1950s and 1960s was and still is interpreted primarily as an achievement of ordoliberal non-interventionism, the commitment to full employment policies is far more weakly established within the German SPD and the unions than in the Austrian or Swedish labor movement (Flanagan et al. 1983: 264–6)[3]—not taking into account here that the institutional preconditions for such a full employment policy are much less developed in Germany anyway than in these two traditional neo-corporatist countries. Being partly unwilling, partly unable to increase the demand for labor through active macroeconomic management, the German government thus tried to reduce its supply. As an immediate response to the recession of the 1970s, the SPD/FDP coalition stopped the inflow of migrant workers and awarded special premiums to those who returned to their home countries.

At the same time, the social insurance schemes turned into an instrument of "negative labor supply policy." Admittedly, even in the heyday of the economic miracle, unemployment and pension schemes had been used to channel older workers out of the labor market in order to avoid the appearance of open unemployment in declining sectors such as mining and steel. However, after the severe recession of the mid-1970s, this strategy became the standard operating procedure in response to economic downturns and external shocks. This "passive" response pattern was accompanied by more active elements, such as work creation programs, mostly in construction, though later on also in social services (Schmid 1990: 403). The number of workers employed under these programs rose from 16,000 in 1975 to 51,000 in 1979. Vocational training had already been at the heart of the 1969 Employment Promotion Act, a law designed in the late 1960s to deal with labor scarcity rather than mass unemployment. Training was seen as an instrument for facilitating structural change and avoiding job losses. The scope of and funding for these measures increased considerably during the recession of 1975, but soon fell victim to the austerity-minded Budget Act mentioned above (Garlichs and Maier 1982: 95–6).

However, the pension insurance became even more important than the unemployment insurance as an instrument of labor market policy. Just months before the onset of the first oil crisis, the pension reform of 1972 had opened up the possibility of "flexible retirement" at age 63 without any actuarial reductions in benefits. Although this measure was introduced for reasons completely unrelated to labor market considerations, unfavorable employment prospects for older

---

[3] "The unions were not likely to be strongly deterred in their choice of a wage policy by potentially adverse output or substitution effects on the employment of such groups as foreigners, college graduates, women seeking part-time employment, school leavers seeking apprenticeships, or even workers past the age of fifty whose share in unemployment was reduced after the 1967 recession by a lowering of the legal retirement age in 1973 and by contractual provision for greater job security [ . . . ] Between 1973 and 1977, the unemployment rates among these demographic groups were substantially higher than the total unemployment rate and with the exception of unemployment of older men increased more rapidly" (Flanagan et al. 1983: 269–70).

workers after the first oil crisis made the flexible retirement option increasingly attractive. The implementation of flexible retirement had an immediate impact on a second route to early retirement, disability pensions for those completely or partially unable to work (*Erwerbsunfähigkeitsrenten*). In part, flexible pensions replaced disability pensions since it proved easier for disabled workers who had fulfilled the specified waiting period to leave the labor market by way of flexible retirement rather than through the cumbersome procedures of the disability scheme. As a result, there was a sharp decline in the number of people entering the disability scheme once flexible retirement had become an option. In the years following the recession, however, the number of "disabled entrants" increased significantly again. This was partly due to two important court rulings (in 1969 and 1976) according to which the definition of "incapacity to work" (*Erwerbsunfähigkeit*) must also take into account the situation on the labor market, that is, the prospects for a person who is less than fully capable of working but not completely disabled finding appropriate part-time employment in his or her respective profession[4] (and at an acceptable distance from his or her home).

The third route to early retirement was known as the "59er rule."[5] This regulation establishes the right for an individual to claim a pension at the age of 60 if he or she has been unemployed for the preceding 12 months. Companies usually offer workers aged 59 or even younger the opportunity to top up their unemployment benefits to the level of their last net earnings until the employee can draw a pension at the age of 60. In large firms this became the primary strategy (after overtime reduction and short-time working) for responding to economic downturns (Russig 1982: 263). It was a policy that met with broad acceptance among workers. Since none of the three routes to early retirement were "actuarially fair," workers had a very strong incentive to retire early (Börsch-Supan 1998, 2000).

If the Kohl government pursued a partly contradictory strategy this was due to the fact that it was simultaneously trying to achieve two partly conflicting goals.

---

[4] Hence, a legal interpretation of disability became dominant which took the situation on the labor market into consideration. In conjunction with this new interpretation, pensions were not only to be granted if an individual's working capacity was reduced by more than a half, but also if his or her working capacity was reduced by less than half but no appropriate part-time job was available for the applicant (within one year *and* in the vicinity of a worker's place of residence; Seidel 1990). This approach (*konkrete Betrachtungsweise*) opened up enormous "moral hazard" opportunities for employers and employees. Pension insurance assumed de facto responsibility for the labor market risks of all insured individuals experiencing any degree of purported reduction in working capacity, while unemployment insurance was only responsible for insured individuals who still had full earning capacity.

[5] This regulation was introduced for white-collar workers in the wake of the Great Depression of 1929 because periods of unemployment were judged to be longer for them than for blue-collar workers. The regulation was extended several times throughout the 1930s and was finally reenacted in West Germany in 1955. Blue-collar workers were also able to benefit from this regulation with the pension reform of 1957, which put them on equal footing with salaried employees in several other important respects as well (Nitsche 1986).

These were, on the one hand, containing social spending and, on the other hand, helping firms cope with the economic crisis by offering them the opportunity to lay off workers almost "painlessly" with the help of the welfare state. The conflict between these two objectives was partly solved by "policy sequencing," which led to the same procyclical policy profile that can be seen in active labor market policy: program cutbacks during economic slumps were followed by considerable expansion of entitlements and eligibility during boom periods. The expansionary measures then became particularly important when the next crisis arrived in the early 1990s. In the meantime, the extension of (contribution-financed) social programs prevented non-wage labor costs from decreasing during the boom as much as they had increased during the recession.

Among the more restrictive measures, the 1983 reduction in unemployment benefits deserves special mention. Where early retirement was concerned, the 1984 budget law tightened eligibility criteria for disability pensions, a restriction that particularly affected women, who tend to have more uneven working careers. As a result we can see a steep decline (of about 50 percent) in the take-up rate for women's disability pensions from 1984 to 1985 (Verband Deutscher Rentenversicherungsträger 1997: 53). At the same time, however, it was made considerably easier for women to obtain a standard old-age pension age 60. Hence, the decline in disability pensions was partly offset by a significant rise in the take-up rate for the standard old-age pension scheme. In 1984, the government also introduced the Pre-Retirement Act (*Vorruhestandsgesetz*). The act was meant to be a substitute for the more costly 59er rule which established the right to pensions due to long-term unemployment (Mares 1997). The Pre-Retirement Act gave employers the opportunity to let workers go at age 58 (therefore dubbed the 58er rule) and pay them between two (women's retirement age was 60) and five years' ("flexible retirement" age for men was 63) income equal to at least 65 percent of their last net wage. At the same time, the law provided a public subsidy of up to 35 percent of the retirement wage in the event that a vacant position be filled for at least two years by a registered unemployed person or trainee. However, pre-retirement did not arouse very much excitement among employers and workers, since it proved more costly to employers and offered less generous benefits to workers. The take-up rate was rather modest, at about 165,000 workers between 1984 and 1988, when the act expired. The substitution rate has been estimated to have been around 80 percent, resulting in a maximum of 135,000 new jobs (Jacobs et al. 1991; see Frerich and Frey 1993 for even lower figures). This is a rather unimpressive number, particularly since the government simultaneously tried to discourage employers from continuing to use the unemployment route to early retirement. As early as 1982, the government had forced firms using the 59er rule to pay back unemployment benefits for workers dismissed at age 59 (if they had been employed by the company for a longer period). Two years later, employers were also forced to repay pension and health insurance contributions made by the Federal Labor Office on behalf of the unemployed. However, firms were quick to challenge this new provision in court. After protracted legal battles, the employers' repayments were ultimately rather insignificant. Thus, while the 59er rule was still frequently used as a route to retirement, the Pre-Retirement Act expired in 1988 (and was succeeded by an even less successful program with a negligible labor market impact). The employers' obligation to pay back social insurance contributions made by the Federal Labor Office was abolished altogether in 1991. The number of unemployment pensions steadily increased from the mid-1980s and skyrocketed in the wake of the unification crisis in the early 1990s. While these attempts to counteract the tendency toward an ever earlier exit from the labor market did not result in very much, the extension of entitlements introduced when the crisis appeared to be over and when social insurance had gone into surplus again had a much greater economic impact.

In the second half of the 1980s, when economic growth had picked up again, one of the more important expansionary measures was certainly the major extension of the drawing period for unemployment benefits, particularly for workers aged 54 and over. Since 1987, these workers have received standard unemployment benefit (*Arbeitslosengeld*) for up to thirty-two months. From the establishment of unemployment insurance in 1927, until as late as 1985, the maximum period for drawing this benefit had been twelve months. Not surprisingly, the almost threefold extension was enacted at a time when economic prospects seemed to be getting brighter and when the unemployment insurance budget had moved back into surplus.[6] The measure was particularly targeted at older workers who had lost their jobs during the preceding crisis and who had only very limited prospects of finding new employment.

Given the longer duration of unemployment benefits, workers could now leave the labor market as early as age 57 and then go on to draw a long-term unemployment pension at age 60. The 59er rule effectively became a 57er rule (Jacobs et al. 1991: 203). The focus of this measure on the older long-term unemployed was underlined by the government's policy of freeing workers at age 58 and above from any obligation to be available for any employment offered by labor offices, the local offices of the Federal Employment Agency. A convenient political side effect was that these hard-to-employ individuals (many of them jobless since the last crisis) no longer even appeared in the unemployment statistics. The overall effect of these various measures on labor force participation for males in the 55–64 age group is depicted in Figure 5.4.

However, there were also more active attempts to address the labor market problems of the 1980s. Overall, participation in active labor market policies

---

[6] The budget of the Federal Employment Agency showed a surplus of DM 3.1 and DM 2.3 billion in 1984 and 1985, respectively, and a marginal deficit of DM 0.2 billion in 1986. Between 1983 and 1988 the government no longer needed to cover Employment Agency deficits with state subsidies.

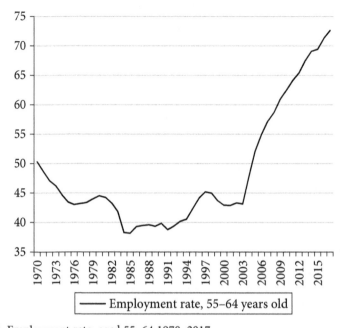

**Fig. 5.4** Employment rate, aged 55–64 1970–2017
*Source*: OECD, Labour Force Statistics (various years).

increased from the late 1970s through the 1980s, albeit with temporary setbacks. Variation in spending was not due to anticyclical policies but, quite to the contrary, followed a procyclical logic dictated by the mode of financing for active labor market measures (Scharpf 1982: 18–19). Unlike in Sweden, where active labor market policy is financed from the general budget, in Germany active labor market policies are funded from unemployment insurance: that is, primarily from contributions. In a recession, the unemployment fund quickly runs into financial difficulties when an increase in legal entitlements to benefits coincides with the erosion of the system's tax base. Politicians are then faced with the choice of either subsidizing the insurance fund from the federal budget or cutting expenditures. Since there is no universal entitlement to training or job-creation measures and since, at the same time, the government is struggling to balance the budget, these programs become an easy first target for spending cuts. This was clearly the case when the Social Democrats curbed spending in the 1975 Budget Act. Once a recession is over, the insurance fund's financial situation improves again and those who are still unemployed and have exhausted their entitlement to *unemployment benefits* are forced to rely on *unemployment assistance* paid from the federal budget and not from contributions. This completely reverses the political incentive structure. Now the government can shift part of the financial burden back to the insurance fund by introducing new job-creation schemes paid by the Federal

Employment Agency (which subsequently entitles participants to receive unemployment benefits again). Such was the case after 1978.

When the next recession hit, the government felt the need to restore the insurance fund's balance by saving on active measures again. It did so by amending the Employment Promotion Act in 1981. By 1985, after the insurance fund had gone back into surplus, the cuts were partly reversed. In spite of these institutional impediments, active labor market policy did make a contribution toward lowering official unemployment. In international comparison, Germany had an unemployment policy that was quite active. However, it remains open to debate whether training measures were effective in providing participants with the right skills. There is uncertainty about the extent to which these measures have reached the low-skilled, for example (Schmid 1990: 399).

Although a better economic situation in the second half of the 1980s allowed for cost shifting and even more generous unemployment insurance and social assistance provisions, significant increases in contribution rates in 1985 and 1986 (when the recession was already over) forced the government to engage in a more fundamental reform of the social insurance system following its electoral victory in 1987. Reforms were necessary if the Kohl government did not want to jeopardize the political and economic benefits that it expected to result from its tax reform (Webber 1989: 269–70). Thus, the government carried out major reforms of the health and pension insurance schemes during Kohl's second term.

When, after massive conflict with pressure groups and tension within the governing coalition, the Health Reform Act was eventually passed, the result fell far short of what had been touted as the "reform of the century." There were some cuts in benefits and co-payments were introduced, while spending for pharmaceuticals was capped. However, the contribution rate was not really stabilized. Rather than bringing financial relief for contribution payers, the health reform paved the way for a significant expansion of the German welfare state. In order to secure the support of the left wing of the Christian Democratic Party, the Party's market-oriented liberals and right wing had to accept a government commitment to introduce at a later point a new branch of social insurance for the frail and elderly (long-term care insurance introduced in 1994).

On the exact day that the Berlin Wall came down, November 9, 1989, the Bundestag passed the pension reform with a broad majority from the governing parties and the Social Democratic opposition. The law changed the long-standing basis for indexing pensions from gross to net wages. Furthermore, a gradual scaling back of early retirement was planned for the period after 2001 (Rüb and Nullmeier 1991: 451–54). Again, the immediate financial effects were rather negligible. The change in the pension indexation formula did not lead to a drop in the replacement ratio but simply prevented that ratio from accelerating further.

Thus, the 1980s were not a time of simple retrenchment. Particularly in the second half of the decade, the welfare state was back on a growth path. In circumstances where neither the federal nor the state government was obligated to pay the welfare bill, the door was open for increased benefits or expanded entitlements or even for the introduction of an entirely new branch of social insurance branch—long-term care insurance. The same holds true for social assistance: after a few years of cuts in social assistance benefits, in which the "standard benefit rate" (*Regelsatz*) continued to decline until it reached its 1970 level (Buhr et al. 1991: 514–24), the losses were offset in 1985 when the indexation mechanism was reformed. From 1985 until after unification, the "standard benefit rate" rose considerably. In the 1980s, the level of social assistance, including housing benefits, rose not only in real terms, but also in relation to average wages (Boss 1999: 38–40). The *Länder*, which initially had been worried about higher costs, did not oppose the reform, but demanded compensation instead. They were ultimately compensated by way of higher transfers from the central budget within the "federal financial equalization scheme" (*Föderaler Finanzausgleich*; Renzsch 1991: 269–73).

Later cuts in the health and pension schemes could not prevent contribution rates to the social insurance schemes from rising further, even though the economic situation had become much more favorable in the second half of the 1980s. Moreover, it is important to note that cuts in entitlements had barely any impact on the various routes to subsidized non-employment during the 1980s. Thus, the economic crises continued to be primarily cushioned by social policy. This allowed unions and business associations to maintain their collaborative relations, and particularly to continue with effective wage coordination. Contrary to many forecasts, the system of semi-central bargaining did not collapse during the crises of the early 1980s and early 1990s. Wage coordination proved to be more than just a "fair weather" phenomenon. In Germany, the wage spread remained low and the coverage of central bargaining arrangements continued to be broad, despite the fact that union membership declined slightly and unemployment skyrocketed (Streeck 1995: 6, 12, 18).

The welfare state was, of course, the most important means of coping with the economic catastrophe in eastern Germany. The lack of coordination between fiscal, monetary, and wage policy had resulted in a labor market disaster for eastern Germany and—with a certain delay—also in a dramatic decline in employment in the west. Ultimately, the brunt of adjustment had to be borne by the welfare state. It is clear that the kind of shock therapy applied to eastern Germany could not have been carried out were it not for the massive West German welfare state acting as a buffer cushioning the impact of unemployment in the east of the country.

When the labor market in eastern Germany began to collapse, a functioning labor market administration simply did not exist. A special provision for the new east German *Länder* treated those who had, in reality, actually lost their jobs as if they were simply working fewer hours. These unemployed people who were officially recognized only as underemployed workers had to claim a special short-time pay (*Kurzarbeitergeld*), since this was administratively easier to handle (Brinkmann et al. 1995: 62–3). After 1991, early retirement became widely used. One pre-retirement provision had already been introduced by the last communist government but was superseded by the Unification Treaty. If an older worker was eligible in the period from February to October 1990, he/she could draw a pre-retirement pension. About 400,000 older workers in post-communist, pre-unification East Germany left the labor market via this route. The Unification Treaty replaced this scheme, which had to be financed from the federal budget, with a "transition allowance" (*Altersübergangsgeld*) funded by the Federal Employment Office, i.e. mainly paid by contributions. For unemployed workers aged 55 or older, the benefit amounted to 65 percent of their last net income and was granted for five years or until the claimant was entitled to draw a regular pension. This scheme was used by around 600,000 workers. Once the preconditions were met in 1991 (at least twelve months of unemployment), the number of people claiming a pension because of long-term unemployment sharply increased, in the 1990s alone from 57,562 (1990) to 294,133 (1995; see Fig. 5.5).

These and other early retirement programs substantially reduced the labor force participation of older workers. In view of the overall catastrophic state of the post-unification east German labor market, early retirement programs alone could do little to relieve the unemployment crisis. The use of active labor market policy was therefore expanded to unprecedented levels. Employment in

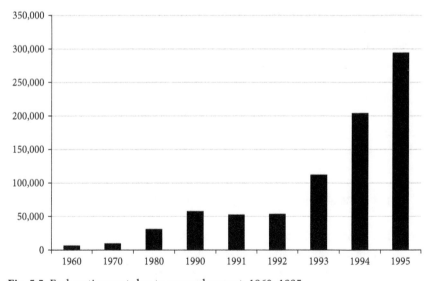

**Fig. 5.5** Early retirement due to unemployment, 1960–1995

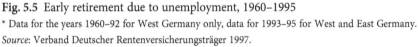

* Data for the years 1960–92 for West Germany only, data for 1993–95 for West and East Germany.
*Source*: Verband Deutscher Rentenversicherungsträger 1997.

work-creation schemes was at least twice as high in the east as in the west every year from 1991, despite the fact that the working-age population in the new *Länder* is only about a fifth the size of the west's: "More than half of all East Germans participated in such schemes from between November 1989 and November 1994" (Carlin et al. 2015: 51). Yet active labor market policies still often developed in a procyclical fashion. In contrast to the situation in the old *Länder*, active labor market measures in the east were often used to improve infrastructure. Since such investment can be quite expensive, the federal government subsidized these schemes in 1991 and 1992. When budgetary pressures intensified, the government curbed spending. Consequently, employment in work-creation schemes dropped by 60 percent in the following years despite a short-lived upturn just before the 1998 elections. Training measures were initially also used extensively, but training also fell victim to the type of competition between active and passive labor market policies (Schmid and Wiebe 1999: 389) that had already been observed in the previous decades.

In the west we find the same basic adjustment pattern that had already existed for the previous two decades. New cohorts of older workers continued to leave the labor market. After 1992, the pension reform of 1989 started to take effect. Workers who wanted to retire early had to accept a somewhat smaller pension. Since this cut was less than would have been predicted by actuarial calculations, the effects were not at all dramatic. Nevertheless, despite all the political attempts to reverse the trend toward an ever earlier retirement, the deteriorating situation on the labor market was the most important driving force behind the increasing tendency toward early exit from work in the 1990s. Figure 5.6 shows that, once again, labor market considerations were among the most prominent reasons for entitlement to disability pensions. The legislative efforts of the early 1980s to block this route to retirement proved to be entirely futile.

In western Germany, despite worsening unemployment during the recession of the 1990s, job-creation programs never regained the importance they had had in the late 1980s. This seems to have been a consequence of the large shift in resources to the east. Vocational training, by contrast, has tended to remain stable in the former Federal Republic.

## 5.3  The Welfare State as a Shock Absorber: Public Finance

In its effort to balance the budget so as to provide voters with tax relief at a later stage, the Kohl government attempted to control growing welfare spending caused by high unemployment and rising healthcare costs. Initially, the government relied mainly on ad hoc measures that raised revenues and curbed expenditures. The 1983 and 1984 budget laws raised contribution rates and broadened the insurance system's tax base beyond regular wages to include vacation allowances

**Fig. 5.6** Early retirement due to reduced working capacity and lack of part-time employment, 1977–1996 (West Germany only), as a share of all pensions due to reduced working capacity

*Source*: Verband Deutscher Rentenversicherungsträger 1997 (see table 5.2.2).

and the annual Christmas bonus. Among the measures preventing additional increases in the cost of welfare were temporary suspensions or delays in the adjustment of pensions to gross wages. The 1984 cuts in unemployment benefit levels (from 68 to 63 percent) and unemployment assistance levels (from 58 to 56 percent of the previous net wage) for single persons had more of a long-term impact. It should be noted that all these schemes have substantial financial support from the federal government, thus expenditure cuts automatically also reduce the government's share of the welfare bill. The financially autonomous sickness funds, by contrast, were burdened with additional expenditures, e.g. the obligation to pay contributions to the pension and unemployment insurance funds on sickness pay and other transfers from health insurance. This lowered the cost burden for schemes receiving financial support from the federal government, while schemes without a state subsidy had to bear an even larger burden. The same mechanism also worked in the opposite direction: the cuts in transfer payments from old-age insurance to health insurance for pensioners were an example of this (Berg 1986: 29–30). In fact, this pattern of burden-shifting between the programs with and without the financial support of the federal

**Table 5.1** Social budget sources, 1970–2017

| Year | Federal government | States | Local authorities | Private households and others |
|------|--------------------|--------|-------------------|-------------------------------|
| 1970 | 23.8 | 13.5 | 6.8 | 55.9 |
| 1975 | 25.5 | 12.2 | 7.8 | 54.5 |
| 1980 | 23.3 | 11.5 | 7.8 | 57.4 |
| 1985 | 21.2 | 11.2 | 8.3 | 59.4 |
| 1990 | 19.3 | 10.3 | 8.5 | 61.9 |
| 1995 | 19.3 | 7.8 | 9.2 | 63.7 |
| 2000 | 20.5 | 9.2 | 8.9 | 61.4 |
| 2005 | 23.0 | 8.9 | 9.5 | 58.6 |
| 2010 | 24.3 | 8.7 | 9.5 | 57.5 |
| 2015 | 24.2 | 8.5 | 9.6 | 60.1 |
| 2017 | 21 | 8.9 | 9.9 | 59.8 |

*Source*: German Federal Ministry of Labor and Social Affairs (BMAS), *Sozialbudget*, various years (own calculations).

government can be seen throughout the 1980s. The upshot was a steady decline in the share of social spending financed from the federal budget—a trend that continued until the late 1990s and was then reversed by, *inter alia*, what were known as Agenda reforms. Recently, however, in economically more favorable times, the federal state again seems to have withdrawn from its financial commitment (see Table 5.1; cf. Chapter 6).

There are other burden-shifting techniques that were employed by both the Schmidt and Kohl governments. The most prominent of these are:

- changes in the definition of program responsibilities (e.g. benefits for the very long-term unemployed are no longer paid by tax-financed social assistance but by contribution-financed unemployment insurance);
- the scaling back of transfers from the federal budget to the social insurance budgets, leading to pressure to increase contributions;
- the introduction of new programs or the extension of existing programs that are primarily or entirely financed from contributions (e.g. the introduction of long-term care insurance which replaces social assistance payments to the frail and elderly; discussed below); and
- contribution rates for schemes receiving financial support from the public budget are augmented so as to increase the share of contribution financing, etc.

Finally, it is possible that programs without government financial support grow faster in terms of spending due to increasing demand or above-average inflation (such as service-dominated healthcare in contrast to transfer-dominated pension insurance).

Table 5.1 also illustrates the effect of German federalism since it shows quite clearly that not only the federal government but also the *Länder* successfully reduced their share of social spending. The states apparently did not use their veto position in the German upper house, or Bundesrat, to advocate and protect the interests of local authorities, which now bear an increasing proportion of social spending. However, the shifts in the relative shares of welfare state financing have been most unfavorable for employers and employees, as shown in Table 5.2. Only after 2000 was the trend toward financing an ever larger share of social spending from social insurance contributions slightly reversed.

Externalizing costs became a particularly important strategy in the wake of German unification. At a time when the government was unable to accrue higher deficits, could not rely heavily on an increase in corporate and personal income taxes (given intensified tax competition), had promised not to raise (indirect) taxes, yet found it impossible to reduce spending on eastern Germany, it was tempting to finance unification through social insurance. This is exactly what happened. At the beginning of the 1990s, the social insurance schemes were in good financial shape, so, initially, they were able to support the growing burden of unification without running up deficits of their own. Unemployment insurance was directly hit by the collapse of the labor market in the former GDR. The government raised the unemployment insurance contribution rate by 2.5 percentage points in 1991—a hike which spared the public budget from having to cover the significant deficit that would otherwise have built up. Additional labor market expenditures for the east that year amounted to some DM 30 billion, of which—thanks to the contribution rate hike—only DM 5 billion had to be met from the federal subsidy. The remaining deficit of DM 25 billion was financed from contributions to the unemployment insurance fund from the west (Deutsche Bundesbank 1991b: 34).

**Table 5.2** Social budget financing structure, 1970–2017

| Year | Contributions | Taxes | Others |
|------|---------------|-------|--------|
| 1971 | 59.2 | 36.0 | 4.8 |
| 1975 | 59.3 | 36.9 | 3.8 |
| 1980 | 63.0 | 34.4 | 2.6 |
| 1985 | 65.1 | 32.5 | 2.5 |
| 1990 | 67.5 | 30.0 | 2.5 |
| 1995 | 68.8 | 28.5 | 2.6 |
| 2000 | 65.8 | 31.8 | 2.3 |
| 2005 | 63.1 | 34.9 | 2.0 |
| 2010 | 61.9 | 36.4 | 1.8 |
| 2015 | 65.1 | 33.2 | 1.8 |
| 2017 | 65.0 | 33.4 | 1.6 |

*Source*: German Federal Ministry of Labor and Social Affairs (BMAS), *Sozialbudget*, various years (own calculations).

Health insurance was also used, albeit indirectly, to cover expenditures that would otherwise have had to be paid from the federal budget. This was achieved in 1995 by reducing transfers from the unemployment insurance fund to the sickness funds for the provision of healthcare to the unemployed. Since the federal government is not involved in financing the health insurance scheme, but does have to cover upcoming deficits in unemployment insurance, this also helped save the government money. Finally, the government shifted some of its financial burden onto the pension scheme. In 1992, the former GDR pension scheme was integrated into the western system, two years ahead of the initial schedule. This meant that pension deficits in eastern Germany resulting from the gap between revenues and generous entitlements were now captured by a pension scheme covering the whole of Germany and including contributions from west Germans. According to calculations, the west German pension schemes would have run a surplus that would even have allowed for a reduction in contribution rates had the money not been spent on covering the revenue gap in the east (Deutsches Institut für Wirtschaftsforschung 1997b: 433–4). In fact, similar statements could be made about unemployment insurance (Deutsches Institut für Wirtschaftsforschung 1997a: 729). A consequence of cost shifting to the detriment of the social insurance schemes was rapidly rising contribution rates, as depicted in Table 5.3. While

**Table 5.3** Social insurance contributions in percent of gross wage, 1950–2018

| Year | Contribution rates (in percent of gross wage)[a] | | | | |
|------|-------|----------------------|---------------------------|---------------------------|-----------------------------|
|      | Total | Pension insurance | Health insurance[b] | Unemployment insurance | Long-term care insurance |
| 1950 | 20.0  | 10.0 | 6.0       | 4.0 |      |
| 1955 | 20.2  | 11.0 | 6.2       | 3.0 |      |
| 1960 | 24.4  | 14.0 | 8.4       | 2.0 |      |
| 1965 | 25.2  | 14.0 | 9.9       | 1.3 |      |
| 1970 | 26.5  | 17.0 | 8.2[b]    | 1.3 |      |
| 1975 | 30.5  | 18.0 | 10.5      | 2.0 |      |
| 1980 | 32.4  | 18.0 | 11.4      | 3.0 |      |
| 1985 | 35.1  | 19.2 | 11.8      | 4.1 |      |
| 1990 | 35.6  | 18.7 | 12.6      | 4.3 |      |
| 1995 | 39.3  | 18.6 | 13.2      | 6.5 | 1.0  |
| 2000 | 41.0  | 19.3 | 13.5      | 6.5 | 1.7  |
| 2005 | 41.5  | 19.5 | 13.8      | 6.5 | 1.7  |
| 2010 | 39.6  | 19.9 | 14.9      | 2.8 | 1.9  |
| 2015 | 39.5  | 18.7 | 15.4      | 3   | 2.4  |
| 2018 | 39.75 | 18.6 | 15.6      | 3   | 2.55 |

[a] Joint contribution rate of both employers and employees.
[b] Average contribution rate across all funds; from 1950 to 1969 blue-collar workers' funds only.

Source: BMA various years.

the total contribution rate to all social insurance schemes was already high at 35.6 percent in 1990, it had risen to 41.7 percent just six years later.

The expansionary trend in social expenditures was not really counteracted by additional cost-cutting in areas such as healthcare (Health Reform Act of 1993), which at best prevented a further increase in healthcare costs and contribution rates. However, despite the precarious state of public finance and poor labor market performance, it was in fact possible to expand social policy to a certain extent in the 1990s. The introduction of long-term care insurance in 1994 appeared to go against the tide of cutting welfare spending, lowering entitlements, and reducing welfare programs' coverage. This expansionary measure, however, placed the main financial burden of social policy back onto contribution payers and led to further cost shifting from the "public" to the "para-public/semi-state purse" in those instances where long-term care insurance replaced social assistance payments to the old and frail, which were previously covered by local authorities. While long-term care insurance had some positive employment effects (an estimated 67,000 new jobs; cf. Pabst 1999), it is questionable to what extent these could offset the detrimental effects of higher non-wage labor costs on private service sector employment.

If we consider the demand for unemployment and pension benefits, which had risen steeply in the wake of German unification, together with the various devices the government used to reshuffle the financial mix in social spending to its own favor, we have a good initial impression of the overall burden placed on the German welfare state by the unification process. Calculations estimate that, all in all, the social insurance schemes shouldered almost one-quarter of the annual public transfers from west to east between 1991 and 1997 (Deutsche Bundesbank 1996). The total net transfer financed from the pension, unemployment, and health insurance budgets amounted to DM 283 billion in the period from 1991 to 1999 (Meinhardt 1999: 817). It goes without saying that contribution rates would have been much lower if the costs of German unification had been paid out of general taxation.

In the following section, I will summarize the argument and discuss the feedback effects of rising non-wage labor costs on labor market performance.

## 5.4 Welfare without Work, Budgets without Balance

How did the German model cope with the more unfavorable economic environment of the 1980s and 1990s? If we take export market shares as an initial rough indicator of German firms' ability to compete on world markets, there is no evidence of a significant deterioration of competitiveness, despite the fact that relative unit labor costs did rise sharply in 1986/87 and again in the early 1990s (Carlin and Soskice 1997: 58). The capability of German industry to respond to high wage costs with increases in productivity had apparently not suffered over these two decades, and German firms had seemingly maintained their high capacity for successful innovation (Carlin and Soskice 1997: 57–61).[7] There was also little evidence of a large-scale exit process where firms relocate production sites outside the German high-wage regime. The level of manufacturing employment remained very high in Germany between 1970 and 2000. A liberal international market was still a blessing rather than a curse for Germany and its export-oriented growth model.

In this chapter, I have argued that Germany's main problem before the introduction of the euro was less the lack of international competitiveness, but rather weak job growth in services. External shocks regularly triggered adjustments in the German political and economic system, with adverse effects on overall employment in the long run, particularly in services with low productivity. This was the reason for the German system's poor labor market performance. I described the interplay between the Bundesbank, state actors, and the social partners, within an institutional and legal setting comprising free collective bargaining (Tarifautonomie) between strong and encompassing social partners, substantial central bank autonomy, fragmented public budgets, and a generous welfare state. This interplay, I argue, is the strategic constellation that has to be held responsible for Germany's low employment equilibrium. In the era of the German economic miracle, full employment and growing affluence were dependent on the manufacturing sector. Structural change has reduced the importance of industry for employment in all developed countries (Iversen and Wren 1998; Wren 2013). For Germany and its "oversized" manufacturing sector (Giersch et al. 1992), the transition to the service economy has not been a smooth process but rather an abrupt and distorted one. Above all, the high labor costs made it difficult to replace jobs lost in manufacturing with new employment opportunities in the service sector. German industrial employment shrank particularly dramatically during the two oil crises in the early and late 1970s. Industrial workers who lost their jobs tended to move into early retirement or unemployment schemes rather than into low-paid employment in the service sector.

As this chapter emphasized, high non-wage labor costs were not caused by unfavorable conditions on the labor market alone. Fiscal policy bears its fair share of responsibility, too. In each of the major crises since the mid-1970s, the Bundesbank urged the federal government to consolidate its budget as a way of

---

[7] The increase in unit labor costs in Germany is partially due to the more important role played by in-company provision of business services. Lower productivity gains in services may lead to higher unit labor costs in manufacturing without an adverse effect on competitiveness—since other firms will have to buy these services at correspondingly higher prices (see Deutsche Bundesbank 1994b). However, the data suggest that the relatively stable export market share cannot be explained by a low price elasticity of the demand for Germany's high quality export goods or by a corresponding decline in profitability (Carlin and Soskice 1997: 59–60).

keeping inflation low. The government's fiscal austerity in line with monetary rigor came partly at the expense of social insurance, where contribution rates were forced up even more. All this placed a heavy burden on social insurance, with respect to both spending and revenue. High contributions to the payroll-financed German welfare state added to the problem of high labor costs. As a consequence, the German employment ratio was low, job growth in low productivity employment was poor, and older workers' labor force participation had fallen consistently since the mid-1970s.

The end of the economic miracle was marked by the first oil shock, when the primary policy response combined a tight-money policy with measures to consolidate the budget. I argue that, once industrial employment plummeted again as a consequence of the second oil crisis, political actors intensified their procyclical strategies of cost externalization instead of addressing the underlying problems of structural change and a high social wage. Consolidation was implemented at the expense of the welfare state against the backdrop of a restrictive monetary policy pursued by the Bundesbank, which tried to impose wage restraint and fiscal discipline on unions and the government, respectively.

The crisis following German unification was no exception in this respect. Although unification posed an unprecedented challenge to the German political economy, the response of the key economic actors strongly resembled their behavior in earlier crises. The Bundesbank insisted on price stability. The government, as in previous recessions, shifted a significant share of the costs of the crisis onto the social partners and economic adjustment took place by way of a "negative labor supply policy" orchestrated by the many passive instruments of the Bismarckian welfare state. Hence, the political system responded in much the same way as it had to the second OPEC crisis a decade earlier. The externalization of the costs of adjustment, both by the state and firms, once again became the routine response to a non-routine situation. The Bundesbank's strict monetary policy elicited by the rapid growth in public debt and by the inflationary tendencies stemming from steep wage increases in the wake of the unification boom was another important factor. Older workers, particularly in east Germany, began to participate in special programs for early retirement. This costly process of dual externalization led to a considerable rise in contribution rates, itself a major obstacle to smoother structural change.

Chapter 6 addresses how the German political economy developed from the sick man of Europe in the early 2000s to the economic *Wunderkind* of today.

# 6

# International Complementarities of National Capitalism

## 6.1 Germany in the Euro Area: A New Equilibrium?

Chapter 4 describes the emergence of Germany's postwar growth model as being predicated on wage coordination and wage moderation, subsequently on low inflation, high productivity, international cost competitiveness, and therefore on export-led growth. Chapter 5 portrays the pathological side effects of this model as a result of the social partners tending to transfer their economic adjustment costs onto the welfare state once the periods of high growth and full employment were over and once manufacturing had ceased to be the employment generator it had been for the first three postwar decades (Wren 2013). In this last empirical chapter I analyze the role that Germany's Bismarckian welfare state has played and continues to play in the country's political economy in the profoundly changed circumstances of the 2000s. As a basis of the analysis in the present chapter, I pose three questions relating to the insights of the two preceding chapters: First, are the German labor market and the German political economy "still adjusting badly" (Eichhorst and Kaiser 2006; see Chapter 5) in the new millennium and, if not, what has changed? I then also refer to Chapter 4 to address, secondly, the question of how German wage setting and, more generally, how Germany's production regime functions in the euro area. This also allows me to compare the German export-led growth model with the French and Italian models, which proved less able to secure wage moderation and therefore could to a lesser degree base their political economies on export-led growth. Prior to the introduction of the euro, this left them dependent on domestic demand generated by government expenditures and on regular currency depreciations. In fact, my answer to the third question, namely why the euro area ties two fundamentally different political economies together, leads us back to the insights presented in Chapter 3, where I describe the extent to which postwar Germany's quasi-corporatism must be understood against the background of the prevailing conflicts during the interwar period. These conflicts themselves reflected a party political constellation in which strong Social and Christian Democracy had successfully marginalized the liberal bourgeois camp. This theme will be taken up again in the conclusion when I compare the German trajectory with developments in France and Italy

*Social Protection, Capitalist Production: The Bismarckian Welfare State in the German Political Economy, 1880–2015.*
Philip Manow, Oxford University Press (2020). © Philip Manow.
DOI: 10.1093/oso/9780198842538.001.0001

(but also Spain and Portugal) and map out a "four worlds of welfare corporatism" framework that situates the conservative continental countries within the world of advanced western capitalisms (Manow et al. 2018).

The present chapter primarily covers the first decade of the new millennium, a time that not only saw the creation of the euro area and, with it, a fundamental transformation of the basic economic parameters within which the German model previously functioned. Starting in 2008 and triggered by the insolvency of Lehman Brothers, the world economy also experienced a profound economic crisis—the Great Recession. Although the comparisons with the Great Depression of the late 1920s and early 1930s that are frequently drawn (Eichengreen 2012; O'Rourke and Taylor 2013; Tooze 2018) appear a bit exaggerated, the depth and impact of the financial crisis seem to render it largely unrivaled by most other post-World War II crashes. The deep economic slump in the wake of the Lehman bankruptcy subsequently spilled over into a dramatic challenge to the euro area, manifested in the severe sovereign debt crisis of some of its member countries and, consequently, in a persistent recession (De Grauwe 2013; Hall 2012; Hancké 2013; Iversen et al. 2016; Iversen and Soskice 2018; Mody 2018; Scharpf 2011; Streeck and Schäfer 2013). This crisis shook the foundations of an economic structure to which Germany had adapted over the previous ten years.

A breakup of the currency zone, today less likely than in 2009–11 but still a possible scenario, would have fundamental and unpredictable repercussions for the German economy and the country's public finances. It will be quite some time before economic normalcy returns, since European recovery would presuppose that the euro area's serious structural defects (EMU as an "incomplete" currency union; see De Grauwe 2013) be repaired. As long as this is not occurring, any "return to normalcy" remains unlikely. A high level of government debt and a low level of competitiveness in southern Europe apparently either require a complete change of the euro area's institutional setup—possibly a split into two different currency zones, one representing the northern export-led growth model under a strong euro, the other the southern demand-driven, consumption-based economic model with continuous depreciations—or will be resolved in a drawn-out process of structural adjustment and a prolonged recessive period in the periphery, possibly eased by massive transfers from the euro area's less burdened northern members (Iversen and Soskice 2018). As gloomy as both scenarios appear in economic terms, it remains wholly uncertain whether either option would even find enough support to render it politically sustainable.

This chapter addresses the question of how the German economy has fared in these new and profoundly challenging times. I will take up the themes of the previous chapters by examining changes in the German wage-bargaining model (see Chapter 4) and in *Modell Deutschland*'s process of pathological adjustment to low growth (see Chapter 5). In this context, I will address the following more specific puzzles.

- If the interplay between an independent central bank with a non-accommodating monetary policy, on the one hand, and a quasi-corporatist system of wage coordination, on the other, was so central to the functioning of *Modell Deutschland* after the breakdown of Bretton Woods (Hall 1994; Hall and Franzese 1998; see Chapter 5; Scharpf 1987), how have unions and employers responded to the new environment where the ECB's monetary policy could no longer be exclusively targeted at German wage settlements, but was set with euro area-wide inflation in mind (Hancké 2013; see Section 6.2)?

- If the generous German welfare state is designed in such a way that the "social partners" could use or, for that matter, often abuse it for their particularistic needs (Streeck 2009, and see Chapter 5), how did this close production–protection nexus survive the fundamental reform of the Bismarckian welfare state through what was known as the Agenda 2010 under Chancellor Schröder? How has Germany managed to avoid the emerging low-wage sector undermining the country's high-skill/high-productivity/high-wage regime—as unions always had feared? In other words: can the German system function under conditions of dualization (Emmenegger et al. 2012; Palier and Thelen 2010)? Apparently the answer is yes, but how exactly?[1] (see Section 6.3).

- Finally, how can we explain Germany's initial economic troubles, which prevailed until around 2005, its quite spectacular subsequent comeback, *plus* its almost complete mirror image—namely the impressive boom in the southern euro area up until the financial crisis and the bust ever since? What can the framework proposed here contribute to such an explanation, particularly with its emphasis on the interaction between social protection and capitalist production in the continental political economies (see Section 6.4)?

In my attempt to answer these questions, I use the label "supply-side corporatism" (Wolfgang Streeck) to help me describe the deeply ingrained mechanisms by which the German political economy adjusts to a high interest rate environment. These mechanisms were employed when the German economy experienced its first adjustment crisis in response to the new monetary regime under the euro. I then address in some detail the profound welfare and labor market reforms that were a central part of this adjustment process (together with wage moderation), namely what was known as the Agenda 2010 (see Section 6.2). Subsequently,

---

[1] I will only briefly touch on the political fallout of these developments. One of the political consequences of the profound welfare reforms was the rise and then firm establishment of a new radical alternative to the left wing of the SPD. This affected the "strategic configuration of parties" (*Kitschelt*) in the German party system (Arndt 2013; Schumacher 2011; see also Schwander and Manow 2017a).

I analyze the changes in Germany's wage-bargaining system under the new monetary opportunity structure, and how the welfare reforms have been conducive to the adjustment of wage coordination (see Section 6.3). Lastly, this gives me the opportunity to compare the *two* political economies in the euro area (the continental and the southern growth models) and to sketch how they function under the single currency (see Section 6.4). I relate my description of the functioning logic of these two political economies to the argument developed in the preceding chapters, i.e., to an account of the interplay between welfare states, types of capitalism, and party competition (cf. Kersbergen and Manow 2009; Manow 2009, 2013, 2015b; Manow et al. 2018). This enables us to locate the German political economy in a broader comparative framework.

## 6.2 The Agenda 2010: The End of the "Bismarckian Promise"

Probably the most significant reform of the German welfare state in recent years was the groundbreaking Agenda 2010 reform, including the highly controversial labor market reforms (Hartz reforms) enacted under the red/green (SPD/Greens) coalition with Gerhard Schröder as Chancellor (Arndt 2013: 99; cf. 99–126; Hassel and Schiller 2010). Given that the relatively peaceful industrial relations in Germany have always been predicated on the welfare consensus between both Social and Christian Democracy, for many Germany in the early 2000s represented the European country where social reform was least likely (Kitschelt 2001)—despite the apparent malfunctioning of the German economy, as was manifested in low growth and high unemployment. Therefore, the comprehensive welfare reforms enacted by the red/green coalition in 2002 and 2003 came as a surprise to many observers.

In the early 2000s, Germany struggled with low growth and high unemployment. It was a time when Germany was labeled the "sick man of Europe." Real GDP growth had plummeted from 2 percent in 1998 and 1999 to 0.5 and 0.4 percent in 2002 and 2003, respectively. In 2005, the German economy was almost stagnant at 0.2 percent. In 2004/2005, unemployment came close to a staggering 12 percent and, in absolute terms, reached the critical five-million threshold.

The fact that Germany faced economic problems almost immediately after the introduction of the new currency was no coincidence, but rather the consequence of the high real interest rates that accompanied the euro (see Krugman and Obstfeld 2012: 767, figure 20.8): "Before 1999, Germany had not only the lowest nominal interest rates, but also the lowest real interest rates. With entry into the Monetary Union, however, these comparative advantages were lost. Since nominal interest rates converged whereas German inflation rates continued to be lower, real interest rates in Germany actually became the highest in the euro area. As a consequence, economic growth was lower in Germany than almost any other EMU member country, unemployment increased dramatically from 2000 to 2005, as did social expenditures, whereas tax revenues fell by 2.4 percentage points between 2000 and 2004" (Scharpf 2011: 13). In the rest of the euro area, credit-fueled higher demand, higher growth, and a housing bubble, particularly in Spain and Ireland, drove inflation and thereby forced real interest rates down (Krugman and Obstfeld 2012). The divergence between higher- and lower-inflation countries that had already been predicted as early as 1992 in the famous Walters Critique of the common currency evolved exactly as anticipated (Carlin 2013; Walters 1992).

The crisis could also be explained by the fact that German capital flowed to the south immediately after the introduction of the common currency. Today we are aware that this movement was driven by the mistaken belief that capital within the euro area—with its uniform interest rate, common fiscal rules, and lack of exchange rate risks—could be safely shifted to where the "economic action" was, i.e., where high growth rates and therefore high returns on investments prevailed.[2] The consumption and construction boom in southern Europe was fuelled by what, from the perspective of the periphery, were exceptionally low interest rates and this attracted German capital, thus reinforcing the boom. The ECB, forced to pursue a "one size fits all" monetary policy in a currency area where both an overheated economy (Spain or Ireland, for instance) and an economy in recession (such as Germany) soon existed side by side, inevitably selected an interest rate that was too low to dampen the Spanish or Irish construction craze, but that was already too high for Germany's bleak economy (and has subsequently been dubbed a "one size fits none" rate). At a time when high growth rates, high employment, and rising real wages in the south seemed to be signs of exactly the economic convergence process that optimists had expected from the single currency Germany had to undergo a politically and economically painful process of structural reform.

At that time, however, Germany's economic slump in the year 2000 was not perceived as having much to do with the euro. A "supply-side diagnosis . . . dominated economic and social policy discourse" (Carlin et al. 2015: 58). Further, even if political actors had been aware of the underlying causes (which in all likeliness they were not), they still had to avoid at all costs delegitimizing the new currency, which had been introduced against the will of the majority of Germans. Instead, the dominant discourse held the prevailing labor market inflexibility and high non-wage labor costs, a dysfunctional welfare state, and, in general, a significant political reform gridlock (*Reformstau*) responsible for the poor state in which Germany's economy found itself at the start of the new millennium (see Chapter 5).

---

[2] Martin Wolf dryly comments: "Why anybody should have imagined that Greek and German government debts were equivalent is not easy to comprehend" (Wolf 2014: 47).

Of course, not all of Germany's poor economic performance at the time can be blamed on the new currency. It is quite apparent that Germany's GDP growth had been sluggish and its labor market performance poor even before the introduction of the euro. This was primarily part of the long-term economic fallout of a set of circumstances that were to repeat themselves after 1999 for the entire country, namely the entry of the former East German states into the new currency zone of unified Germany at an exchange rate that was far too high.[3] It was also due to the fact that the German production model in general and the German welfare state in particular were tailored to the needs of a manufacturing sector that now, at best, produced stagnant employment, while the German growth model seemed much less well adjusted to the needs of the increasingly important service economy (Wren 2013).

When unemployment finally surpassed the four-million mark in 2002, politicians and the public were alarmed. Yet unemployment continued to increase: in 2005, 4.86 million people were without employment. This was the annual average, but in the early months of that year the total number of unemployed had actually passed the symbolically important five-million mark. What is more, long-term unemployment was also a pressing problem. This pointed to the need to reform the job placement program of the unemployment insurance and to reconsider whether the passive character of German labor market policies did not actually provide the unemployed with rather perverse incentives: "A full 32.8 percent of jobless workers between 1995 and 1999 had been on the rolls for more than a year, reflecting the ineffectiveness of the BA's [Federal Labor Office's] job placement services" (Vail 2010: 104) and also reflecting the dependency trap inherent in generous benefit levels and long drawing periods so typical of Germany's social insurance system, a system tailored to insider interests and specifically to preserving their labor market and income status. Moreover, poorly camouflaged by the fact that many jobseekers were channeled through expensive work-creation schemes or training courses of highly dubious usefulness was the fact that not only was unemployment high, but employment was also low. The high number of early retirees completes this rather gloomy picture (see Chapter 5).

Various labor market stimuli failed to tackle these problems. Efforts to find solutions in tripartite negotiations with the social partners—the traditional corporatist approach that both the outgoing Kohl government and the incoming Schröder government had attempted—proved wholly inadequate. Kohl's belated and half-hearted reform attempts were a far cry from the "radical retrenchment" as it has been labeled in the literature (Beramendi et al. 2015a: 40), anyway. The

---

[3] What subsequently developed was high unemployment, a massive increase in public spending (active and passive labor market policies), a unification boom, and the Bundesbank's harsh monetary reaction, which led to a prolonged period of poor economic growth and low employment (Carlin et al. 2015).

social partners were more interested in protecting their position within Germany's corporatist political economy than in responding to the virulent labor market crisis. During the red/green coalition's second term (after a narrowly won election in 2002), the failure to confront these problems within a tripartite framework was ultimately the catalyst for a bold attempt to enact profound labor market and welfare reforms without the social partners' consent. The reforms were designed to "wrest authority from neocorporatist labor market institutions, which had failed to devise effective responses" to the severe employment and unemployment problems of the times (Vail 2010: 102). This is what the Agenda 2010 and the Hartz reforms accomplished. They therefore decisively withdrew from the corporatist model that had dominated the German political economy for the last fifty years and in important respects reneged on the "Bismarckian promise" that had prevailed in the previous five decades.

I refrain here from providing a detailed account and full evaluation of the Agenda 2010 measures—given that there are already a plethora of detailed assessments (Arndt 2013; Carlin et al. 2015; Clasen 2005; Clegg and Clasen 2006a, 2006b; Eichhorst and Kaiser 2006; Hassel 2014b; Hassel and Schiller 2010; Schwander and Manow 2017a; Vail 2010). A simple outline of the major reform measure must suffice. The first two Hartz laws, enacted in 2003, placed a stronger emphasis on labor market activation through the introduction of personnel service agencies (*Personalservice Agenturen*, PSA), and opened activation measures, previously limited to recipients of earnings-related benefits, up to everyone (Carlin et al. 2015: 63). At the same time, benefit requirements were tightened: once a spell of unemployment lasts longer than 18 months, the unemployed are now forced to accept any available job, regardless of their qualifications and previous pay (Koch et al. 2009). Availability and entitlement criteria were also tightened, and the annual adjustment of benefits was abolished (Eichhorst and Kaiser 2006). Additionally, the reforms comprised a number of smaller policy measures promising to increase labor supply and to make accepting employment worthwhile. Measures included the reduction of social contributions on low-paid jobs and marginal employment (what were known as "minijobs"). Another activation measure was the introduction of what were dubbed "Me Inc." or "Ich-AGs," i.e. a measure facilitating the creation of small (also single person) enterprises. The third Hartz law reformed the public placement agency (Public Employment Service) in order to improve its case management and the placement of jobseekers.

The last and by far the most controversial and important part of the reform, the Hartz IV law, sharply reduced the drawing period for the generous earnings-related unemployment benefit (*Arbeitslosengeld I*) from a maximum of 32 to 12 months (18 months for older unemployed persons). After this period, the unemployed have to rely on the flat-rate, means-tested benefit, *Arbeitslosengeld II* (also known as Hartz IV), which corresponds roughly to the level of the former social assistance, i.e., it does not take the level of prior earnings into account, and by consequence also not the length of the prior period of employment and contribution payment.

As a consequence, the reform fused the previously separated systems of social assistance and unemployment insurance. "This meant that status protection of the long-term unemployed was abolished in favor of a joint flat-rate benefit for all jobseekers not entitled to unemployment insurance benefit, i.e., with prior employment shorter than the waiting period or after expiry" of *Arbeitslosengeld I* (Eichhorst and Kaiser 2006: 9). It cannot be stressed too much that this represented a very substantial attack on insider interests. At the same time, due to the reform, benefit recipients have to accept any job offer to prove their willingness to work, even jobs paid so poorly that the wage will remain below the social assistance level. Wages are then topped up by transfer payments.

Considering that the "old" welfare system had been geared primarily to the protection of status, income, and the qualifications of skilled workers (see Chapter 5), these measures clearly represented a major break with Germany's "Bismarckian tradition" and violated the interests of the workers in the industrial core—a traditional SPD support base. The reform qualifies as a "dramatic shift from the status-preserving earnings-related principle to the means-tested basic-income principle for the long-term unemployed" (Carlin et al. 2015: 62). These reforms therefore represent a significant break with cherished principles of Germany's welfare system, and qualify as a "path-breaking transformation of labour market and social policy" (Carlin et al. 2015: 61). It is no surprise then that they met with vehement union protest and were highly contested within the Social Democratic Party. In fact, they were enacted against a sizeable intraparty opposition of "traditionalists" clinging passionately to Germany's established Bismarckian ways. From this it also becomes clear that one of the key aims of the Agenda 2010 was precisely *not* to "sharpen the lines between social *insurance* (for those who had paid the social contributions) and social *assistance* and in-work benefits for those excluded from the normal labor market and for whom the state was asked to take responsibility" (Palier and Thelen 2010: 122). The objective was the exact opposite, namely *to blur* these lines. To interpret the welfare reforms, as Palier and Thelen do, as an attempt to protect the industrial core model of the German political economy is misguided (see also Beramendi et al. 2015a: 40; Carlin et al. 2015: 66).

Despite the reforms—or because of them (see following discussion)—Germany violated the Maastricht 3 percent budget deficit criterion in the years 2002 to 2005, in the midst of the recession. "There was not just a little irony in this fact, since in the early 1990s it had been German negotiators who had pushed to include an Excessive Deficit Procedure in the Maastricht Treaty" (Eichengreen 2007: 372). In the ensuing conflict with the European Commission, Germany and France successfully negotiated a less restrictive application of the Stability and Growth Pact.

In retrospect, many interpret this as the euro area's "original sin" (cf. James 2012: 18), which paved the way for a period of low fiscal discipline and which ultimately—in the wake of the financial crisis in 2008/2009—allegedly led to the profound sovereign debt crisis that threatened and still threatens to tear the euro area apart. Although Greece's entry into the euro area, based on forged budget data, is certainly a serious contender for the "original sin" award, and although the crisis of the Eurozone only later turned into a sovereign debt crisis in some countries (Baldwin and Giavazzi 2015), it is true that the outcome of the conflict between France and Germany, on the one side, and the Commission, on the other, made future sanctions against other euro area members who violate the Maastricht criteria hard to justify and quite unlikely to be imposed. In fact, in 2005 "the disciplinary mechanism was softened, many processes became merely discretionary, and new procedural provisions made it harder to take action against noncompliant states" (James 2012: 18). As Paul De Grauwe dryly states: "For all practical purposes, the Pact had become a dead letter" (De Grauwe 2014: 227).[4]

Politically, the German government saw its violation of the Stability and Growth Pact as the *consequence* of the pending welfare state reforms. As Chancellor Schröder later explained, the red/green coalition was confronted with a dilemma:[5] embarking upon a policy of structural reform by pursuing a highly unpopular welfare reform *and* simultaneously aggravating the recession with a strict policy of fiscal consolidation would have simply spelt political disaster and certain electoral suicide. Forced to choose, the Schröder government opted for the long-term structural change: welfare reform. In retrospect, it is probably fair to say that Schröder was proven right—economically, if not politically—since he was voted out of office in 2005 anyway.

The combination of structural reforms, rationalization in firms, and the wage moderation practiced by unions ultimately led Germany out of the recession, particularly in combination with the much higher growth and more specifically

---

[4] De Grauwe also caustically comments on the regulations of the old and the new Stability and Growth Pact: "Up to now, these sanctions have never been applied. The reader will be surprised at so much political naiveté from the drafters of the Stability and Growth Pact when they believed that such sanctions could ever be enforced" (De Grauwe 2014: 217).

[5] Spiegel: "The ECB accuses you of having softened the criteria of the Stability and Growth Pact." Schröder: "This critique has to be taken seriously. But one has to put it into perspective. We strengthened the growth aspect of the Pact with that reform. Specific burdens, such as the costs related to German reunification, now had to be taken into account. More importantly however, countries which undertook difficult structural reforms had more leeway to stimulate growth. For us Germans, this was key, since we had initiated the Agenda 2010. In Germany, we were confronted with a stagnating economy. At the same time we were very determined to push this reform through and to adjust the welfare state to the changed circumstances. Hence, we needed to emerge from stagnation with the help of an economic stimulus package. In this situation we were forced, also because of the welfare reforms, to emphasize the growth component of the Pact. In the end this proved to be successful. We did our homework with the Agenda 2010. This is one of the reasons why we came through the crisis better than others. Countries such as France or Italy are now forced to catch up under much more unfavorable circumstances" (Spiegel, "Europa muss aufwachen," September 5, 2011).

the much higher wage growth in Europe's south. German GDP grew at an impressive rate of 4.1 and 3.1 percent in 2006 and 2007, respectively, before the financial crisis hit the German export-based economy unusually hard. However, even the Lehman crisis only temporarily interrupted the revival of *Modell Deutschland*. As soon as global demand returned, German companies were able to overcome the massive external shock caused by the financial crisis. The country came out of the recession much faster than the UK or most other euro area members—although the subsequent recession in Europe's periphery did not leave German growth unaffected, of course.

The labor market also weathered the storm remarkably well (Burda and Hunt 2011; Eichhorst and Tobsch 2014b: 3). The level of unemployment sank steadily and today (August 2019) is at around 4.9 percent (national figures; according to the ILO definition the German unemployment rate is 3.4 percent)—less than half of the 12 percent unemployment that was recorded at the peak of the crisis in 2005. Today's figure of around 2.2 million unemployed and 800,000 open jobs is close to a full employment scenario (see Fig. 6.1).[6]

Significantly, the higher labor market flexibility resulting from the Agenda 2010 reforms did not—as reform critics had claimed—come at the cost of undermining the "normal" segment of the labor market. In the private sector there is a relatively high probability that people will transfer from the nonstandard segment of the labor market to its regular core. This regular core appears to have been

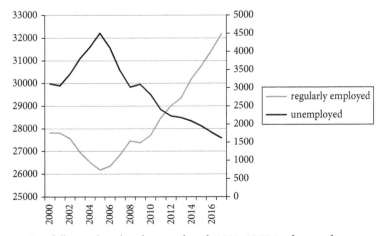

**Fig. 6.1** Gainfully employed and unemployed, 2000–2017, in thousands
*Source*: Annual statistical yearbook of the Federal Statistical Office (regularly employed left y-axis, unemployed right y-axis).

---

[6] Of course, the massive influx of over one million immigrants in 2015/2016, most of them poorly qualified, changes this picture substantially.

strengthened rather than weakened by the reform. The number of "regularly employed," meaning those subject to mandatory social insurance contributions, even increased significantly from its low point of slightly more than 26 million in 2005 to 33.4 million in August 2019 (cf. Fig. 6.1). Inequality, which had been steadily increasing since the 1990s, has been on the decline since 2006 and poverty rates have decreased, too. For instance, the GINI coefficient fell from 32.8 (2006) to 30.1 (2011) and has dropped further since (29.1 in 2018), and the poverty rate fell from 9.1 to 7.8 between 2007 and 2013 (e.g. OECD 2015: 56).[7] By far the largest increase in inequality had happened, from comparatively low levels, *before* the reform between 1995 and 2005. The claim that the Agenda reforms increased "German inequality quite dramatically" (Blyth 2015: 269) is unsubstantiated.[8]

Total employment is also at a record high of around 45.28 million people. With an employment rate of 76 percent, in Europe, Germany today has become quite unlike its conservative homologues, France and Italy (Eichhorst and Tobsch 2014b: 6–7), with 65.3 and 58.7, respectively, and much closer to Sweden with its 77.5 (cf. https://data.OECD.org). It was this high employment rate which then also helped fuel domestic demand during the crisis when export demand collapsed. Full-time, non-temporary employment is still the dominant form in the German labor market, specifically for 40 percent of working-age individuals and for 60 percent of those in gainful employment (Eichhorst and Tobsch 2014a: 10). The overall job growth, however, came at the cost of an increase in nonstandard employment. Yet, if we want to bemoan this development, we should bear in mind how high structural unemployment had been previously. We also should take into account that "nonstandard jobs contribute to better labor market access and additional job creation, which generates additional income from work. Flexible types of contracts also contribute to wage moderation in collective agreements and to overall competitiveness" (Eichhorst and Tobsch 2014b: 4; Klinger et al. 2013). Moreover, for many, particularly mothers, part-time employment is the preferred form of employment, and does not lead to an accumulation of social risks (Böhnke et al. 2015). And overall, the increase in so-called "atypical employment," i.e. on a temporary contract and/or as part-time employment (with less than 20 hours a month) has been modest, from about 20 percent in 2000 to about 23 percent in 2017 (from 6 to 7.7 million; Statistical Yearbook, various years).

With these more flexible forms of employment the Agenda 2010 managed to reduce the inactivity rate, which was their biggest achievement (Klinger et al. 2013). Inactivity, widespread in the 1990s, "is no longer a problem of the German labour market" (Hassel 2014b: 68). While the overall flexibility of the

---

[7] See for instance, World Bank: http://data.worldbank.org/indicator/SI.POV.GINI?locations=DE or OECD (2015).

[8] Also, the share of total social expenditure as a percentage of GDP did not change substantially. It was at 25.4 in the year 2000 and is at 25.1 today (in 2018).

labor market has clearly increased, average job tenure has not only remained stable but also even increased, from 10.3 to 11.5 years between 2000 and 2011 (Eichhorst and Tobsch 2014b: 13)—mainly due to the fact that the Agenda 2010 and subsequent reforms rendered many routes to early retirement much less attractive, but also because in 2007, another deeply unpopular reform measure raised the retirement age to 67. It is important to note, however, that high employment, low inactivity etc. were as much due to a favorable economic climate (weak euro, eastern enlargement of the EU, and low interest rates) as to the flexibility of the labor market promoted by the reforms.

At the same time, the rapidly increasing low-wage sector (see Rhein 2013) is the more worrying development for many, but even here opinions vary. Some emphasize that "the liberalization of non-standard contracts has contributed to the expansion of overall labour market inclusion and job growth in Germany and that at least some forms of nonstandard work provide stepping stones into permanent regular jobs. Atypical contracts do not necessarily undermine the dominance of standard employment relationships and job quality in this primary segment but rather form a supplementary part of employment in sectors that depend on more flexible and maybe cheaper forms of labour" (Eichhorst and Tobsch 2014b: 2). Not surprisingly, the reforms also created the need for some reregulation, and the introduction in 2014 of a binding wage floor (minimum wage) for many labor market sectors is one of these reregulating measures. Interventions like these moved the German political economy further away from one of its formerly sacred principles—that of *Tarifautonomie* or autonomy of the social partners in wage bargaining. Germany became less corporatist.

There is no doubt that the welfare reforms created real "losers"—in fact, they were designed to do precisely that, but those were, contrary to the expectations of many, rather the labor market insiders. Some categories of households benefit substantially from higher transfers (Koch et al. 2009: 249–50) and overall spending on social assistance significantly increased after the reform: "Hartz IV—widely considered the harshest of the recent reforms—actually provided a boost for an estimated one-third of those who were previously in the lowest tier of the old social assistance system," particularly single mothers"(Palier and Thelen 2010: 138).[9] Whereas these former "outsiders" benefited, insiders lost out considerably. Against all conclusions of

---

[9] Combining unemployment insurance and Germany's social assistance scheme involved a huge cost shifting game between the municipalities, which were responsible for social assistance, and the social insurance schemes (Hassel and Schiller 2010). The process conformed to the pattern described in Chapter 5: the political incentive to substitute social insurance contributions for taxes. Municipalities had an incentive to declare as many recipients of social assistance as "employable" as possible. In some instances, comatose patients miraculously turned into active "jobseekers." Whereas the federal government had anticipated less than 3.5 million employable recipients of ALG II/Hartz IV, in the end it was more than 5 million. The welfare state "retrenchment measure," the Agenda 2010, increased social assistance spending dramatically to 25 billion euros—11 billion more than anticipated.

"dualization," the reform "clearly and most drastically cut the benefits for well-insured labor market insiders" (Beramendi et al. 2015a: 41).[10]

Not surprisingly, the reforms were highly controversial, and this is reflected in the conflicting assessments of these reforms still found in the literature today. It is beyond doubt that other factors—like eastern enlargement, unions' wage moderation, an undervalued euro, and the growth in the south—contributed to pulling Germany out of the slump after 2005 as well, but newer economic studies agree on the view that the labor market reforms share a substantial part of the responsibility for the impressive reduction in unemployment in the second half of the decade (Hochmuth et al. 2018): "absent the reform, Germany's unemployment rate would be 50% higher today" (Hartung et al. 2018: 37; much more skeptical is Mody 2018: 637).

Given the substantial pathologies of Germany's prior "welfare without work" model (see Chapter 5) even critics of the Agenda 2010 can hardly deny the urgent need for reform in the early 2000s. Labor market performance since then also tends to discredit some of the initially very critical assessments of the Agenda: higher flexibility apparently *did* contribute to the employment growth that reformers had wished for, and so far without undermining the core of regular employment. It therefore appears rather questionable to accuse the Agenda 2010 of having strengthened "dualization" (Thelen 2014) without at the same time referring to the disheartening and unacceptable exclusion of a very high number of long-term unemployed under the *status quo ante*. To put it more specifically: a prior "dualization" between those in and those not in employment has been substituted by today's "dualization" between those in stable and those in marginal employment, and it seems strange to assess the one without alluding to the other (or to describe only the latter as "dualization"). Moreover, most labor market indicators prove the higher employment dynamics today as compared to pre-reform times.

If we try to evaluate comparatively, it appears as though Germany has neither moved in the direction of Anglo-Saxon liberalism nor copied Scandinavian-style activation, but has managed to reform and liberalize the continental regime, a "partial liberalization" (Carlin et al. 2015) following rather a sectoral pattern: liberalized service sectors exist side by side with traditional economic coordination in manufacturing. However, in an evaluation of the reforms from a political point of view, both critics and proponents would probably concur that the labor market after the Agenda 2010 reforms is in a situation that is "fundamentally different from the situation in the late 1990s and early 2000s" (Eichhorst and Tobsch 2014b). According to established performance criteria such as employment and unemployment, youth unemployment, female labor market participation, and

---

[10] An assessment which then stands in strange contradiction to the overall summary of the very same authors (cf. Beramendi et al. 2015a: 43): "The dominant response by governments has been an increase in the levels of segmentation at the expense of outsiders."

average retirement age, it can be stated that Germany today is no longer "adjusting badly" (Manow and Seils 1999; see Chapter 5). Again, this overall assessment would not only have to make reference to the domestic reforms, but also be put into the context of the new monetary environment, which became much more favorable for the German political economy after 2005 (see following discussion).

However, the return of growth, the turnaround of the German economy, and the substantial reduction in the number of unemployed and inactive persons came too late for the red/green government. In 2005, Schröder was forced to call new elections after having lost the large state of North Rhine-Westphalia, which had been traditionally Social Democratic. With this state now in the hands of the oppositional Christian Democrats, a two-thirds majority of the opposition in the Bundesrat, Germany's second chamber, became a likely scenario. With such a majority, the CDU/CSU-FDP opposition would have been able to block *any* government initiative.[11] Schröder decided that attack was the best form of defense. In the early federal elections of 2005, the share of the vote of the red/green coalition suffered. However, the opposition, which in the meantime had decided to rally around an even more radical reform platform than what the Agenda had brought, also lost vote shares (see Table 6.1).

While voters apparently punished the Social Democrats for their reform agenda, they showed little enthusiasm for the CDU's attempt to position itself as even more "de-regulative" than the Schröder government. As a consequence, the race was extremely close, and neither a center-right (CDU/CSU/FDP) nor a center-left (SPD and Greens) coalition gained a majority of seats. The upshot was that a Grand Coalition then ruled from 2005 to 2009. The Christian Democrats, however, had learned their lesson: in 2009, Chancellor Angela Merkel moved the Christian Democrats' program back to the center. Given that in 2009 the genuine "left-wing,"

**Table 6.1** Bundestag elections, overview of results, 1994–2017, in percent

|  | 1994 | 1998 | 2002 | 2005 | 2009 | 2013 | 2017 |
|---|---|---|---|---|---|---|---|
| SPD | 36.4 | 40.9 | 38.5 | 34.2 | 23 | 25.7 | 20.5 |
| CDU/CSU | 41.5 | 35.1 | 38.5 | 35.2 | 33.8 | 41.5 | 32.9 |
| FDP (Liberals) | 6.9 | 6.2 | 7.4 | 9.8 | 14.6 | 4.8 | 10.7 |
| Grüne (Greens) | 7.3 | 6.7 | 8.6 | 8.1 | 10.7 | 8.4 | 8.9 |
| PDS/Die Linke | 4.4 | 5.1 | 4 | 8.7 | 11.9 | 8.6 | 9.2 |
| AfD (right-wing populists) |  |  |  |  |  |  | 12.6 |
| Turnout | 79 | 82.2 | 79.1 | 77.7 | 70.8 | 71.5 | 76.2 |

*Source*: http://www.bundeswahlleiter.de (Federal Returning Office).

[11] According to Article 77, Section 4 of the Basic Law for the Federal Republic of Germany, i.e. the German constitution. Parliament can only override a two-thirds majority veto of the second chamber by finding a two-thirds majority itself, which is a completely unrealistic prospect.

orthodox anti-reform position was occupied by *Die Linke*, a party which had easily surpassed the German legal 5 percent threshold in the 2005 election thanks to the lack of popularity of the Agenda 2010 in the traditionalist left milieu, the Social Democrats were crushed from two sides. There was little room left in the political center for a Social Democracy that under Schröder had once claimed—in imitation of Blair's New Labour—to represent the New Center (*Die neue Mitte*) after Merkel ultimately decided to abandon her short flirtation with a neoliberal agenda.

In hindsight, the SPD's electoral disaster was predictable, partly because a Social Democratic minister of labor had not only been responsible for important labor market reforms between 2002 and 2005, but also for another hugely unpopular measure: the decision in 2007 to increase the retirement age to 67. However, the onset of the global financial crisis in 2009 also played into the hands of the CDU chancellor, since German voters are known to become more conservative in times of economic crisis (Anderson and Ward 1996).

## 6.3 German Wage Bargaining within the Euro Area

In order to put the Agenda 2010 reforms into a broader economic context, we need to examine them in relation to the changed monetary incentive structure in the euro area. With respect to the nexus between monetary policy and industrial relations, it is important to note that relatively high interest rates and their recessive consequences had not been perceived as the prime cause of Germany's economic troubles in the early 2000s. It appeared that poor economic performance pointed instead to the lack of competitiveness of German firms and products as the root cause of all the country's economic troubles.

Having been "socialized" with the implicit supply-side logic of *Modell Deutschland* in the post-Bretton Woods world where the Bundesbank's independence and its hard currency policy ruled supreme (Franzese 1999; Hall and Franzese 1998; Scharpf 1987), the relevant German actors, in both the political and economic spheres, believed that interest rates were not too high, but wages and welfare benefits were. Subsequently, monetary policy did not have to be adjusted, but German wage costs did. Adjusting monetary policy was considered a taboo, at any rate, given the independence of the European Central Bank, which had been modeled on the Bundesbank (James 2012).

Initially, the immediate post-euro recession thus seemed to present German unions, employers, and politicians with a familiar challenge. The well-established interplay between wage bargaining and monetary policy could not be continued under the new circumstances of the euro, given that the ECB would not and could not target its monetary policy exclusively on pilot agreements between German employers and unions—as the Bundesbank had done in the past (see Chapter 5). However, in the high interest rate environment of the early 2000s, German social partners felt that the circumstances they found themselves in were, if not comfortable, then at least familiar (Hall and Franzese 1998). What has been succinctly labeled Germany's "supply-side corporatism" (Wolfgang Streeck) kicked in: Germany experienced wage moderation and productive company-level pacts concluded by the social partners, productivity-enhancing rationalization and, in part, relocation of firms, and finally the welfare reforms enacted by a Social Democratic government. It is worth highlighting that this latter aspect of the adjustment process, namely the profound welfare reform enacted by the red/green coalition, was a rather new element, something from which the CDU under Helmut Kohl had largely shied away. Thus it signified a major deviation from the course of earlier politics and also from the established approaches of social policy.

By creating space for the emergence of a large low-wage sector, the labor market and welfare reforms themselves subsequently exerted pressure on the unions and thereby further contributed to the wage restraint of the social partners. Of course, the boom in Europe's periphery and the ensuing significant increase in labor unit costs there helped restore the cost competitiveness of German industry as well— while the cost pressures stemming from eastern enlargement also helped keep German wages under control. The new, much poorer members of the European Union provided Germany with new product markets, but in particular with a supply of cheap production factors. Business relocation to the East or the threat of it helped German firms to keep their wage costs under control, as did the import of cheap labor under the EU Posting of Workers Directive.

The monetary parameters for the German model changed profoundly again when the banking crisis eventually translated into a sovereign debt crisis for some of euro area member states. The subsequent expansionary policy of the European Central Bank, the low interest rate environment, the (from a German perspective) undervalued euro, the massive repatriation of capital from the periphery to the center: taken together, all this boosted German investment and production substantially (Wolf 2014: 63). Germany's recent record-high trade surplus (see Fig. 6.2) is therefore to some extent the *result* of the euro crisis, not its cause, which also means that it cannot be explained by only referring to superior economic performance.[12] Just as everything that was wrong with *Modell Deutschland* in the early 2000s could not be blamed on the new currency, it is also impossible to explain today's economic revival of the German economy by exclusively citing the inherent strengths of *Modell Deutschland*.

One component of this situation is undoubtedly that German euro area partners can no longer devalue their currency in order to rebalance their current

---

[12] To the extent that the German current account surplus has to be explained by interest rates that were too low and a euro that was undervalued, at least from a German perspective, both of which were the result of the ECB's rather accommodating monetary policy, the European critique of Germany's current account imbalances appears contradictory.

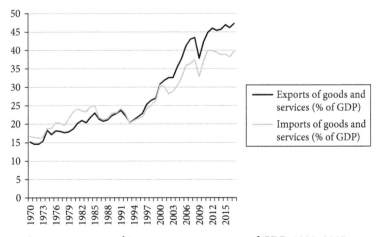

**Fig. 6.2** German exports and imports as a percentage of GDP, 1980–2017
*Source*: World Bank.

accounts vis-à-vis Germany—rendering strategies of wage moderation by German employers and unions now even more effective than they had been under the flexible or fixed, but adjustable exchange rates of the past (Höpner and Lutter 2014). Painful and unpopular "internal devaluation" is the only option left to Germany's euro partners (De Grauwe 2013, 2014; Iversen and Soskice 2018). While countries like France or Italy had hoped that the EMU would replace the Bundesbank's de facto monetary hegemony within the EMS with a more lenient European monetary policy, at the same time, the common currency exposed their economies to full, unfettered competition from German industry and foreclosed the devaluation option in response to inflationary wage settlements at home.

Yet, it is important to emphasize that this very situation had been an antici-pated, intended, and welcome consequence of monetary union. Italian and French government representatives hoped that the disciplinary effects of the common currency would help them keep wage inflation under control, given that national monetary and political authorities in the past had tended to give in too quickly to unions' aggressive wage demands (see De Grauwe 2014). These self-binding effects of the currency union were quite obvious from the beginning, as, for instance, Daniel Gros and Niels Thygesen had already remarked in 1998 in what was to become one of the classic textbooks on monetary union: "In sum, labour market flexibility is always useful and if EMU forces labour market reforms that are needed anyway, the economy of EU can only gain" (Gros and Thygesen 1998: 288). Bemoaning the euro's deregulatory effect on southern European industrial relations seems therefore to be rather a case of "dynamic inconsistency."

The absence of a devaluation instrument within the euro area certainly made German (Nordic) wage restraint more effective. Wage constraint, "combined with heavy investment in training...propelled northern Europe—Germany in particular—to a hegemonic trade position within Europe" (Iversen and Soskice 2018: 271). This has contributed to an erosion of the industrial base in the euro area periphery, the converse being the slight reversal of the long-term decline of employment in manufacturing in Germany. German industrial production increased by 8.7 percent from 2010 to 2014, whereas in Italy and Spain, it declined over the same period by 7.7 and 7.2 percent, respectively. The manufacturing sector in 2013 accounted for 22 percent of German GDP and 10 percent of French GDP, and for 28 and 22 percent of total employment in Germany and France, respectively.

Generally, since the introduction of the common currency, the labor markets in the center and in the periphery developed in a countercyclical fashion. German unemployment was high when it was low in the rest of the euro area and started to decline when it rose in the south—one of the many asymmetries indicating that the euro area is anything but an Optimal Currency Area (see Fig. 6.3).

As we have seen, during the first years of the euro area the monetary environment for German unions and employers' associations was not completely unfamiliar. The traditional German model could work reasonably under the ECB's high interest rate regime (that is, high for sluggish Germany). What about the period after 2005 though, when the ECB's interest rates became too low and accordingly the euro too weak for the booming German economy? If the German export-led growth model presupposes wage moderation, but the ECB cannot substitute the Bundesbank's disciplinary monetary policy, how do unions and employers secure a moderate development of wages? The answer to these questions can be divided into several components. First, it is possible that the erosion of the German wage-bargaining system (Streeck 2009), i.e., its increasing devolution to the company level, actually explains its continuing capacity to

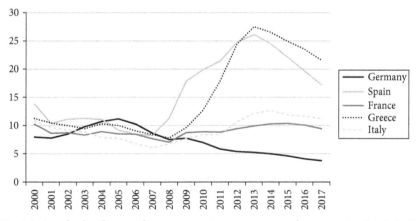

**Fig. 6.3** Standardized unemployment rates in euro area member countries, 2000–2017
*Source*: World Bank.

deliver wage moderation. Second, the disciplining effect of the Agenda 2010 labor market reforms is also worth mentioning. Further, the moderating effect of eastern enlargement and of the currency union itself, and finally the disciplinary consequences of crisis-induced immigration should also be acknowledged. Let me briefly elaborate on these points.

Ironically, the more limited coverage of wage negotiations, due to the erosion of membership both of the unions and of the employers' associations, could turn out to be an explanation for the continuing capacity of the German political economy to moderate wages. Since the 1990s, German collective wage agreements have been largely substituted with company-level agreements or what are known as firm-level "productivity pacts" (Rehder 2003). They trade employment guarantees by employers with workers' consent to rationalization, partial relocations, increased labor flexibility, and so on. If we are looking for an explanation for how the German economy continued to deliver wage moderation during times when the familiar strategic interaction between social partners and the central bank had ceased to function, it is important to emphasize the fact that the "control of labour costs in the German industrial relations system shifted over time from the dominance of coordinated wage setting institutions to competitiveness-driven plant level adjustment" (Hassel 2014a: 26; see also Hancké 2002; Hassel 2017). The erosion of Germany's wage coordination system would then not be an indication of a fundamental change of *Modell Deutschland* (Streeck 2009), but a necessary precondition for the model to function as it had previously, albeit under profoundly different circumstances.

This insight helps us to explain a second, *prima facie* puzzling aspect of Germany's economic recovery after 2004. Whereas the poor labor market dynamic in the 1990s was due to particularly weak job growth in the (low-skill, low-productivity) service sector, the recent strong increase in the employment rate (Germany's labor market miracle; Hartung et al. 2018) and the corresponding low degree of inactivity were to a large extent due to the substantial expansion of the low-wage labor market segment, primarily in services. This labor market dynamic had previously been hindered by union wage coordination, restrictive employment protection rules, and the high "replacement rates" implicit in the generous regulations of the unemployment insurance scheme, which were tailored to insider interests (Rueda 2005, 2006). Once the Agenda 2010 reforms removed these protective features, low union density and low productivity in the service sector combined to bring about unforeseen job growth, also keeping costs of living down and thereby supporting wage moderation in manufacturing, too (Carlin et al. 2015).

Further, the wage discipline of German workers in the 2000s is certainly also due to monetary union itself, since regional economic integration, admittedly evolved over many decades, substantially intensified under the EMU and further increased with European enlargement in 2004. Both events lend momentum to the establishment of a new economic region that integrates new member states from Central and Eastern Europe with the German economy, but also increases integration with the Baltic and Benelux states. German trade "with the new member states of the EU increased from 2 percent to more than 7 percent of GDP between 1994 and 2006. During that period, intra-firm trade represented about 21.6 percent of imports from Eastern Europe" (Hassel 2014b: 63). Some observers even maintain that the new ways of "organising production by slicing up the value chain has been more important for Germany's lower unit labour costs than German workers' wage restraint. According to estimates, German offshoring to Eastern Europe boosted not only the productivity of its subsidiaries in Eastern Europe by almost threefold compared to local companies, but it also increased the productivity of the parent companies in Germany by more than 20%" (Marin 2010).

Wage development within this emerging, larger economic region *could* be taken into account by the ECB's monetary policy. To the extent that the ECB *did* take German wages into account, while "Germany's neighbours effectively targeted [these German wages] to hold down their own wages...the northern European countries could pursue the export-led growth strategies to which they had long been accustomed with considerable success" (Hall 2012: 358–9).

Now that (relatively) high growth and low unemployment have returned to Germany, we should therefore not expect that unit labor costs will increase as steeply as they did during the boom in southern Europe. They will increase, but it seems safe to predict that they will remain largely in line with productivity and international competitiveness, since functional equivalents to the monetary signals of the Bundesbank and the traditional system of pattern wage bargaining seem to have been put in place: competitive firm-level pacts, the relocation and regional economic integration of firms, the liberalization of the service sector, etc. With the anticipated inflation firmly anchored around 2 percent or lower, German unions do not need strong monetary signals to figure out which wage hikes are likely to harm the international competitiveness of industries, sectors, or companies.

Finally, the crisis itself appears to contribute to German wage restraint: while the labor inflow from Europe's periphery in the wake of the crisis is insufficient to bring relief to southern labor markets, it is apparently enough to ensure that labor supply meets Germany's increased labor demand. In 2013, Germany welcomed around 400,000 new immigrants, a number only surpassed by the US—and in 2015 more than a million migrants arrived, with similarly high numbers in 2016.[13]

---

[13] In this respect, a parallel between the early 1950s and the 2010s can also be observed: a steady inflow of qualified workers enabled Germany to combine full employment with low inflation (see Chapter 5). However, the massive inflow of refugees in 2015 and 2016 (estimated at 1.3 million) is quite another issue. This will translate into a huge quasi-Keynesian push for domestic demand—and integration into the labor market of these mainly poorly skilled people will take a rather long time. Employment rate after 10 years is estimated to be 10 percent lower than for the German population.

In sum, even if the ECB were to pursue a much more accommodating monetary policy, this would be unlikely to result in German wage inflation to the extent that the boom in southern Europe did after 2000. It is more likely that the strength of German industry would be reinforced under a lax monetary policy (due to what would then be a weak external value of the euro). This points to the systematic differences in wage-setting regimes in the coordinated "hard currency" north of the euro area as compared to the largely uncoordinated "soft currency" south (Hancké 2013; Höpner and Lutter 2014; Iversen and Soskice 2018; Mody 2018), which have been at the heart of the crisis. These differences will be addressed in the next section.

## 6.4 One Currency, Two Political Economies

The fact that in pre-crisis times German unit labor costs remained stagnant or even decreased (see Fig. 6.4), whereas in most other countries of the euro area they increased, was something that had initially been interpreted as a welcome

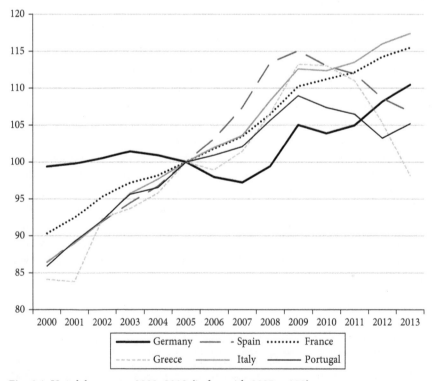

**Fig. 6.4** Unit labor costs, 2000–2013 (index with 2005 = 100)
*Source*: ECB.

economic convergence, given that wage levels in the south were significantly below the German level at first (Illing et al. 2012). In retrospect, Germany's European neighbors have severely criticized the country's economic and political adjustments to the slump of the early 2000s as a strategy of unfair labor cost dumping as the cause of the widening competitiveness gap between the center and the periphery in the currency zone.

From a "northern" perspective, in turn, Italian, Spanish, or French labor had simply become too expensive, a trend concealed for some time by massive capital inflows (Hall 2014). Unable to moderate wages, fragmented and militant unions in these countries successfully pushed for wage settlements significantly above productivity growth plus inflation, thereby steadily undermining their industry's competitiveness. Because of their incapacity to correct for this through (nominal) currency depreciations within the euro area, countries in the periphery are now forced to pursue a painful process of real depreciation.

Whether German wages are "too low" or southern wages "too high" is a debate in which it is not necessary to take sides (in fact, both assessments are accurate and tautologically have to be accurate if the comparison is restricted to the euro area only). With very different degrees of export dependency, also with respect to exports outside the eurozone, German employers (and policy-makers) have to be more sensitive about German wages than, say, French or Italian employers and policy-makers (Scharpf 2017). However, what is more central to my argument is the fact that the discussion about deflation in the south or reflation in the north points to profound differences in the two political economies, particularly with respect to their different abilities to deliver wage moderation. In fact, these differences explain why countries such as France and Italy pushed for a single European currency in the first place—it was intended to represent the ultimate credible commitment to break with the inflationary cycles inherent to their political economies.[14]

Before the euro, the "typical situation in the high-inflation countries usually involved powerful (or, at the very least, highly militant) labour unions that managed to extract high wages from employers, both in the public and in the private sector (high wages are defined here as wages that grow faster than labour productivity). Since employers passed on these wage increases through higher prices (or rising budgets), higher wages led into the next inflationary cycle, where they would be raised again to reflect higher inflation, and so on, ad infinitum" (Hancké 2013: 16). High inflation rates then regularly triggered devaluations to regain price competitiveness (Höpner and Spielau 2016). Yet these devaluations could only provide temporary relief. A weaker currency translates into increased

[14] It is therefore not true that the founders of the EMU were insufficiently aware of the profound differences between the political economies of the EMU members (see Hall 2014). They were simply over-optimistic about how smoothly the anticipated adjustment process would take place.

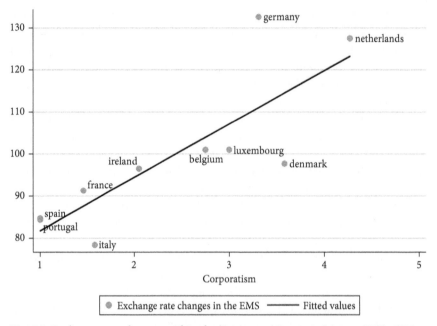

**Fig. 6.5** Exchange rate changes within the European Monetary System, 1979–1999
*Source*: Own calculations based on European Commission (2005); Siaroff (1999).

costs of living through higher prices for imported goods, and unions, both strong and militant ones, are then eager to compensate for the decrease in workers' real wages with higher (nominal) wages, which, in turn, initiates the next round of inflationary wage–price dynamics (Carlin and Soskice 1990: ch. 12; De Grauwe 2013). The competitive advantage of each devaluation quickly dissipated in the next inflationary wage–price spiral.

It is striking to see that the pattern of de- and revaluations in the European Monetary System (EMS) from 1979 to 1999 almost perfectly predicts which countries were going to have problems with the fixed regime of the euro that replaced the EMS (cf. Höpner and Spielau 2016). Figure 6.5 plots the overall changes of the exchange rates for the countries participating in the exchange rate system (except the UK) against their corporatism scores (Siaroff 1999) which capture, *inter alia*, their degrees of wage coordination.

Over the entire period, the Italian Lira devalued around 50 percent vis-à-vis the Deutschmark or the Dutch Gulden, whereas countries like Belgium, Luxembourg, or Denmark stayed relatively close to their initial parities from 1979.

It was the desire to break out of this inflationary cycle and to credibly commit to a low inflation equilibrium, with the anticipated consequences for domestic wage-bargaining regimes, that motivated countries such as Italy and France to pursue the single currency strategy, since the EMS, already described by Stanley Fisher as an "arrangement by France and Italy to accept German leadership, imposing constraints on their domestic monetary and fiscal policies" (quoted in James 2012: 208), had failed to fully deliver low inflation and exchange rate stability (cf. Eichengreen 2007: 283).[15] That France and Italy were forced to devalue the Franc and the Lira several times was something which—apart from the fact that depreciations provided only temporal economic relief—was perceived as damaging national prestige.[16] In an asymmetric strategic situation, in which the undervalued currency saw much less need for appreciation than the overvalued saw for depreciation, the Bundesbank and the German government could simply wait until others took the necessary steps. The view that periodic devaluations were (and are) an essential precondition for the functioning of the soft currency political economies in Europe's south thus does not seem to be fully accurate (Scharpf 2011). It was precisely the intention to overcome these recurrent episodes that motivated key Italian and French actors to opt for a common currency. It is unsurprising then that these actors have not proven to be particularly eager to regain the devaluation option, but are more interested in expanding their *fiscal* leeway (Iversen et al. 2016).

What the relevant political actors in the south did not anticipate, however, was that the much stricter constraint, the "irrevocable" commitment to a common currency, would still not be sufficient to constrain domestic wage bargaining—at least not instantly. This commitment would only become binding at a later point and then with much more harmful consequences, namely, only *after* the southern economies (except Italy) had gone through a substantial boom period. This then made the necessary real devaluation, particularly the wage decreases, much more painful than before, both economically and politically (Manow 2017).

The initial surge in the south was indeed just the complement of the later crisis: with higher wage- and therefore higher price inflation, the southern euro area benefited from very low, partly negative real interest rates in the first five years of the monetary union. As wages then increased at a consistently higher rate than wages in the north (Höpner and Lutter 2014), southern industry quickly lost its cost competitiveness.[17] This translated into growing current account deficits,

---

[15] That the effects of the EMU on domestic wage bargaining regimes were not only anticipated, but also intended, is indicated, for instance, by the view of monetary economist Niels Thygesen, member of the Delors Committee. Monetary union, he stated, would be "a way of 'reducing the scope for the kind of lax and divergent monetary policies' that characterized Europe in the 1970s" (James 2012: 7).

[16] Of course, it is important to emphasize that devaluations were not always due to wage growth differentials, but sometimes also reflected domestic imperatives of Germany's monetary policy. One example of this was the increased interest rates with which the Bundesbank wanted to cool down an overheating economy in the wake of Germany's post-unification boom. Also, the status of the Deutschmark as a reserve currency sometimes forced the French or the Italians to devalue vis-à-vis the Deutschmark during periods when the US dollar was weak.

[17] In fact, every year since the introduction of the euro, unit labor costs have increased more dramatically in Italy and France than in Germany (Höpner and Lutter 2014). The lack of wage moderation is partly due to unions' strategies, partly due to highly inflexible labor markets:

which could only be sustained by massive capital inflows. Once these stopped in the wake of the Lehman bankruptcy and capital even started to flow in the reverse direction, the crisis fully and dramatically unfolded.

With respect to wage bargaining, the southern high-inflation equilibrium and the German low-inflation equilibrium seem to be opposites (Iversen et al. 2016; Iversen and Soskice 2018). In this context, Bob Hancké speaks of the "two Europes," "one with orderly wage-determination systems, where low wage and price inflation targets were internalized by the trade unions by means of inter-sectoral wage coordination, and another, where wages rose faster relative to productivity, competitiveness collapsed, and trade balances deteriorated sharply" (Hancké 2013: 13; Hassel 2014c; Iversen and Soskice 2018; Mody 2018).[18] The challenge, therefore, is not to explain why the euro area is not an optimal currency area, but why it is almost the exact opposite, why the single currency binds together two rather different types of political economies—a hard currency, export-led growth model, on the one hand, with a soft currency, i.e. inflation-prone, consumption-based growth model, on the other (Iversen et al. 2016; Mody 2018).

One key motive for currency union was certainly a geopolitical consideration: committing unified Germany irreversibly to the European project. In addition, the currency union represented a *quid pro quo* of low inflation and low interest rates for the south and therefore a boost of credit-based growth there, in exchange for abandoning the option of devaluation in order to regain competitiveness vis-à-vis the northern export industry (Iversen et al. 2016). But low interest rates presupposed low price inflation, and that in turn meant low wage inflation. Thus, in addition to these two important factors, EMU came about not *despite* the profound differences between the northern and the southern political economy, but *because* of them: as the ultimate commitment to the "German" low inflation equilibrium in order to break with the inflationary tendencies inherent in the southern model.

This explanation of the euro crisis is also in line with several other recent explanations for the crisis (Hancké 2013; Hassel 2014c; Höpner and Lutter 2014;

---

"productivity growth was correspondingly weak...The most important reason for the relatively inflexible labour markets of southern Europe was legislation, which made it extremely difficult to lay-off long-term workers" (Wolf 2014: 63). But it "really did *not* make sense for countries whose industries were competing with those of China to allow their labour costs to rise faster than in countries like Germany, whose industries were complementary to those of China" (Wolf 2014: 293–4).

[18] This bifurcation into two groups of countries had already occurred in the 1970s under the European Monetary System: "The first group, made up of Germany, the Benelux countries, and Denmark, had succeeded in limiting inflation to the mid to high single digits and in keeping their exchange rates stable...In fact, this was a deutschmark-based arrangement, since Germany was the lowest-inflation country and accounted for more than two-thirds of the collective GDP of this group. The second set of countries—France, Italy, and the United Kingdom, and Ireland—had more difficulty restraining inflation and were therefore unable to keep their currencies within the margins of the Snake" (Eichengreen 2007: 283).

Iversen et al. 2016; Iversen and Soskice 2018).[19] Differences between the continental and the southern wage-bargaining regimes can explain both the political motives behind the strong push for a common currency in the 1990s—as a means of breaking the domestic inflationary cycles in the soft currency countries (mainly Italy and France) and as the ultimate proof of reunified Germany's commitment to Europe—and what were then divergent dynamics of the two political economies under the euro, which finally culminated in the dramatic crisis of 2008/2009 and the subsequent recession and sovereign debt crisis. Somewhat ironically, or tragically, therefore, the export of the German low-inflation regime to the European level, triggered the real divergence between the north and the south of the currency zone (Palier et al. 2018), and it rather reinforced than weakened central traits of the German political economy, in particular its strong export dependence.

In the final chapter I summarize the argument of the book and draw conclusions for the comparative study of Europe's political economies.

[19] This contradicts Martin Wolf's diagnosis, however: the euro crisis is not (or at least no longer) a "financial crisis with fiscal consequences" (Wolf 2014: 302), but has since turned into a competitiveness crisis with fiscal consequences. My position also diverges from Scharpf's analysis, in which he emphasizes the fiscal problem of euro member states running a public debt in a "foreign" currency. With Draghi's "whatever it takes" guarantee the ECB has, in fact, become lender of last resort. Further, with historically low interest rates, debt service is cheaper than ever before. However, (the lack of) private competitiveness remains a problem and, with sluggish growth, these states then also inevitably have a fiscal problem.

# 7

# Conclusion

The preceding chapters have traced the impact of the Bismarckian welfare state on the German political economy over a time span of more than 130 years, from the 1880s to the 2010s. The study set out to show in three longer historical chapters how the German welfare state shaped class-formation and provided a blueprint for the solution of industrial conflict (Chapter 2), how it acted as a catalyst for the formation of political camps and how it contributed to the formation of political conflict lines in Weimar Germany (Chapter 3), and—finally—how these conflicts became critical for the definition of the regulatory role and the redistributive powers of the central state within Germany's postwar political economy. Chapters 4, 5, and 6 then investigated the German welfare state's contribution to the rise, demise, and resurrection of *Modell Deutschland* over the 1950s and 1960s (rise), the 1970s to 1990s (demise), and finally in the new millennium (resurrection). Chapter 4 emphasized how important the welfare state was for the establishment and stability of long-term economic coordination among employers and employees after 1945, in particular for the mutual deferral of wages and profits throughout the 1950s and 1960s (cf. Eichengreen 1996a, 1996b, 2007). Chapter 5 analyzed how the welfare state functioned as a buffer for the labor market distortions caused by external shocks starting with the first OPEC crisis in 1973. It also highlighted how the welfare state was used to ease the fiscal strain caused by the combination of decreasing revenue in times of low economic growth rates and sharply increased spending demands in times of high unemployment. The central claim of this chapter was that its role as a "shock absorber" has made the welfare state more and more expensive, with adverse effects for job growth, labor market dynamism, and smooth structural change. The welfare state helped stabilize the German political economy in times of "diminished expectations" (Krugman) and of increased economic volatility, yet it stabilized an economic model whose economic performance has steadily deteriorated since the mid-1970s. And an ever more expensive welfare state in combination with sluggish employment growth was one of the main reasons for that deterioration.

Chapter 6 finally analyzed the causes and effects of the crucial reform of the German labor market and its unemployment and pension system in the early 2000s. It sketched how economic coordination German style carried over to completely new circumstances under Europe's single currency. This is described as a process of adaption that maintained high productivity in the manufacturing sector, but allowed for a "selective liberalization" (Kathleen Thelen) of the labor

*Social Protection, Capitalist Production: The Bismarckian Welfare State in the German Political Economy, 1880–2015.*
Philip Manow, Oxford University Press (2020). © Philip Manow.
DOI: 10.1093/oso/9780198842538.001.0001

market, namely one largely confined to the low-wage labor market segment. This then became mainly relevant for job growth in the service sector. The particular strengths of the German political economy, namely wage restraint, re-investment of profits in the firm and therefore constant productivity gains, peaceful industrial relations, premiums on long-term economic coordination, etc. seem rather to have been reinforced under the euro. But this then also contributes to the increasing imbalance between the two different political economies of the euro-zone, the (formerly) hard-currency, export-led growth countries of the North versus the (formerly) soft-currency, domestic demand models of the South.

I do not claim that my study gave an exhaustive account of the interplay between Germany's "protection regime" and its "production system." In order to keep the empirical material manageable and the study readable I had to focus on *specific* paths of influence. For instance, the argument could have been made more complete by taking the welfare state's crucial role within Germany's system of industry-wide vocational training into account (Busemeyer and Iversen 2011; Busemeyer and Trampusch 2011; Crouch et al. 1999; Culpepper and Finegold 1999; Estevez-Abe et al. 1999). With respect to vocational training one could have pointed out the importance of both strict employment protection and generous unemployment protection for a production system that is based on a combination of workers' general and firm-specific skills (Estevez-Abe et al. 1999). In this context one could also have mentioned the critical contribution of the welfare state for the stability of Germany's industry-wide vocational training system, in particular via its support for industry-sector wage bargaining and equal wages within industrial sectors (Manow 2001b).

The same holds true for the question of how Germany's system of secondary and tertiary education meets the skill demands of the German economy (but see Ansell 2008, 2010; Ansell and Gingrich 2013). In particular one could have explained why Scandinavian social democracy together with the center parties managed to introduce comprehensive schooling in the late 1960s and early 1970s and how they found a consensus on strong public spending for higher education, and how all this contributed to a much smoother transition from an industrial to a service economy in the Nordic countries. In contrast to this, German Social Democrats attempted very similar reforms around the same time, but met with strong resistance by the Christian Democrats, and therefore finally failed. An explanation for this striking divergence of the Scandinavian and the continental models would have had to point to the imperative for a party like the Christian Democrats that mobilizes a socio-economically diverse electorate to balance between worker, middle-, and upper-class interests. And the differentiation between *Hauptschule* (elementary), *Realschule* (secondary school), and *Gymnasium* (college-track secondary school) strikes exactly such a compromise between the different socio-economic strata within the Christian Democratic electorate. And it would have been also a story, similar to my above emphasis on the importance of fiscal federalism in Germany, of how the federal structure of the German polity restricts party-political room for maneuver (Manow 2005).

Yet, all these additional perspectives would have just provided further empirical support for the study's central claim—without altering its basic thrust, namely that we have to get at a better understanding of the systematic relationship between national welfare states and distinct national forms of capitalism if we want to explain the functioning of the political economy of advanced industrial countries (Ebbinghaus and Manow 2001). This at least is true for the institutionally "dense" political economies and welfare regimes of continental Europe and Scandinavia in which long-term economic coordination critically depends upon the interplay between "market and state." Here the state—to a large extent—means "welfare state" (cf. Iversen and Pontusson 2000). This study argued that we cannot accurately assess current welfare state developments or comprehend the differences in economic performance among the OECD countries without having first reached such an understanding.

What can one gain from this analysis of the "political construction of a coordinated political economy"? And do any of the insights generated with respect to the institutional and political genealogy of the German political economy travel beyond this single case? Let me address these two questions in turn.

When it comes to what we learned with a view to the German political economy and its genealogy, my study provides, I believe, answers to several questions that continue to puzzle students of German capitalism. First of all, the preceding chapters offered a response to the often posed question of how Germany managed to combine low inflation with low unemployment without embarking on "that kind of tripartite macroconcertation and political exchange [ ... ] that establishes the constituent principle of corporatist policy making" (Traxler and Kittel 2000: 1161; cf. Thelen 1991: 3). To put it in more economic terms: the study offered an answer to the question of why German unions since the mid-1950s continued exerting wage restraint despite high growth rates and full employment and despite the fact that the official union rhetoric became much more strident in favor of large-scale redistribution in the course of the 1950s. The answer at the same time provides an explanation for the puzzle left by the "wage coordination – central bank independence" argument (Franzese 1999; Hall 1994; Hall and Franzese 1997; Iversen 1996, 1998a, 1998b, 1999, 2000; Scharpf 1991), namely how to explain wage restraint in a period in which the German central bank could not have played its non-accommodating role, as interest rates were a blunt monetary instrument under the Bretton Woods system of fixed exchange rates (Holtfrerich 1998).

As we saw in Chapter 4, the importance in the 1950s of, first, mobilization with a view to pending legislative questions of industrial relations and then, second, welfare state reform helped unions to overcome collective action problems and to strike a balance between different economic sectors: exposed versus sheltered, small and medium enterprises versus large firms, the Ruhr area's heavy industry versus shipbuilding in the north and the automobile industry in the south. Once the leadership of the metalworker union was established in the wake of the massive strikes in the late 1950s on issues of social policy (in particular sickness pay), the unions could be forced into a system of coordinated wage bargaining by Germany's employer association in the early 1960s. And once a system of pattern wage bargaining proved beneficial for both sides, it lasted for the next decade and a half, until it came under stress after the end of the Bretton Woods system.

Why was wage coordination stable? It seems warranted to stress again that it contributed to an exceptional position of the German political economy in comparative terms, namely providing a big country with the economic profile of a small country. How unlikely economic coordination and a very large export share are in a big country becomes clear once we compare the German case with France, Italy, or the UK. An export-led growth model becomes unlikely not only because the domestic market is large enough so that an export orientation is not without alternatives, but also because coordination becomes more unlikely the bigger a country is. Germany thus represents an anomaly that calls for an explanation.

While the extraordinary size of Germany's export sector is a rather recent phenomenon, the result of the unusually lenient monetary policy of the ECB and the—for Germany—strongly undervalued euro, export-led growth has been a key ingredient of *Modell Deutschland* since the 1950s, initially supported by an undervalued Deutschmark within the Bretton Woods system. This growth model, in turn, depends on a particular type of economic coordination, namely a decentralized one, as it could not have worked through conventional neo-corporatist channels as in the Nordic model or in the smaller continental political economies (Belgium, Netherlands, Austria, Switzerland). A central element in this whole intricate balance is that the German welfare state provided a functional equivalent to the full-employment guarantee of the Scandinavian model there issued by the central, Social Democratic government. The German functional equivalent included (a) generous unemployment entitlements that guaranteed that possible episodes of unemployment would not endanger a worker's relative income position, and (b) "dynamic" pensions that were adjusted to current wages and thereby prolonged a worker's relative income position into retirement. These provisions supported strategies of long-term skill acquisition, the investment into a mixture of firm- and sector-specific skills, unions' policy of wage moderation and a common pact of re-channeling firms' profit into productivity-increasing investments. They provided these productivity-enhancing practices with a micro-foundation, i.e. with a rationale reflected in an individual person's lifelong income profile. On the employer side the strong expansion of the welfare state kept the growth of company welfare schemes under control, as one potential manifestation of wage drift in times of high growth and full employment, which would have undermined collective bargaining.

This then also answers the question of how the German political economy could be so highly coordinated if a particular brand of liberal tradition of economic thinking, ordoliberalism, allegedly became so dominant in postwar Germany (Blyth 2015; Brunnermeier et al. 2016; Hien and Joerges 2017). The answer, laid out particularly in Chapter 3, came in two parts: first, ordoliberalism was never really liberal; second, it was also not very influential with respect to Germany's postwar economic order. What emerged in postwar Germany as a distinct political economy was much less influenced by (ordo-)liberal doctrine than by the reconstruction of the German welfare state—which ordoliberals had vigorously opposed. And it was the welfare state that enabled economic coordination between labor and capital which also was anything but well received in ordoliberal thinking. To the contrary: ordoliberalism was fully allergic towards any collusion between labor and capital as it had been Weimar's neo-corporatist complex against which ordoliberalism had initially been formulated (see Chapter 3).

The preceding chapters argued that in Germany the Bismarckian, occupationalist, corporatist welfare state thus provided capital and labor with the infrastructure necessary to uphold a complex form of long-term economic coordination.[1] It is rather ironic that the basis for this coordination between capital and labor seems to have been critically reneged in 2005, when crucial status guarantees for workers were revoked with the Agenda 2010 reforms (see Chapter 6). And it appears quite paradoxical that exactly this revocation of crucial provisions of *Modell Deutschland* should have started the spectacular comeback of the German economy in the second half of the decade. The most important measure of the labor market reforms was the substantial shortening of the drawing period for unemployment assistance from a maximum of 32 to a maximum of 12 months. After that period, unemployed only qualify for unemployment support, which is roughly at the level of social assistance, irrespective of prior income, the level of qualification, and the duration of former employment—and therefore the period in which contributions to the social insurance schemes had been paid. This seriously undermines the "Bismarckian promise," namely "status preservation," especially since spells of unemployment then also extend to old age—given that periods of low contributions translate into low pensions. While there has not been an immediate negative effect of the Agenda reforms on the stability of the German production model, and while the reforms' beneficial job growth effects *did* contribute to its subsequent quite spectacular revival, it is still important to note that this signifies a clear break with the previous logic of *Modell Deutschland*. The main

---

[1] Moreover, the reconstruction of Weimar's political conflicts over social policy and their distributive and institutional consequences also shed light on the exact relationship between political consociationalism and economic corporatism in Germany. While a close nexus between both phenomena has often been noted and empirically confirmed (Crepaz and Lijphart 1995; Lijphart and Crepaz 1991), the literature, so far, has not provided any account of the exact *causal* nature of their relationship—something which Chapter 3 did.

reaction to this, up to now, was however rather political than economic, as the advent first of the left-protest party *Die Linke* and then, second, of the right-populist movement must be seen in the light of the profound changes to the implicit contract on which the postwar German social model had been based (Manow 2018; Schwander and Manow 2017a, 2017b).

Relatedly, the preceding analysis also addressed the question of how the German system functioned under the profoundly changed circumstances of the eurozone when the strategic interaction between capital and labor under the supervision of a non-accommodating central bank, which was so central for Germany's post-Bretton Woods equilibrium, had ceased to function. In particular Chapter 6 thereby also shed light on the role that Germany played in the euro crisis from 2009/2010 onwards. As I argue in that chapter, German unions continued to deliver wage restraint even after introduction of the common currency, first and not so surprisingly in the quasi familiar high-interest rate environment up to the crisis, but—much more remarkably—then also after 2010 in times of high growth and high (low) employment (unemployment). Several causes seem to be responsible for Germany's continuing capability to moderate wages even in times in which the Bundesbank had lost its disciplinary function: the wage pressure through (a) strong immigration, or (b) through the EU's eastern enlargement in 2004, which eased business relocation or at least made the threat of it more credible, (c) the decline in union membership as well as in firms' membership in employer associations, with both developments leading to a lesser coverage of collective labor agreements,[2] and last but not least (d) the Agenda reforms themselves, which *inter alia* motivated unions or works councils to rather bargain for job security than for major wage hikes, as well as (e) the continuing fiscal incapacity of the German state to engage in major economic steering—except perhaps in real emergencies like the immediate demand shock in the wake of the Lehman bankruptcy.

This might then also help explain the stance of the German government on the politics of the eurozone after the crisis broke out, a position which had no particularly ordoliberal traits (Feld et al. 2015)—not to mention that the common currency had not been an ordoliberal or even German project in the first place. Again, blaming ordoliberalism or some irrational German inflation angst, allegedly stemming from 1923/24, for either the refusal of the German government to underwrite euro bonds or for its insistence on the Maastricht criteria seems not particularly enlightening—nor are speculations about a grandiose German "vision of a long-term reordering of Europe's society and economy" (unconvincing in this and other interpretations of the German position; Tooze 2018: 518 and passim). There are much more straightforward explanations for

---

[2] Which then were substituted with firm-level "productivity pacts," exchanging workplace guarantees by employers for wage restraint and higher working hour flexibility by unions.

this, for instance: fear of fiscal moral hazard, emphasis on national democratic accountability for national budgets, lack of interest for a low-debt country to be made liable for high-debt countries (a position that was not "German" in any sense, but shared by all other low-debt euro-countries, i.e. Finland, the Baltic states, and the Netherlands), and not the least: protection of a relatively well-functioning economic model that is based upon wage restraint plus fiscal restraint (see Chapter 6).

This then, finally, allows us to also address the second of the above questions, namely what we might have learned *beyond* the German case, to what extent a better understanding of the German political economy helps us with a view to a *Comparative* Political Economy perspective. It has become clear, I think, that those welfare regimes usually subsumed under the label conservative-continental do in fact represent two very different political economies (see Chapter 6). We therefore should extend Esping-Andersen's original analysis (1990) towards a "four worlds of welfare capitalism" perspective (Beramendi et al. 2015b; Manow et al. 2018). Economically speaking, the main difference between a continental and a southern model seems to lie in their different capacities to deliver wage restraint, with all the consequences with respect to inflation, international competitiveness, size of the export sector, relative importance of demand-led growth, fiscal policy of the state, etc. that follow from this. Politically speaking the main difference seems to lie in the relative strengths of a reformist versus a radical left, which in turn (historically) reflects different, either moderate or radical stances of political Catholicism (Manow 2015b; Watson 2015), and ultimately the different situation of Catholicism as either a religious minority in the continental European countries or as the religious monopoly in the South. The political difference, in turn, can explain the economic differences: if parties on the left as well as trade unions are split between a reformist and a revolutionary current, wage coordination becomes very unlikely—because unions try to outbid each other in wage bargaining and because it is also unlikely to find a social democratic party in government that could motivate and underpin neo-corporatist exchanges.

The German case, which can stand for the other coordinated economies of the continent like Austria, Switzerland, and the Benelux as well, then also becomes "readable" in a consistent Comparative Political Economy framework, instead of being depicted as an odd outlier in a CPE perspective that takes the US and Sweden as polar cases on a liberal market vs. Keynesian welfare state continuum. Instead, a framework based upon the history of "party-political class coalitions" would emphasize for the political economies of the continental countries the importance of a moderate political Catholicism in the form of center-right Christian Democracy, a party that does not fit so easily in a traditional progressive/left versus conservative/right spectrum.

My analysis in the preceding chapters was predicated upon a basic syllogism. This syllogism consists of, first, stating that the welfare state is "the principal institution in the construction of post-war capitalism" (Esping-Andersen 1990: 5); second, stating that different parties or rather party coalitions in power led to different welfare state regimes (Kersbergen and Manow 2009)—that "countries cluster on policy because they cluster on politics" (Shalev 2007: 289); and there-fore, third, of arguing that it then makes sense to link basic features of the western European political economies to basic features of their respective party systems, in particular to long-term patterns of party coalitions (Manow 2009, 2015b). The latter, in turn, point back to the cleavage structures that emerged historically with the advent of the modern nation state and its full democratization.

Within such a comparative framework the specific profile of the continental variant of economic coordination might then also be better appreciated than under the dualistic worldview dominant in much of the recent and contemporary CPE literature, centered on the juxtaposition of the left, Keynesian, centrally coordinated Scandinavian model and the right, liberal, decentralized, pure-market model of the Anglo-Saxon world (see Chapter 1). What this then also brings to the fore is a certain weakness of recent CPE scholarship, which either focuses on economic outcome instead of political input, or—if it starts with political input—only looks at the impact of single party families like Christian Democracy or Social Democracy (Huber et al. 1993; Huber and Stephens 2000, 2001). For the West European countries, countries that host the most advanced welfare states of the world, with their proportional electoral rules and thus multi-party systems and coalition governments, such an approach appears to be analytically inadequate.

Under a less dualistic CPE perspective, then finally, Germany's economic crisis management in the wake of the Great Recession would also appear less as the wholly unexplainable folly as depicted in many of the contributions to the recent literature, and rather as a quite consistent attempt to defend core elements of its—relatively well-functioning—political economy. It is in a sense both ironic and tragic that it was the euro, initially conceived as an instrument of Europe's economic convergence, which has brought these differences between a southern and a continental model into very sharp relief.

# References

Abelshauser, Werner (1984a), "The First Post-Liberal Nation: Stages in the Development of Modern Corporatism in Germany," *European History Quarterly*, 14, 285–318.

Abelshauser, Werner (1984b), "Wirtschaftliche Wechsellagen, Wirtschaftsordnung und Staat: Die deutschen Erfahrungen," in Dieter Grimm (ed.), *Staatsaufgaben* (Frankfurt am Main: Suhrkamp), 199–232.

Abelshauser, Werner (1997), "Erhard oder Bismarck? Die Richtungsentscheidung der deutschen Sozialpolitik am Beispiel der Reform der Sozialversicherung in den Fünfziger Jahren," *Geschichte und Gesellschaft* 22, 376–92.

Adamsen, Heiner R. (1981), *Investitionshilfe für die Ruhr. Wiederaufbau, Verbände und Soziale Marktwirtschaft 1948-1952* (Wuppertal: Peter Hammer).

Alber, Jens (1989a), "Das Gesundheitswesen der Bundesrepublik im internationalen Vergleich. Analyse ausgewählter Indikatoren aus 21 Ländern," *NGM*, 1989 (1), 140–9.

Alber, Jens (1989b), *Der Sozialstaat in der Bundesrepublik 1950-1983* (Frankfurt am Main: Campus).

Albert, Götz (1998), *Wettbewerbsfähigkeit und Krise der deutschen Schiffbauindustrie 1945-1990* (Frankfurt: Peter Lang).

Alecke, Björn (1999), *Deutsche Geldpolitik in der Ära Bretton Woods* (Münster: Lit. Verlag).

Allen, Christopher S. (1989), "The Underdevelopment of Keynesianism in the Federal Republic of Germany," in Peter A. Hall (ed.), *The Political Power of Economic Ideas: Keynesianism across Nations* (Princeton, NJ: Princeton University Press), 264–89.

Althaus, Paul (1931), *Staatsgedanke und Reich Gottes* (4. Auflage edn.; Langensalza: H. Beyer).

Althaus, Paul (1934), *Theologie der Ordnungen* (Gütersloh: Bertelsmann).

Anderson, Christopher J. and Ward, Daniel S. (1996), "Barometer Elections in Comparative Perspective," *Electoral Studies*, 15 (4), 447–60.

Anderson, John A. (1973), *The European Administrative Elite* (Princeton, NJ: Princeton University Press).

Ansell, Ben (2008), "University Challenges: The Trilemma of Higher Education Policy in Advanced Industrial States," *World Politics*, 60 (2), 189–230.

Ansell, Ben (2010), *From the Ballot to the Blackboard: The Redistributive Political Economy of Education* (Cambridge: Cambridge University Press).

Ansell, Ben and Gingrich, Jane (2013), "A Tale of Two Dilemmas: Varieties of Higher Education and the Service Economy," in Anne Wren (ed.), *The Political Economy of the Service Transition* (Oxford: Oxford University Press), 195–224.

Arbeitgeberverbände [BDA] [Bundesverband Deutscher] (1956), "Probleme der Sozialreform Entwurf" (Köln, mimeo).

Arndt, Christoph (2013), *The Electoral Consequences of Third Way Welfare State Reforms: Social Democracy's Transformation and Its Political Costs* (Amsterdam: Amsterdam University Press).

Bähr, Johannes (1989), *Staatliche Schlichtung in der Weimarer Republik. Tarifpolitik, Korporatismus und industrieller Konflikt zwischen Inflation und Deflation 1919-1932* (Berlin: Colloquium).

Baldwin, Richard and Giavazzi, Francesco (eds.) (2015), *The Eurozone Crisis: A Consensus View of the Causes and a Few Possible Solutions* (London: CEPR Press).

Bankverein (1954), *Wer gehört zu wem?* (No place: no publisher).

Baumeister, Martin (1987), *Parität und katholische Inferiorität. Untersuchungen zur Stellung des Katholizismus im Deutschen Kaiserreich* (Paderborn: Schöningh).

BDA (1956a), "Niederschrift über die Sitzung des Ausschusses für Sozialversicherung und betriebliche Sozialfürsorge am 30. Juli 1956 in Köln" (Köln).

BDA (1956b), *Stellungnahme und Vorschläge der Bundesvereinigung der Deutschen Arbeitgeberverbände zur Rentengestaltung* (Köln, mimeo).

Beramendi, Pablo, Häusermann, Silja, Kitschelt, Herbert, and Kriesi, Hanspeter (2015a), "Introduction: The Politics of Advanced Capitalism," in Pablo Beramendi, Silja Häusermann, Herbert Kitschelt, and Hanspeter Kriesi (eds.), *The Politics of Advanced Capitalism* (New York: Cambridge University Press), 1–64.

Beramendi, Pablo, Häusermann, Silja, Kitschelt, Herbert, and Kriesi, Hanspeter (eds.) (2015b), *The Politics of Advanced Capitalism* (New York: Cambridge University Press).

Berg, Heinz (1986), *Bilanz der Kostendämpfungspolitik im Gesundheitswesen 1977–1984* (Bonn: Asgard).

Biebricher, Thomas (2013), "Europe and the Political Philosophy of Neoliberalism," *Contemporary Political Theory*, 12 (4), 338–75.

Biechele, Eckhard (1972), "Der Kampf um die Gemeinwirtschaftskonzeption des Reichswirtschaftsministeriums im Jahre 1919." Dissertation, Berlin.

Billerbeck, Ulrich (1982), "Soziale Selbstverwaltung und Gewerkschaftsbewegung," *Jahrbuch Arbeiterbewegung* (Frankfurt am Main: Campus), 39–71.

Blackbourn, David (1997), *Fontana History of Germany, 1780–1918: The Long Nineteenth Century* (London: Fontana).

Blödner, Paul (1934), "Preis- und Produktstabilisierung durch Kartelle. Eine Untersuchung ihrer Problematik am Beispiel der deutschen Großeisenindustrie" (Martin-Luther University Halle/Saale).

Blyth, Mark (2015), *Austerity: The History of a Dangerous Idea* (2nd edn.; Oxford: Oxford University Press).

Böhnke, Petra, Zeh, Janina, and Link, Sebastian (2015), "Atypische Beschäftigung im Erwerbsverlauf: Verlaufstypen als Ausdruck sozialer Spaltung?," *Zeitschrift für Soziologie*, 44 (4), 234–52.

Bonoli, Guiliano (1997), "Classifying Welfare States: A Two-Dimension Approach," *Journal of Social Policy*, 26 (3), 351–72.

Bordo, Michael D. (1993), "The Bretton Woods International Monetary System: A Historical Overview," in Michael D. Bordo and Barry Eichengreen (eds.), *A Retrospective on the Bretton Woods System: Lessons for International Monetary Reform* (Chicago, IL: University of Chicago Press), 3–108.

Börsch-Supan, Axel (1998), "Germany: A Social Security System on the Verge of Collapse," in Horst Siebert (ed.), *Redesigning Social Security* (Tübingen: Mohr Siebeck), 129–59.

Börsch-Supan, Axel (2000), "A Model Under Siege: A Case Study of the German Retirement Insurance System," *The Economic Journal*, 110, F24–F45.

Boss, Alfred (1999), "Sozialhilfe, Lohnabstand und Leistungsanreize," *Kieler Arbeitspapier* 912 (Kiel: Institute of World Economics).

Brinkmann, Christian, Emmerich, Knut, Gottsleben, Volkmar, Müller, Karin, and Völkel, Brigitte (1995), "Arbeitsmarktpolitik in den neuen Bundesländern," in Hartmut Seifert (ed.), *Reform der Arbeitsmarktpolitik. Herausforderung für Politik und Wirtschaft* (Köln: Bund Verlag), 59–87.

Brose, Eric D. (1985), *Christian Labor and the Politics of Frustration in Imperial Germany* (Washington, DC: Catholic University of America Press).

Brunnermeier, Markus K, James, Harold, and Landau, Jean-Pierre (2016), *The Euro and the Battle of Ideas* (Princeton, NJ: Princeton University Press).

Buchheim, Christoph (1989), "Die Währungsreform in Westdeutschland im Jahre 1948. Einige ökonomische Aspekte," in Wolfgang Fischer (ed.), *Währungsreform und Soziale Marktwirtschaft. Erfahrungen und Perspektiven nach 40 Jahren. Jahrestagung des Vereins für Socialpolitik. Gesellschaft für Wirtschafts- und Sozialwissenschaften in Freiburg i. Br. 1988* (Berlin: Duncker & Humblot), 391–402.

Buhr, Petra, Leisering, Lutz, Ludwig, Monika, and Zwick, Michael (1991), "Armutspolitik und Sozialhilfe in vier Jahrzehnten," in Bernhard Blanke and Hellmut Wollmann (eds.), *Die alte Bundesrepublik. Kontinuität und Wandel* (Opladen: Westdeutscher Verlag), 503–46.

Bulmer, Simon (2014), "Germany and the Eurozone Crisis: Between Hegemony and Domestic Politics," *West European Politics*, 37 (6), 1244–63.

Bulmer, Simon and Paterson, William E. (2013), "Germany as the EU's Reluctant Hegemon? Of Economic Strength and Political Constraints," *Journal of European Public Policy*, 20 (10), 1387–405.

Burda, Michael C. and Hunt, Jennifer (2011), "What Explains the German Labor Market Miracle in the Great Recession?," *Brookings Papers on Economic Activity* (Spring).

Burgin, Angus (2012), *The Great Persuasion: Reinventing Free Markets since the Depression* (Cambridge, MA: Harvard University Press).

Burkhart, Simone (2005), "Parteipolitikverflechtung. Über den Einfluss der Bundespolitik auf Landtagswahlentscheidungen von 1976–2000," *Politische Vierteljahresschrift*, 46 (1), 14–38.

Busemeyer, Marius R. (2014), *Skills and Inequality: Partisan Politics and the Political Economy of Education Reforms in Western Welfare States* (New York: Cambridge University Press).

Busemeyer, Marius R. and Iversen, Torben (2011), "Collective Skill Systems, Wage Bargaining, and Labor Market Stratification," in Marius Busemeyer and Christine Trampusch (eds.), *The Political Economy of Collective Skill Formation* (Oxford: Oxford University Press), 205–33.

Busemeyer, Marius R. and Trampusch, Christine (eds.) (2011), *The Political Economy of Collective Skill Formation* (Oxford: Oxford University Press).

Calmfors, Lars and Driffill, John (1988), "Bargaining Structure, Corporatism and Macroeconomic Performance," *Economic Policy*, 3, 13–61.

Cameron, David (1984), "Social Democracy, Corporatism, Labor Quiescence, and the Representation of Economic Interest in Advanced Capitalist Societies," in John H. Goldthorpe (ed.), *Order and Conflict in Contemporary Capitalism* (New York: Oxford University Press), 143–78.

Carlin, Wendy (2013), "Real Exchange Rate Adjustment, Wage-Setting Institutions, and Fiscal Stabilization Policy: Lessons of the Eurozone's First Decade," *CESifo Economic Studies*, 59 (3), 489–519.

Carlin, Wendy, Hassel, Anke, Martin, Andrew, and Soskice, David (2015), "The Transformation of the German Social Model," in Jan Erik Dolvik and Andrew Martin (eds.), *European Social Models from Crisis to Crisis: Employment and Inequality in the Era of Monetary Integration* (Oxford: Oxford University Press), 49–104.

Carlin, Wendy and Soskice, David (1990), *Macroeconomics and the Wage Bargain: A Modern Approach to Employment, Inflation and the Exchange Rate* (Oxford: Oxford University Press).

Carlin, Wendy and Soskice, David (1997), "Shocks to the System: The German Political Economy Under Stress," *National Institute Economic Review*, 159, 57–76.

Chandler, Alfred D. Jr. (1990), *Scale and Scope: The Dynamics of Industrial Capitalism* (Cambridge, MA: Belknap Press).

Childers, Thomas (1985), "Interest and Ideology: Anti-System Politics in the Era of Stabilization 1924–1928," in Elisabeth Mueller-Luckner and Gerald D. Feldman (eds.), *Die Nachwirkungen der Inflation auf die deutshe Geschichte 1924–1933. Schriften des Historischen Kollegs* (Kolloquien 6; München: Oldenbourg), 1–20.

Clasen, Jochen (2005), *Reforming European Welfare States: Germany and the United Kingdom Compared* (Oxford: Oxford University Press).

Clegg, Daniel and Clasen, Jochen (2006a), "Beyond Activation: Reforming Unemployment Protection Systems in Post-Industrial Labour Markets," *European Societies*, 8 (4), 555–81.

Clegg, Daniel and Clasen, Jochen (2006b), "New Labour Market Risks and the Revision of Unemployment Protection Systems in Europe," in Klaus Armingeon and Guiliano Bonoli (eds.), *The Politics of the Post-Industrial Welfare State* (London: Routledge), 192–210.

Cooper, Russell W. (1999), *Coordination Games: Complementarities and Macroeconomics* (New York: Cambridge University Press).

Crepaz, Markus M. L. and Lijphart, Arend (1995), "Linking and Integrating Corporatism and Consensus Democracy: Theory, Concepts and Evidence," *British Journal of Political Science*, 2 (25), 281–5.

Crouch, Colin (1986), "Sharing Public Space: States and Organized Interest in Western Europe," in John A. Hall (ed.), *States in History* (Oxford: Basil Blackwell), 177–210.

Crouch, Colin, Finegold, David, and Sako, Mari (1999), *Are Skills the Answer? The Political Economy of Skill Creation in Advanced Industrial Countries* (Oxford: Oxford University Press).

Crüger, Hans, Parisius, Ludolf, and Crecelius, Adolf (1924), *Das Reichsgesetz, Betreffend die Erwerbs- und Wirtschaftsgenossenschaften Kommentar zum praktischen Gebrauch für Juristen und Genossenschaften* (Berlin: de Gruyter).

Culpepper, Pepper D. and Finegold, David (eds.) (1999), *The German Skills Machine: Sustaining Comparative Advantage in a Global Economy* (New York: Berghahn Books).

Cusack, Thomas, Iversen, Torben, and Soskice, David (2007), "Economic Interests and the Origins of Electoral Systems," *American Political Science Review*, 101, 373–91.

Czada, Roland (1995), *Der Kampf um die Finanzierung der deutschen Einheit*, ed. Max-Planck-Institut für Gesellschaftsforschung. *MPIfG Discussion Paper* 95/1 (Köln: Max-Planck Institute for the Study of Societies).

De Grauwe, Paul (2013), "The Political Economy of the Euro," *Annual Review of Political Science*, 16, 153–70.

De Grauwe, Paul (2014), *Economics of Monetary Union* (9th edn.; Oxford: Oxford University Press).

Deutsche Bundesbank (1991a), "Überprüfung des Geldmengenziels 1991," *Monatsbericht der Deutschen Bundesbank*, 43 (7), 14–17.

Deutsche Bundesbank (1991b), "Die westdeutsche Wirtschaft unter dem Einfluß der Vereinigung Deutschlands," *Monatsbericht der Deutschen Bundesbank*, 43 (10), 15–21.

Deutsche Bundesbank (1992), "Überprüfung des Geldmengenziels 1992 und Anhebung des Diskontsatzes," *Monatsbericht der Deutschen Bundesbank*, 44 (8), 15–21.

Deutsche Bundesbank (1994a), "Die Finanzen der Treuhandanstalt," *Monatsbericht der Deutschen Bundesbank*, 46 (4), 17–31.

Deutsche Bundesbank (1994b), "Reale Wechselkurse als Indikatoren der internationalen Wettbewerbsfähigkeit," *Deutsche Bundesbank Monatsbericht*, 46 (5), 47–60.

Deutsche Bundesbank (1996), "Fiskalische Hemmnisse bei der Aufnahme einer regulären Erwerbstätigkeit im unteren Lohnsegment," *Monatsbericht der Deutschen Bundesbank*, 48 (2), 61–6.

Deutsches Institut für Wirtschaftsforschung [DIW] (1997a), "Vereinigungsfolgen belasten Sozialversicherung," *Wochenbericht*, 40, 725–9.

Deutsches Institut für Wirtschaftsforschung [DIW] (1997b), "Gesetzliche Rentenversicherung: Senkung des Rentenniveaus nicht der richtige Weg," *Wochenbericht*, 24–25, 433–42.

Diegmann, Albert (1993), "American Deconcentration Policy in the Ruhr Coal Industry," in Jerry M. Diefendorf, Axel Frohn, and Hermann-Josef Rupieper (eds.), *American Policy and the Reconstruction of West Germany, 1945–1955* (New York: Cambridge University Press), 197–215.

Djelic, Marie-Laure (1998), *Exporting the American Model: The Post-War Transformation of European Business* (Oxford: Oxford University Press).

Döhler, Marian and Manow, Philip (1997), *Strukturbildung von Politikfeldern. Das Beispiel bundesdeutscher Gesundheitspolitik seit den fünfziger Jahren* (Opladen: Leske + Budrich).

Drewes, Günter (1958), *Die Gewerkschaften in der Verwaltungsordnung* (Heidelberg: Verlagsgesellschaft Recht und Wirtschaft).

Dulien, Sebastian and Guérot, Ulrike (2012), "The Long Shadow of Ordoliberalism: Germany's Approach to the Euro Crisis," *European Council on Foreign Relation Policy Brief*, 22, 1–16.

Dyson, Kenneth (2009), "German Bundesbank: Europeanization and the Paradoxes of Power," in Kenneth Dyson and Martin Marcussen (eds.), *Central Banks in the Age of the Euro: Europeanization, Convergence, and Power* (Oxford: Oxford University Press), 131–59.

Ebbinghaus, Bernhard and Manow, Philip (eds.) (2001), *Varieties of Welfare Capitalism: Social Policy and Political Economy in Europe, Japan and the USA* (London: Routledge).

Eichengreen, Barry (1992), *Golden Fetters: The Gold Standard and the Great Depression 1919–1939* (New York: Oxford University Press).

Eichengreen, Barry (1996a), "Institutions and Economic Growth: Europe after World War II," in Nicholas Crafts and Gianni Toniolo (eds.), *Economic Growth in Europe since 1945* (Cambridge: Cambridge University Press), 38–72.

Eichengreen, Barry (1996b), *Globalizing Capital: A History of the International Monetary System* (Princeton, NJ: Princeton University Press).

Eichengreen, Barry (2007), *The European Economy since 1945: Coordinated Capitalism and Beyond* (Princeton, NJ: Princeton University Press).

Eichengreen, Barry (2012), *Hall of Mirrors: The Great Depression, the Great Recession, and the Uses—and Misuses—of History* (Oxford: Oxford University Press).

Eichhorst, Werner and Kaiser, Lutz C. (2006), "The German Labor Market: Still Adjusting Badly?," *IZA Discussion Paper* 2215. IZA Institute of Labor Economics, Bonn.

Eichhorst, Werner and Tobsch, Verena (2014a), "Flexible Arbeitswelten," *IZA Research Report* 59. IZA Institute of Labor Economics, Bonn.

Eichhorst, Werner and Tobsch, Verena (2014b), "Not So Standard Anymore? Employment Duality in Germany," *IZA Discussion Paper* 8155. IZA Institute of Labor Economics, Bonn.

Emmenegger, Patrick, Häusermann, Silja, Palier, Bruno, and Seeleib-Kaiser, Martin (eds.) (2012), *The Age of Dualization: The Changing Face of Inequality in Deindustrializing Societies* (Oxford: Oxford University Press).

Eschenburg, Theodor (1966), "Die Verbände," in Theodor Eschenburg (ed.), *Zur politischen Praxis in der Bundesrepublik. Band II. Kritische Betrachtungen 1961–1965* (München: Piper), 167–86.

Esping-Andersen, Gøsta (1990), *The Three Worlds of Welfare Capitalism* (Cambridge: Polity Press).

Esping-Andersen, Gøsta (1996), "Welfare States without Work: The Impasse of Labour Shedding and Familialism in Continental European Social Policy," in Gøsta Esping-Andersen (ed.), *Welfare States in Transition: National Adaptations in Global Economies* (London: Sage), 66–87.

Esping-Andersen, Gøsta (1999), *Social Foundations of Postindustrial Economies* (Oxford: Oxford University Press).

Esping-Andersen, Gøsta and Korpi, Walter (1984), "Social Policy as Class Politics in Post-War Capitalism: Scandinavia, Austria and Germany," in J. H. Goldthorpe (ed.), *Order and Conflict in Contemporary Capitalism* (Oxford: Clarendon Press), 179–208.

Estevez-Abe, Margarita, Iversen, Torben, and Soskice, David (1999), "Social Protection and the Formation of Skills: A Reinterpretation of the Welfare State." Presentation at the 95th American Political Science Association Meeting (Atlanta).

Eucken, Walter (1932), "Staatliche Strukturwandlungen und die Krisis des Kapitalismus," *Weltwirtschaftliches Archiv*, 36, 297–321.

European Commission (2005), "Towards Economic and Monetary Union (EMU): A Chronology of Major Decisions, Recommendations or Declarations in this Field," *Occasional Papers, Directorate-General for Economic and Financial Affairs*, 13.

Fear, Jeffrey (1997), "August Thyssen and German Steel," in Thomas McCraw (ed.), *Creating Modern Capitalism: How Entrepreneurs, Companies and Countries Triumphed in the Three Industrial Revolutions* (Cambridge, MA: Harvard University Press), 185–226.

Feld, Lars P., Köhler, Ekkehard A., and Nientiedt, Daniel (2015), "Ordoliberalism, Pragmatism and the Eurozone Crisis: How the German Tradition Shaped Economic Policy in Europe," *European Review of International Studies*, 2 (3), 48–61.

Feldman, Gerald D. (1977), *Iron and Steel in the German Inflation 1916–1923* (Princeton, NJ: Princeton University Press).

Feldman, Gerald D. (1992 [1966]), *Army, Industry and Labor in Germany, 1914–1918* (Providence, RI and Oxford: Berg Publishers).

Feldman, Gerald D. (1993), *The Great Disorder: Politics, Economics, and Society in the German Inflation, 1914–1924* (New York and Oxford: Oxford University Press).

Feldman, Gerald D. (1998), *Hugo Stinnes: Biographie eines Industriellen 1870–1924* (München: Beck).

Feldman, Gerald D. and Nocken, Ulrich (1975), "Trade Associations and Economic Power: A Comparison of Interest Group Development in the German Iron and Steel and Machine Building Industries 1900–1933," *Business History Review*, 49, 413–45.

Ferragina, Emanuele and Seeleib-Kaiser, Martin (2011), "The Welfare Regime Debate: Past, Present, Future?," *Policy and Politics*, 39 (4), 583–611.

Ferrera, Maurizio (1996), "The 'Southern Model' of Welfare in Social Europe," *Journal of European Social Policy*, 6 (1), 17–37.

Ferrera, Maurizio (2010), "The South European Countries," in Francis G. Castles, Stephan Leibfried, Jane Lewis, Herbert Obinger, and Christopher Pierson (eds.), *The Oxford Handbook of the Welfare State* (Oxford: Oxford University Press), 616–29.

Finanzen, BMF (Bundesministerium der) (various years), "Finanzbericht," ed. Bundesministerium der Finanzen (Bonn: Bundesministerium der Finanzen).

Flanagan, Robert, Soskice, David, and Ulman, Lloyd (1983), *Unionism, Economic Stabilization and Incomes Policies: European Experiences* (Washington, DC: Brookings Institution Press).

Flora, Peter and Alber, Jens (1981), "Modernization, Democratization, and the Development of the Welfare States in Western Europe," in Peter Flora and Arnold J. Heidenheimer (eds.), *The Development of Welfare States in Europe and America* (New Brunswick, NJ: Transaction Books), 37–80.

Franz, Wolfgang (1990), "Fiscal Policy in the Federal Republic of Germany," *Empirical Economics*, 15, 17–54.

Franzese, Robert J. Jr. (1999), "Partially Independent Central Banks, Politically Responsive Governments, and Inflation," *American Journal of Political Science*, 43 (3), 681–706.

Frerich, Johannes and Frey, Martin (1993), *Handbuch der Geschichte der Sozialpolitik in Deutschland, Bd. 3: Sozialpolitik in der Bundesrepublik Deutschland bis zur Herstellung der deutschen Einheit* (München: Oldenbourg).

Frieden, Jeffrey and Rogowski, Ronald (1996), "The Impact of International Economy on National Policies," in Robert Keohane and Helen Milner (eds.), *Internationalization and Domestic Politics* (Cambridge: Cambridge University Press), 25–47.

Gal, John (2010), "Is There an Extended Family of Mediterranean Welfare States?," *Journal of European Social Policy*, 20 (October), 283–300.

Garlichs, Dietrich and Maier, Friederike (1982), "Die arbeitsmarktpolitische Wirksamkeit der beruflichen Weiterbildung," in Fritz W. Scharpf, Marlene Brockmann, Manfred Groser, Friedhart Hegner, and Günther Schmid (eds.), *Aktive Arbeitsmarktpolitik. Erfahrungen und neue Wege* (Frankfurt am Main: Campus), 89–118.

Garrett, Geoffrey (1989), "Government Partisanship and Economic Performance: When and How Does 'Who Governs' Matter?," *Journal of Politics*, 51 (3), 676–93.

Garrett, Geoffrey (1998), *Partisan Politics in the Global Economy* (Cambridge: Cambridge University Press).

Garrett, Geoffrey and Lange, Peter (1996), "Internationalization, Institutions and Political Change," in Robert Keohane and Helen Milner (eds.), *Internationalization and Domestic Politics* (Cambridge: Cambridge University Press), 48–75.

Garrett, Geoffrey and Way, Christopher (1999), "Public Sector Unions, Corporatism, and Macroeconomic Performance," *Comparative Political Studies*, 32 (4), 411–34.

Geyer, Martin H. (1987), *Die Reichsknappschaft. Versicherungsreformen und Sozialpolitik im Bergbau* (München: Beck).

Geyer, Martin H. (1991), "Soziale Rechte im Sozialstaat: Wiederaufbau, Krise und konservative Stabilisierung der deutschen Rentenversicherung 1924–1937," in Klaus Tenfelde (ed.), *Arbeiter im 20. Jahrhundert* (Stuttgart: Klett-Cotta), 406–34.

Geyer, Martin H. (1992), "The Miner's Insurance and the Development of the German Social State," in Klaus Tenfelde (ed.), *Towards a Social History of Mining in the 19th and 20th Centuries* (München: Beck), 1046–65.

Giersch, Herbert, Paqué, Karl-Heinz, and Schmieding, Holger (1992), *The Fading Miracle: Four Decades of Market Economy in Germany* (New York: Cambridge University Press).

Gillingham, John (1991), *Coal, Steel and the Rebirth of Europe, 1945–1955: The Germans and French from Ruhr Conflict to Economic Community* (New York: Cambridge University Press).

Glasman, Maurice (1996), *Unnecessary Suffering: Managing Market Utopia* (London: Verso).

Goldthorpe, John H. (ed.) (1984), *Order and Conflict in Contemporary Capitalism: Studies in the Political Economy of Western European Nations* (Oxford: Clarendon Press).

Gordon, Andrew (1985), *The Evolution of Labor Relations in Japan: Heavy Industry, 1853-1955* (Cambridge, MA: Harvard University Press).

Gordon, Colin (1994), *New Deals: Business, Labor and Politics in America, 1920-1935* (New York: Cambridge University Press).

Gros, Daniel and Thygesen, Niels (1998), *European Monetary Integration: From the European Monetary System to Economic and Monetary Union* (London: Prentice Hall).

Grünthal, Günter (1968), *Reichsschulgesetz und Zentrumspartei in der Weimarer Republik* (Düsseldorf: Droste).

Hacke, Jens (2018), *Existenzkrise der Demokratie: Zur politischen Theorie des Liberalismus in der Zwischenkriegszeit* (Berlin: Suhrkamp).

Hall, Peter A. (1994), "Central Bank Independence and Coordinated Wage Bargaining: Their Interaction in Germany and Europe," *German Politics and Society*, 31, 1–23.

Hall, Peter A. (1997), "The Role of Interests, Institutions, and Ideas in the Comparative Political Economy of Industrialized Nations," in Mark I. Lichbach and Alan S. Zuckerman (eds.), *Comparative Politics: Rationality, Culture, and Structure* (Cambridge: Cambridge University Press), 174–207.

Hall, Peter A. (2012), "The Economics and Politics of the Euro Crisis," *German Politics*, 21 (4), 355–71.

Hall, Peter A. (2014), "Varieties of Capitalism and the Euro Crisis," *West European Politics*, 37 (6), 1223–43.

Hall, Peter A. and Franzese, Robert J. (1997), *Mixed Signals: Central Bank Independence, Coordinated Wage Bargaining, and European Monetary Union*, ed. Wissenschaftszentrum Berlin für Sozialforschung. Forschungsschwerpunkt Arbeitsmarkt und Beschäftigung. Abteilung: Wirtschaftswandel und Beschäftigung (discussion paper, FS I 97–307; Berlin: Wissenschaftszentrum Berlin für Sozialforschung).

Hall, Peter A. and Franzese, Robert J. (1998), "Mixed Signals: Central Bank Independence, Coordinated Wage Bargaining, and European Monetary Union," *International Organization*, 52 (3), 505–35.

Hall, Peter A. and Gingerich, Daniel W. (2009), "Varieties of Capitalism and Institutional Complementarities," in Bob Hancké (ed.), *Debating Varieties of Capitalism: A Reader* (Oxford: Oxford University Press), 135–79.

Hall, Peter A. and Soskice, David (2001a), "An Introduction to Varieties of Capitalism," in Peter A. Hall and David Soskice (eds.), *Varieties of Capitalism: The Institutional Foundations of Comparative Advantage* (Oxford: Oxford University Press), 1–68.

Hall, Peter A. and Soskice, David (eds.) (2001b), *Varieties of Capitalism: The Institutional Foundations of Comparative Advantage* (Oxford: Oxford University Press).

Hancké, Bob (2002), "The Political Economy of Wage-Setting in the Eurozone," in Philippe Pochet (ed.), *Wage Policy in the Eurozone* (Brussels: Peter Lang), 131–48.

Hancké, Bob (2013), *Unions, Central Banks, and EMU: Labor Market Institutions and Monetary Integration in Europe* (Oxford: Oxford University Press).

Hancké, Bob, Rhodes, Martin, and Thatcher, Mark (2009), "Beyond Varieties of Capitalism," in Bob Hancké (ed.), *Debating Varieties of Capitalism: A Reader* (Oxford: Oxford University Press), 273–300.

Hanow, H. (1927), "Gesetz über Wahlen nach der RVO, dem AVG und dem RKG," *Monatsschrift für Arbeiter- und Angestelltenversicherung*, 15 (Heft 7/8), 369–83.

Hartung, Benjamin, Jung, Philip, and Kuhn, Moritz (2018), "What Hides Behind the German Labor Market Miracle? Unemployment Insurance Reforms and Labor Market Dynamics," *CEPR Discussion Paper* DP13328.

Haselbach, Dieter (1991), *Autoritärer Liberalismus und Soziale Marktwirtschaft. Gesellschaft und Politik im Ordoliberalismus* (Baden-Baden: Nomos).

Hassel, Anke (2007), *Wage Setting, Social Pacts and the Euro: A New Role for the State* (Amsterdam: Amsterdam University Press).

Hassel, Anke (2014a), "Three Sources for Germany's Export Dependency: Industrial Relations, Social Insurance and Fiscal Federalism." Manuscript.

Hassel, Anke (2014b), "The Paradox of Liberalization: Understanding Dualism and the Recovery of the German Political Economy," *British Journal of Industrial Relations*, 52 (1), 57–71.

Hassel, Anke (2014c), "Adjustments in the Eurozone: Varieties of Capitalism and the Crisis in Southern Europe." Manuscript, Hertie School of Governance.

Hassel, Anke (2017), "No Way to Escape Imbalances in the Eurozone? Three Sources for Germany's Export Dependency: Industrial Relations, Social Insurance and Fiscal Federalism," *German Politics*, 26 (3), 360–79.

Hassel, Anke and Schiller, Christof (2010), *Der Fall Hartz IV: wie es zur Agenda 2010 kam und wie es weitergeht* (Frankfurt am Main: Campus).

Heidenheimer, Arnold (1980), "Unions and Welfare State Development in Britain and Germany: An Interpretation of Metamorphoses in the Period 1910–1950," *Berlin: Wissenschaftszentrum, IIVG Papers 1980*, 209.

Heller, Hermann (1933), "Autoritärer Liberalismus," *Die Neue Rundschau*, 44 (1), 289–98.

Hemerijck, Anton, Unger, Brigitte, and Visser, Jelle (2000), "How Small Countries Negotiate Change: Twenty-Five Years of Policy Adjustment in Austria, the Netherlands, and Belgium," in Fritz Scharpf and Vivian A. Schmidt (eds.), *Welfare and Work in the Open Economy, Volume II: Diverse Responses to Common Challenges* (Oxford: Oxford University Press), 175–63.

Hennis, Wilhelm (1961), "Verfassungsordnung und Verbandseinfluß. Bemerkungen zu ihrem Zusammenhang im politischen System der Bundesrepublik," *Politische Vierteljahresschrift*, 2, 23–35.

Hentschel, Volker (1996), *Ludwig Erhard: Ein Politikerleben* (Munich: Olzog).

Herbst, Ludolf (1982), *Der Totale Krieg und die Ordnung der Wirtschaft: die Kriegswirtschaft im Spannungsfeld von Politik, Ideologie und Propaganda, 1939–1945* (Stuttgart: Deutsche Verlags-Anstalt).

Herrigel, Gary (1996), *Industrial Constructions: The Sources of German Industrial Power* (New York: Cambridge University Press).

Herrigel, Gary (2000), "American Occupation, Market Order, and Democracy: Reconfiguring the Steel Industry in Japan and Germany after the Second World War," in Jonathan Zeitlin and Gary Herrigel (eds.), *Americanization and its Limits: Reworking US Technology and Management in Post-War Europe and Japan* (Oxford: Oxford University Press), 340–99.

Herrmann, Walther (1936), *Intermediäre Finanzgewalten. Eine Analyse deutscher hilfsfiskalischer Gebilde im ersten Jahrzehnt nach der Stabilisierung* (Jena: Gustav Fischer).

Hickey, S. H. F. (1985), *Workers in Imperial Germany: The Miners of the Ruhr* (Oxford: Clarendon Press).

Hicks, Alexander and Kenworthy, Lane (2003), "Varieties of Welfare Capitalism," *Socio-Economic Review*, 1 (1), 27–61.

Hien, Josef and Joerges, Christian (eds.) (2017), *Ordoliberalism, Law and the Rule of Economics* (Oxford: Hart Publishing).

Hiepel, Claudia (1997), "'Zentrumsgewerkverein' oder autonome Interessenvertretung? Zur Frühgeschichte des Gewerkvereins Christlicher Bergarbeiter im Ruhrgebiet," in Jochen-Christoph Kaiser and Wilfried Loth (eds.), *Soziale Reform im Kaiserreich. Protestantismus, Katholizismus und Sozialpolitik* (Stuttgart: Kohlhammer), 155–73.

Hillebrand, Rainer (2015), "Germany and Its Eurozone Crisis Policy: The Impact of the Country's Ordoliberal Heritage," *German Politics & Society*, 33 (1–2), 6–24.

Hochmuth, Brigitte, Kohlbrecher, Britta, Merkl, Christian, and Gartner, Herrmann (2018), "Hartz IV and the Decline of German Unemployment: A Macroeconomic Evaluation." Manuscript.

Hockerts, Hans Günter (1980), *Sozialpolitische Entscheidungen im Nachkriegsdeutschland. Alliierte und deutsche Sozialversicherungspolitik 1945 bis 1957* (Stuttgart: Klett-Cotta).

Hockerts, Hans Günter (1983), "Sicherung im Alter. Kontinuität und Wandel der gesetzlichen Altersversicherung 1889–1979," in Werner Conze and M. Rainer Lepsius (eds.), *Sozialgeschichte der Bundesrepublik Deutschland* (Stuttgart: Kohlhammer), 296–323.

Hoffmann, Eduard (1928), "Die Organisation der Verbindung der Eisen schaffenden und der Eisen verarbeitenden Industrie." Manuscript, University of Munich.

Holtfrerich, Carl-Ludwig (1998), "Geldpolitik bei festen Wechselkursen (1948–1970)," in Deutsche Bundesbank (ed.), *Fünfzig Jahre Deutsche Mark. Notenbank und Währung in Deutschland seit 1948* (München: C. H. Beck), 347–437.

Hong, Young-Sun (1998), *Welfare, Modernity, and the Weimar State* (Princeton, NJ: Princeton University Press).

Höpner, Martin and Lutter, Mark (2014), "One Currency and Many Modes of Wage Formation: Why the Eurozone Is Too Heterogeneous for the Euro," *MPIfG Discussion Paper* 14 (Köln: Max-Planck Institute for the Study of Societies).

Höpner, Martin and Lutter, Mark (2018), "The Diversity of Wage Regimes: Why the Eurozone Is Too Heterogeneous for the Euro," *European Political Science Review*, 10 (1), 71–96.

Höpner, Martin and Lutter, Mark (2019), "The German Undervaluation Regime under Bretton Woods: How Germany became the Nightmare of the World Economy," *MPIfG Discussion Paper* 19 (Köln: Max-Planck Institute for the Study of Societies).

Höpner, Martin and Spielau, Alexander (2016), "Besser als der Euro? Das Europäische Währungssystem 1979–1998," *Berliner Journal für Soziologie*, 26 (2), 273–96.

Hubatsch, Wolfgang (1978), *Enstehung und Entwicklung des Reichswirtschaftsministeriums von 1918 bis 1933* (Berlin: Duncker & Humblot).

Huber, Ernst Rudolf (1978), *Deutsche Verfassungsgeschichte seit 1789.* Band V.: Weltkrieg, Revolution und Reichserneuerung 1914–1919 (Stuttgart: Kohlhammer).

Huber, Evelyne, Ragin, Charles, and Stephens, John D. (1993), "Social Democracy, Christian Democracy, Constitutional Structure, and the Welfare State," *American Journal of Sociology*, 3, 711–49.

Huber, Evelyne and Stephens, John D. (2000), "Partisan Governance, Women's Employment, and the Social Democratic Service State," *American Sociological Review*, 65, 323–42.

Huber, Evelyne and Stephens, John D. (2001), *Development and Crisis of the Welfare State: Parties and Politics in Global Markets* (Chicago, IL: University of Chicago Press).

Hunt, James C. (1982), "'Die Parität in Preußen' (1899): Hintergrund, Verlauf und Ergebnis eines Aktionsprogramms der Zentrumspartei," *Historisches Jahrbuch*, 102, 418–34.

Illing, Gerhard, Jauch, Sebastian, and Zabel, Michael (2012), "Die Diskussion um den Euro," *Leviathan*, 40 (2), 156–72.

Iversen, Torben (1996), *The Political Economy of Inflation: Bargaining Structure or Central Bank Independence?* (Discussion Paper FS I 96-315; Berlin: Wissenschaftszentrum Berlin für Sozialforschung. Forschungsschwerpunkt: Arbeitsmarkt und Beschäftigung. Abteilung: Wirtschaftswandel und Beschäftigung).

Iversen, Torben (1998a), "Wage Bargaining, Hard Money and Economic Performance: Theory and Evidence for Organized Market Economics," *British Journal of Political Science*, 28, 31-61.

Iversen, Torben (1998b), "Wage Bargaining, Central Bank Independence and the Real Effects of Money," *International Organization*, 52 (3), 469-505.

Iversen, Torben (1999), *Contested Economic Institutions: The Politics of Macroeconomics and Wage Bargaining in Advanced Democracies* (New York: Cambridge University Press).

Iversen, Torben (2000), "Decentralization, Monetarism, and the Social Democratic Welfare State," in Torben Iversen, Jonas Pontusson, and David Soskice (eds.), *Unions, Employers, and Central Banks: Macroeconomic Coordination and Institutional Change in Social Market Economies* (Cambridge: Cambridge University Press), 205-31.

Iversen, Torben (2006), "Capitalism and Democracy," in Barry R. Weingast and Donald Wittman (eds.), *The Oxford Handbook of Political Economy* (New York: Oxford University Press), 601-23.

Iversen, Torben and Pontusson, Jonas (2000), "Comparative Political Economy: A Northern European Perspective," in Torben Iversen, Jonas Pontusson, and David Soskice (eds.), *Unions, Employers, and Central Banks: Macroeconomic Coordination and Institutional Change in Social Market Economies* (Cambridge: Cambridge University Press), 1-37.

Iversen, Torben, Pontusson, Jonas, and Soskice, David (eds.) (2000), *Unions, Employers, and Central Banks: Macroeconomic Coordination and Institutional Change in Social Market Economies* (Cambridge: Cambridge University Press).

Iversen, Torben and Soskice, David (2015), "Democratic Limits to Redistribution. Inclusionary versus Exclusionary Coalitions in the Knowledge Economy," *World Politics*, 67 (2), 185-225.

Iversen, Torben and Soskice, David (2018), "A Structural-Institutional Explanation of the Eurozone Crisis," in Philip Manow, Bruno Palier, and Hanna Schwander (eds.), *Welfare Democracies & Electoral Politics: Explaining Electoral Dynamics in Times of Changing Welfare Capitalism* (Oxford: Oxford University Press), 257-80.

Iversen, Torben, Soskice, David, and Hope, David (2016), "The Eurozone and Political Economic Institutions," *Annual Review of Political Science*, 19, 163-85.

Iversen, Torben and Stephens, John D. (2008), "Partisan Politics, the Welfare State, and Three Worlds of Human Capital Formation," *Comparative Political Studies*, 41 (5), 600-37.

Iversen, Torben and Wren, Anne (1998), "Equality, Employment and Budgetary Restraint: The Trilemma of the Service Economy," *World Politics*, 50, 507-46.

Jacobs, Klaus, Kohli, Martin, and Rein, Martin (1991), "Germany: The Diversity of Pathways," in Martin Kohli, Martin Rein, Anne-Marie Guillemard, and Herman van Gunsteren (eds.), *Time for Retirement: Comparative Studies of Early Exit from the Labor Force* (New York: Cambridge University Press), 181-221.

Jacoby, Sanford M. (1999), *Modern Manors: Welfare Capitalism since the New Deal* (Princeton, NJ: Princeton University Press).

James, Harold (2012), *Making the European Monetary Union* (Cambridge, MA: Belknap Press).

Janssen, Hauke (1998), *Nationalökonomie und Nationalsozialismus. Die deutsche Volkswirtschaftslehre in den dreißiger Jahren* (Marburg: Metropolis).

Jochem, Sven and Siegel, Nico A. (1999), "Zwischen Sozialstaats-Status quo und Beschäftigungswachstum: das Dilemma des Bündnisses für Arbeit im Trilemma der Dienstleistungsgesellschaft," *Zentrum für Sozialpolitik, ZeS-Arbeitspapier* 17 (Bremen).

Jones, Larry Eugene (1985), "In the Shadow of Stabilization: German Liberalism and the Legitimacy Crisis of the Weimar Party System, 1924–1930," in Elisabeth Mueller-Luckner and Gerald D. Feldman (eds.), *Die Nachwirkungen der Inflation auf die deutsche Geschichte 1924–1933. Schriften des Historischen Kollegs* (Kolloquien 6; München: Oldenbourg), 21–41.

Kaiser, Jochen-Christoph (1996), "Die Formierung des protestantischen Milieus. Konfessionelle Vergemeinschaftung im 19. Jahrhundert," in Olaf Blaschke and Frank-Michael Kuhlemann (eds.), *Religion im Kaiserreich. Milieus—Mentalitäten—Krisen* (Gütersloh: Chr. Kaiser), 257–88.

Kaiser, Jochen-Christoph (1997), "Protestantismus und Sozialpolitik. Der Ertrag der 1890er Jahre," in Jochen-Christoph Kaiser and Martin Greschat (eds.), *Sozialer Protestantismus und Sozialstaat. Diakonie und Wohlfahrtspflege in Deutschland 1890 bis 1938* (Stuttgart: Kohlhammer), 94–113.

Kalbitz, Rainer (1978), "Biographie über den Streik der IG Metall in Schleswig-Holstein 1956/57," in IG Metall (ed.), *Streik der Metaller Schleswig-Holstein 1956/57, Dokumentation* (Frankfurt: IG Metall), 181–217.

Kalbitz, Rainer (1979). *Aussperrung in der Bundesrepublik* (Köln: EVA).

Katz, Lawrence F. and Summers, Lawrence H. (1989), "Industry Rents: Evidence and Implications," *Brookings Papers on Economic Activity*, 20, 209–75.

Katzenstein, Peter J. (1984), *Corporatism and Change: Austria, Switzerland and the Politics of Industry* (Ithaca, NY: Cornell University Press).

Katzenstein, Peter J. (1987), *Policy and Politics in West Germany: The Growth of a Semi-Sovereign State* (Philadelphia, PA: Temple University Press).

Kaufmann, Franz-Xaver (1988), "Christentum und Wohlfahrtsstaat," *Zeitschrift für Sozialreform*, 34, 65–89.

Kaufmann, Franz-Xaver (1999), "Der Begriff Sozialpolitik und seine wissenschaftliche Deutung," in BMA und Bundesarchiv (eds.), *Geschichte der Sozialpolitik in Deutschland seit 1945* (Baden-Baden: BMA und Bundesarchiv).

Kaufmann, Hugo M. (1969), "A Debate over Germany's Revaluation 1961: A Chapter in Political Economy," *Weltwirtschaftliches Archiv*, 103 (2), 181–212.

Kersbergen, Kees van (1995), *Social Capitalism: A Study of Christian Democracy and the Welfare State* (London: Routledge).

Kersbergen, Kees van and Manow, Philip (eds.) (2009), *Religion, Class Coalitions and Welfare States* (New York: Cambridge University Press).

Kipping, Matthias (1996), *Zwischen Kartellen und Konkurrenz. Der Schuman-Plan und die Ursprünge der europäischen Einigung 1944–1952* (Berlin: Duncker & Humblot).

Kitschelt, Herbert (2001), "Partisan Competition and Welfare State Retrenchment: When Do Politicians Choose Unpopular Policies?," in Paul Pierson (ed.), *The New Politics of the Welfare State* (Oxford: Oxford University Press), 265–302.

Kitschelt, Herbert, Lange, Peter, Marks, Gary, and Stephens, John D. (eds.) (1999), *Continuity and Change in Contemporary Capitalism* (New York: Cambridge University Press).

Klinger, Sabine, Rothe, Thomas, and Weber, Enzo (2013), "Makroökonomische Perspektive auf die Hartz-Reformen: Die Vorteile überwiegen," *IAB-Kurzbericht*, 11, 1–8.

Koch, Susanne, Kupka, Peter, and Steinke, Joss (2009), *Aktivierung, Erwerbstätigkeit und Teilhabe. Vier Jahre Grundsicherung für Arbeitssuchende* (Bielefeld: Bertelsmann).

Kocka, Jürgen (1981), "Class Formation, Interest Articulation, and Public Policy: The Origins of the German White-Collar Class in the Late Nineteenth and Early Twentieth Centuries," in Suzanne Berger (ed.), *Organizing Interests in Western Europe: Pluralism, Corporatism, and the Transformation of Politics* (Cambridge: Cambridge University Press), 63–81.

Kolb, Karl (1928), *Kapitalbildung und Kapitalanlage in der deutschen Sozialversicherung (in den Zeiträumen 1910-1913, 1914-1917, 1924-1927)* (Leipzig: Universitätsverlag).

Korpi, Walter (2006), "Power Resources and Employer-Centered Approaches in Explanations of Welfare States and Varieties of Capitalism: Protagonists, Consenters, and Antagonists," *World Politics*, 58, 167–206.

Kreile, Michael (1978), "West Germany: The Dynamics of Expansion," in Peter J. Katzenstein (ed.), *Between Power and Plenty: Foreign Economic Policies of Advanced Industrial States* (Madison, WI: University of Wisconsin Press), 191–224.

Kriesi, Hanspeter (2019), "Conclusion: A Critical Juncture for the Structuration of Party Systems?," in Hanspeter Kriesi (ed.), *European Party Politics in Times of Crisis* (New York: Cambridge University Press), 355–82.

Kriesi, Hanspeter and Hutter, Swen (2019), "Crises and the Transformation of the National Political Space in Europe," in Hanspeter Kriesi (ed.), *European Party Politics in Times of Crisis* (New York: Cambridge University Press), 3–32.

Krohn, Claus-Dieter (1981), *Wirtschaftstheorien als politische Interessen. Die akademische Nationalökonomie in Deutschland 1918-1933* (Frankfurt am Main: Campus).

Krugman, Paul and Obstfeld, Maurice (2012), *Internationale Wirtschaft. Theorie und Politik der Außenwirtschaft* (München: Pearson).

Kuckuk, Peter (1998), "Westdeutscher Schiffbau in der Nachkriegszeit. Ein Überblick," in Peter Kuckuk (ed.), *Unterweserwerften in der Nachkriegszeit. Von der Stunde Null zum Wirtschaftswunder* (Bremen: Edition Temmen), 11–36.

Lange, Peter (1984), "Unions, Workers, and Wage Regulation: The Rational Bases of Consent," in John H. Goldthorpe (ed.), *Order and Conflict in Contemporary Capitalism* (New York: Oxford University Press), 98–123.

Langner, Albrecht (1998), *Katholische und evangelische Sozialethik im 19. und 20. Jahrhundert. Beiträge zu ideengechichtlichen Entwicklungen im Spannungsfeld von Konfession, Politik und Ökumene* (Paderborn: Schöningh).

LaPorta, Rafael (1996), "Law and Finance," *NBER Working Paper* 5661 (Cambridge, MA: National Bureau of Economic Research).

Lapp, Susanne and Lehment, Harmen (1997), "Lohnzurückhaltung und Beschäftigung in Deutschland und in den Vereinigten Staaten," *Die Weltwirtschaft*, 1, 67–83.

Leckebusch, Günther (1963), *Die Beziehungen der Deutschen Seeschiffswerften zur Eisenindustrie an der Ruhr in der Zeit von 1850 bis 1930*. Schriften zur Rheinisch-Westfälischen Wirtschaftsgeschichte (Köln: Rheinisch-Westfälisches Wirtschaftsarchiv zu Köln).

Lehmbruch, Gerhard (1977), "Liberal Corporatism and Party Government," *Comparative Political Studies*, 10 (1), 91–126.

Lehmbruch, Gerhard (1987), "Administrative Interessenvermittlung," in Adrienne Windhoff-Héritier (ed.), *Verwaltung und ihre Umwelt. Festschrift für Thomas Ellwein zum 60. Geburtstag* (Opladen: Westdeutscher Verlag), 11–43.

Lehmbruch, Gerhard (1991), "The Organization of Society, Administrative Strategies and Policy Networks: Elements of a Developmental Theory of Interest Systems," in Roland

M. Czada and Adrienne Windhof-Héritier (eds.), *Political Choice: Institutions, Rules, and the Limits of Rationality* (Boulder, CO: Westview Press), 121–58.

Lehmbruch, Gerhard (1995), "Ressortautonomie und die Konstitution sektoraler Netzwerke. Administrative Interessenvermittlung in Japan," in Karlheinz Bentele, Bernd Reissert, and Ronald Schettkat (eds.), *Die Reformfähigkeit von Industriegesellschaften. Fritz W. Scharpf—Festschrift zu seinem 60. Geburtstag* (Frankfurt am Main: Campus), 64–100.

Lehmbruch, Gerhard (1996a), "Der Beitrag der Korporatismusforschung zur Entwicklung der Steuerungstheorie," *Politische Vierteljahresschrift*, 37, 735–51.

Lehmbruch, Gerhard (1996b), "Die korporative Verhandlungsdemokratie in Westmitteleuropa," *Schweizerische Zeitschrift für Politische Wissenschaft*, 2, 19–41.

Lehmbruch, Gerhard (1997), "From State of Authority to Network State: The German State in Developmental Perspective," in Michio Muramatsu and Frieder Naschold (eds.), *State and Administration in Japan and Germany: A Comparative Perspective on Continuity and Change* (Berlin: de Gruyter), 39–62.

Lehmbruch, Gerhard (2000 [1976]), *Parteienwettbewerb im Bundesstaat* (3., erweiterte Auflage; Opladen: Westdeutscher Verlag).

Lehmbruch, Gerhard and Schmitter, Philippe C. (eds.) (1982), *Patterns of Corporatist Policy-Making* (London: Sage).

Leibfried, Stephan (1993), "Towards a European Welfare State? On Integrating Poverty Regimes into the European Community," in Catherine Jones (ed.), *New Perspectives on the Welfare State in Europe* (London: Routledge), 120–43.

Liefmann, Robert (1938), *Cartels, Concerns and Trusts* (New York: Dutton).

Lijphart, Arend and Crepaz, Markus M. L. (1991), "Corporatism and Consensus Democracy in Eighteen Countries: Conceptual and Empirical Linkages," *British Journal of Political Science*, 2 (21), 235–56.

Lindlar, Ludger and Scheremet, Wolfgang (1998), *Germany's Slump: Explaining the Unemployment Crisis of the 1990s* (Amsterdam: Duitsland Instituut, Universiteit van Amsterdam).

Lipset, Seymour M., Trow, Martin, and Coleman, James S. (1956), *Union Democracy: The Internal Politics of the International Typographical Union* (New York: Free Press).

Loth, Wilfried (1997), "Der Volksverein für das Katholische Deutschland," in Jochen-Christoph Kaiser and Wilfried Loth (eds.), *Soziale Reform im Kaiserreich. Protestantismus, Katholizismus und Sozialpolitik* (Stuttgart: Kohlhammer), 142–54.

Maier, Charles S. (1975), *Recasting Bourgeois Europe: Stabilization in France, Germany, and Italy in the Decade after World War I* (Princeton, NJ: Princeton University Press).

Maier, Charles S. (1987), *In Search of Stability: Explorations in Historical Political Economy* (Cambridge: Cambridge University Press).

Manow, Philip (1997a), "Social Insurance and the German Political Economy," *MPIfG Discussion Paper* 2 (Köln: Max-Planck Institute for the Study of Societies).

Manow, Philip (1997b), "Entwicklungslinien ost- und westdeutscher Gesundheitspolitik zwischen doppelter Staatsgründung, deutscher Einigung und europäischer Integration," *Zeitschrift für Sozialreform*, 43, 101–31.

Manow, Philip (2000), "'Modell Deutschland' as an Inter-denominational Compromise," *Discussion Paper* 1/2000. Minda-de-Gunzburg Center for European Studies, Harvard University, Cambridge, MA.

Manow, Philip (2001a), "Comparative Institutional Advantages of Welfare State Regimes and New Coalitions in Welfare State Reforms," in Paul Pierson (ed.), *The New Politics of the Welfare State* (New York: Oxford University Press), 146–64.

Manow, Philip (2001b), "Business Coordination, Collective Wage Bargaining and the Welfare State: Germany and Japan in Historical-Comparative Perspective," in Bernhard Ebbinghaus and Philip Manow (eds.), *Comparing Welfare Capitalism: Social Policy and Political Economy in Europe, Japan and the USA* (London: Routledge), 27–11.

Manow, Philip (2001c), "Ordoliberalismus als ökonomische Ordnungstheologie," *Leviathan*, 29, 179–98.

Manow, Philip (2001d), "Crisis and Change in Pension Finance: Germany and Japan Compared," *MPIfG Working Paper* (Köln: Max-Planck Institute for the Study of Societies).

Manow, Philip (2004), "The Good, the Bad, and the Ugly: Esping-Andersen's Regime Typology and the Religious Roots of the Western Welfare State," *MPIfG Working Paper* 3 (Köln: Max-Planck Institute for the Study of Societies).

Manow, Philip (2005), "Germany – Cooperative Federalism and the Overgrazing of the Fiscal Commons," in Herbert Obinger, Stephan Leibfried, and Francis G. Castles (eds.), *Federalism and the Welfare State* (Cambridge, MA: Cambridge University Press), 222–62.

Manow, Philip (2009), "Electoral Rules, Class-Coalitions and Welfare State Regimes – or How to Explain Esping-Andersen with Stein Rokkan," *Socio-Economic Review*, 7 (1), 101–21.

Manow, Philip (2013), "Religious Cleavages, Divisions on the Left and the Political Economy of Southern Europe," *International Journal of Social Quality*, 3 (2), 78–105.

Manow, Philip (2015a), "'Proporz' or Polarization? The Religious Cleavage, the Division on the Left and the Party Systems of Southern Europe," in Volker Schneider and Burkhard Eberlein (eds.), *Complex Democracy: Varieties, Crises, and Transformations* (Berlin: Springer), 51–68.

Manow, Philip (2015b), "Workers, Farmers, and Catholicism: A History of Political Class Coalitions and the South-European Welfare State Regime," *Journal of European Social Policy*, 25 (1), 32–49.

Manow, Philip (2017), "Uniform Monetary Policy, Non-Uniform Wage Policy: How Rules and Discretion get into Conflict in the Eurozone (and what—if anything—Ordoliberalism has to do with it)," in Josef Hien and Christian Joerges (eds.), *Ordoliberalism, Law and the Rule of Economics* (Oxford: Hart Publishing), 301–16.

Manow, Philip (2018), *Die Politische Ökonomie des Populismus* (Berlin: Suhrkamp).

Manow, Philip, Palier, Bruno, and Schwander, Hanna (eds.) (2018), *Worlds of Welfare Capitalism and Electoral Politics* (Oxford: Oxford University Press).

Manow, Philip and Seils, Eric (1999), "Adjusting Badly: The German Welfare State, Structural Change and the Open Economy," in Fritz W. Scharpf and Vivien A. Schmidt (eds.), *From Vulnerability to Competitiveness: Welfare and Work in the Open Economy* (New York: Oxford University Press), 264–304.

Manow, Philip and Seils, Eric (2000a), "Adjusting Badly: The German Welfare State, Structural Change, and the Open Economy," in Fritz W. Scharpf and Vivien A. Schmidt (eds.), *Welfare and Work in the Open Economy, Volume 2: Diverse Responses to Common Challenges* (New York: Oxford University Press), 264–307.

Manow, Philip and Seils, Eric (2000b), "The Unemployment Crisis of the German Welfare State," in Martin Rhodes and Maurizio Ferrera (eds.), *West European Politics*, special issue on "Restructuring European Welfare States" (April), 138–60.

Manow, Philip, Palier, Bruno and Schwander, Hanna (eds.) (2018), *Welfare Democracies and Party Politics: Explaining Electoral Dynamics in Times of Changing Welfare Capitalism* (Oxford: Oxford University Press).

Mares, Isabela (1997), "Business (Non) Coordination and Social Policy Development: The Case of Early Retirement." Presentation at the "Varieties of Capitalism" conference (Berlin: Wissenschaftszentrum Berlin).

Marin, Dalia (2010), "Germany's Super Competitiveness: A Helping Hand from Eastern Europe," *VOX—CEPR's Policy Portal*, June 20. http://www.voxeu.org/article/germany-s-super-competitiveness.

Markovits, Andrei S. (1986), *The Politics of the West German Trade Unions: Strategies of Class and Interest Representation in Growth and Crisis* (New York: Cambridge University Press).

Marks, Gary (1989), *Unions in Politics: Britain, Germany, and the United States in the Nineteenth and Early Twentieth Century* (Princeton, NJ: Princeton University Press).

Martiny, Martin (1975), "Die politische Bedeutung der gewerkschaftlichen Arbeitersekretariate vor dem Ersten Weltkrieg," in Heinz O. Vetter (ed.), *Vom Sozialistengesetz zur Mitbestimmung* (Köln: Bund Verlag), 153–74.

Matsaganis, Manos, Ferrera, Maurizio, Capucha, Luis, and Moreno, Luis (2003), "Mending Nets in the South: Anti-Poverty Politics in Greece, Italy, Portugal and Spain," *Social Policy and Administration*, 37, 639–55.

Meier-Rust, Kathrin (1993), *Alexander Rüstow—Geschichtsdeutung und liberales Engagement* (Stuttgart: Klett-Cotta).

Meinhardt, Volker (1999), "Weiterhin hohe Transfers an die ostdeutschen Sozialversicherungsträger," *DIW Wochenbericht*, DIW Berlin, German Institute for Economic Research, 66 (45), 813–17.

Metall, IG (ed.) (1978), *Streik der Metaller Schleswig-Holstein 1956/57, Dokumentation* (Frankfurt: IG Metall).

Michels, Rudolf (1928), *Cartels, Combines and Trusts in Postwar Germany* (New York: Columbia University Press).

Milgrom, Paul and Roberts, John (1990), "Rationalizability, Learning and Equilibrium in Games with Strategic Complementarities," *Econometrica*, 58, 1255–78.

Milgrom, Paul and Roberts, John (1994), "Complementarities and Systems: Understanding Japanese Economic Organization," *Estudios Economicos*, 9, 3–42.

Mody, Ashoka (2018), *Euro-Tragedy: A Drama in Nine Acts* (Oxford: Oxford University Press).

Moene, Karl Ove and Wallerstein, Michael (1995), "How Social Democracy Worked: Labor-Market Institutions," *Politics & Society*, 23, 185–211.

Mörschel, Richard (1990), "Die Finanzierungsverfahren in der Geschichte der gesetzlichen Rentenversicherung," *Die Deutsche Rentenversicherung* (September/October), 619–61.

Müller, Dirk H. (1996), *Arbeiter, Katholizismus, Staat. Der Volksverein fuer das katholische Deutschland und die katholischen Arbeiterorganisationen in der Weimarer Republik* (Bonn: Dietz).

Müller-Armack, Alfred (1932), *Entwicklungsgesetze des Kapitalismus. Ökonomische, geschichtstheoretische und soziologische Studien zur modernen Wirtschaftsverfassung* (Berlin: Junker und Dünnhaupt).

Müller-Armack, Alfred (1948), *Das Jahrhundert ohne Gott: zur Kultursoziologie unserer Zeit* (Münster: Regensberg).

Müller-Armack, Alfred (1950), "Soziale Irenik. Über die Möglichkeit einer die Weltanschauungen verbindenden Sozialidee," *Weltwirtschaftliches Archiv* 64. (Cited from the reprint in Alfred Müller Armack, *Religion und Wirtschaft. Geistesgeschichtliche Hintergründe unserer europäischen Lebensform* [Bern/Stuttgart: Paul Haupt], 559–78.)

Mundell, Robert A. (1960), "The Monetary Dynamics of International Adjustment under Fixed and Flexible Exchange Rates," *Quarterly Journal of Economics*, 74, 227–57.

Mundell, Robert A. (1963), "Capital Mobility and Stabilization Policy under Fixed and Flexible Exchange Rates," *Canadian Journal of Economics and Political Science*, 29, 475–85.

Nedergaard, Peter and Snaith, Holly (2015), "'As I Drifted on a River I Could Not Control': The Unintended Ordoliberal Consequences of the Eurozone Crisis," *Journal of Common Market Studies*, 53 (5), 1094–109.

Nicholls, Anthony James (1990), "Ludwig Erhard and German Liberalism: An Ambivalent Relationship?," in Konrad H. Jarausch and Larry Eugene Jones (eds.), *In Search of a Liberal Germany: Studies in the History of German Liberalism from 1789 to the Present* (New York and Oxford: Berg), 389–416.

Nicholls, Anthony James (1994), *Freedom with Responsibility: The Social Market Economy in Germany, 1918–1963* (Oxford: Clarendon Press).

Nickell, Stephen and Layard, Richard (1999), "Labor Market Institutions and Economic Performance," in Orley Ashenfelter and David Card (eds.), *Handbook of Labor Economics* (3rd edn.; Amsterdam: Elsevier), 3029–84.

Niethammer, Lutz (1975), "Strukturreform und Wachstumspakt. Westeuropäische Bedingungen der einheitsgewerkschaftlichen Bewegung nach dem Zusammenbruch des Faschismus," in Heinz Oskar Vetter (ed.), *Vom Sozialistengesetz zur Mitbestimmung* (Köln: Bund Verlag), 303–58.

Nipperdey, Thomas (1993), *Deutsche Geschichte 1866–1918* (Bd. II: Machtstaat vor der Demokratie; München: Beck).

Nitsche, Michael (1986), *Die Geschichte des Leistungs- und Beitragsrechts der gesetzlichen Rentenversicherung von 1889 bis zum Beginn der Rentenreform* (Frankfurt am Main: Peter Lang).

Nocken, Ulrich (1977), "Inter-Industrial Conflicts and Alliances as Exemplified by the AVI-Agreement," in D. Petzina, B. Weisbrod, and H. Mommsen (eds.), *Industrielles System und politische Entwicklung in der Weimarer Republik* (Dusseldorf: Droste), 693–704.

Noé, Claus (1970), *Gebändigter Klassenkampf. Tarifautonomie in der Bundesrepublik Deutschland. Der Konflikt zwischen Gesamtmetall und IG Metall vom Frühjahr 1963* (Berlin: Duncker & Humblot).

Nörr, Knut W. (1993), *An der Wiege deutscher Identität nach 1945: Franz Böhm zwischen Ordo und Liberalismus* (Schriftenreihe der Juristischen Gesellschaft zu Berlin, Heft 129; Berlin: de Gruyter).

Nörr, Knut W. (1998), "Im Wechselbad der Interpretationen: Der Begriff der Wirtschaftsverfassung im ersten Jahrzwölft der Bonner Republik," in Karl Acham, Knut W. Nörr, and Bertram Schefold (eds.), *Erkenntnisgewinne, Erkenntnisverluste. Kontinuitäten und Diskontinuitäten in den Wirtschafts-, Rechts- und Sozialwissenschaften zwischen den 20er und 50er Jahren* (Stuttgart: Franz Steiner), 356–79.

Novy, Klaus and Prinz, Michael (1985), *Illustrierte Geschichte der Gemeinwirtschaft. Wirtschaftliche Selbsthilfe in der Arbeiterbewegung von den Anfängen bis 1945* (Bonn: Dietz).

Nowak, Kurt (1997), "Sozialpolitik als Kulturauftrag. Adolf von Harnack und der evangelisch-soziale Kongreß," in Jochen-Christoph Kaiser and Wilfried Loth (eds.), *Soziale Reform im Kaiserreich. Protestantismus, Katholizismus und Sozialpolitik* (Stuttgart: Kohlhammer), 79–93.

O'Rourke, Kevin and Taylor, Alan M. (2013), "Cross of Euros," *Journal of Economic Perspectives*, 27 (3), 167–92.

Obinger, Herbert and Wagschal, Uwe (1998), "Drei Welten des Wohlfahrtsstaates? Das Stratifizierungskonzept in der clusteranalytischen Überprüfung," in Stephan Lessenich and Ilona Ostner (eds.), *Welten des Wohlfahrtskapitalismus: Der Sozialstaat in vergleichender Perspektive* (Frankfurt am Main and New York: Campus), 109–35.

OECD [Organisation for Economic Co-operation and Development] (1983), *OECD Economic Surveys: Germany* (Paris: OECD).

OECD [Organisation for Economic Co-operation and Development] (2015), *In It Together: Why Less Inequality Benefits All* (Paris: OECD).

Offe, Claus (1981), "The Attribution of Public Status to Interest Groups: Observations of the West German Case," in Suzanne D. Berger (ed.), *Organizing Interests in Western Europe: Pluralism, Corporatism, and the Transformation of Politics* (Cambridge: Cambridge University Press), 123–58.

Pabst, Stefan (1999), "Mehr Arbeitsplätze für Geringqualifizierte nach Einführung der Pflegeversicherung?," *WSI-Mitteilungen*, 4, 234–40.

Palier, Bruno, Rovny, Alison, and Rovny, Jan (2018), "The Dual Dualization of Europe: Economic Convergence, Divergence, and their Political Consequences," in Philip Manow, Bruno Palier, and Hanna Schwander (eds.), *Worlds of Welfare Capitalism and Electoral Politics* (Oxford: Oxford University Press), 281–97.

Palier, Bruno and Thelen, Kathleen A. (2010), "Institutionalizing Dualism: Complementarities and Change in France and Germany," *Politics & Society*, 38 (1), 119–48.

Paqué, Karl-Heinz (1995), "How Cooperative Was the Spirit? A Note on the 'Eichengreen-View' of Europe after World War II," *Kiel Working Paper* 701. Institut für Weltwirtschaft an der Universität Kiel.

Paqué, Karl-Heinz (1996), "Unemployment and the Crisis of the German Model: A Long-Term-Interpretation," in Herbert Giersch (ed.), *Fighting Europe's Unemployment in the 1990s* (Berlin and New York: Springer), 123–55.

Paqué, Karl-Heinz (1998), "Zur Zumutbarkeit von Arbeitsplätzen: Bestandsaufnahme und Reformvorschlag," in Eckhard Knappe and Norbert Berthold (eds.), *Ökonomische Theorie der Sozialpolitik* (Heidelberg: Physica), 71–89.

Patch, William L. (1985), *Christian Trade Unions in the Weimar Republic, 1918–1933* (New Haven, CT and London: Yale University Press).

Pierson, Paul (1994), *Dismantling the Welfare State? Reagan, Thatcher, and the Politics of Retrenchment* (Cambridge: Cambridge University Press).

Pierson, Paul (1996), "The New Politics of the Welfare State," *World Politics*, 48 (2), 143–79.

Pirker, Theo (1979), *Die blinde Macht. Die Gewerkschaftsbewegung in Westdeutschland, Teil 2: 1953–1960* (Berlin: Olle & Wolter).

Polk, Jonathan T. and Rovny, Jan (2018), "Welfare Democracies and Multidimensional Party Competition in Europe," in Philip Manow, Bruno Palier, and Hanna Schwander (eds.), *Welfare Democracies & Party Politics: Explaining Electoral Dynamics in Times of Changing Welfare Capitalism* (Oxford: Oxford University Press), 29–60.

Pollmann, Klaus-Erich (1997), "Weltanschauungskampf an zwei Fronten. Der Sozialprotestantismus 1890–1914," in Jochen-Christoph Kaiser and Wilfried Loth (eds.), *Soziale Reform im Kaiserreich. Protestantismus, Katholizismus und Sozialpolitik* (Stuttgart: Kohlhammer), 56–78.

Powell, Walter W. and DiMaggio, Paul J. (eds.) (1991), *The New Institutionalism in Organizational Analysis* (Chicago, IL: University of Chicago Press).

Preiss, Kurt (1933), "Das System der Ausfuhrrückvergütungen in der deutschen Eisen- und Metallindustrie." Manuscript, University of Kiel.

Preller, Ludwig (1978), *Sozialpolitik in der Weimarer Republik* (Düsseldorf: Droste).

Prinz, Michael (1991), "Die Arbeiterbewegung und das Modell der Angestelltenversicherung. Zu einigen Bedingungen für die besondere Bürgerlichkeit des Wohlfahrtsstaats der Bundesrepublik," in Klaus Tenfelde (ed.), *Arbeiter im 20. Jahrhundert* (Stuttgart: Klett-Cotta), 435–60.

Przeworski, Adam and Sprague, John (1986), *Paper Stones: A History of Electoral Socialism* (Chicago, IL: University of Chicago Press).

Rabenschlag-Kräusslich, Jutta (1983), *Parität statt Klassenkamp? Zur Organisation des Arbeitsmarktes und Domestizierung des Arbeitskampfes in Deutschland und England 1900 bis 1918* (Frankfurt am Main: Peter Lang).

Rehder, Britta (2003), *Betriebliche Bündnisse für Arbeit in Deutschland. Mitbestimmung und Flächentarif im Wandel* (Frankfurt am Main: Campus).

Reichsarbeitsministerium [RAM] (1929), *Deutsche Sozialpolitik 1918-1928. Erinnerungsschrift des Reichsarbeitsministeriums* (Berlin: Mittler).

Renzsch, Wolfgang (1991), *Finanzverfassung und Finanzausgleich. Die Auseinandersetzungen um ihre politische Gestaltung in der Bundesrepublik zwischen Währungsreform und deutscher Vereinigung 1948-1990* (Bonn: Dietz).

Reulecke, Jürgen (1996), "Vorgeschichte und Entstehung des Sozialstaats in Deutschland bis ca. 1930. Ein Überblick," in Jochen-Christoph Kaiser and Martin Greschat (eds.), *Sozialer Protestantismus und Sozialstaat. Diakonie und Wohlfahrtspflege in Deutschland 1890 bis 1938* (Stuttgart: Kohlhammer), 57-71.

Rhein, Thomas (2013), "Erwerbseinkommen. Deutsche Geringverdiener im europäischen Vergleich," *IAB Kurzbericht—Aktuelle Analysen aus dem Institut für Arbeitsmarkt- und Berufsforschung*, 15.

Rhodes, Martin (ed.) (1997), *Southern European Welfare States: Between Crisis and Reform* (London: Routledge).

Rieger, Elmar and Leibfried, Stephan (1998), "Welfare State Limits to Globalization," *Politics & Society*, 26 (3), 363-90.

Ritter, Gerhard (1983), *Sozialversicherung in Deutschland und England. Entstehung und Grundzüge im Vergleich* (München: Beck).

Ritter, Gerhard A. (1996 [1994]), "Die Enstehung des Räteartikels 165 der Weimarer Reichsverfassung," in Gerhard A. Ritter (ed.), *Arbeiter, Arbeiterbewegung und soziale Idee in Deutschland. Beiträge zur Geschichte des 19. und 20. Jahrhunderts* (München: Beck), 227-52.

Ritter, Gerhard A. and Tenfelde, Klaus (1996 [1976]), "Der Durchbruch der Freien Gewerkschaften Deutschlands zur Massenbewegung im letzten Viertel des 19. Jahrhunderts," in Gerhard A. Ritter (ed.), *Arbeiter, Arbeiterbewegung und soziale Idee in Deutschland. Beiträge zur Geschichte des 19. und 20. Jahrhunderts* (München: Beck), 131-82.

Rodrik, Dani (1997), "What Drives Public Employment?," *NBER Working Paper* 6141 (Cambridge, MA: National Bureau of Economic Research).

Rohe, Karl (1992), *Wahlen und Wählertraditionen in Deutschland* (Frankfurt am Main: Suhrkamp).

Röpke, Wilhelm (1956), "Probleme der kollektiven Altersvorsorge," *Frankfurter Allgemeine*, February 25.

Röpke, Wilhelm (1962 [1932]), "Epochenwende?," in Wilhelm Röpke (ed.), *Wirrnis und Wahrheit. Ausgewählte Aufsätze* (Stuttgart: E. Rentsch), 105-24.

Röpke, Wilhelm (1976), *Briefe, 1934-1966. Der innere Kompaß* (Erlenbach-Zürich: E. Rentsch).

Ross, Ronald J. (1988), "Catholic Plight in the Kaiserreich: A Reappraisal," in Jack R. Dukes and Joachim Remak (eds.), *Another Germany: A Reconsideration of the Imperial Era* (Boulder, CO: Westview Press), 73-94.

Rothfels, Hans (1927), *Theodor Lohmann und die Kampfjahre der deutschen Sozialpolitik* (Berlin: Mittler).

Rothstein, Bo (1992), "Labor-Market Institutions and Working-Class Strength," in Sven Steinmo, Kathleen Thelen, and Frank Longstreth (eds.), *Structuring Politics: Historical Institutionalism and Comparative Analysis* (Cambridge: Cambridge University Press), 33–56.

Rüb, Friedbert W. and Nullmeier, Frank (1991), "Alterssicherungspolitik in der Bundesrepublik Deutschland," in Bernhard Blanke and Hellmut Wollmann (eds.), *Die alte Bundesrepublik. Kontinuität und Wandel* (Opladen: Westdeutscher Verlag), 437–62.

Rueda, David (2005), "Insider–Outsider Politics in Industrialized Democracies: The Challenge to Social Democratic Parties," *American Political Science Review*, 99 (1), 61–74.

Rueda, David (2006), "Social Democracy and Active Labour-Market Policies: Insiders, Outsiders and the Politics of Employment Protection," *British Journal of Political Science*, 36, 385–406.

Ruggie, John Gerard (1982), "International Regimes, Transactions, and Change: Embedded Liberalism in the Postwar Economic Order," *International Organization*, 36 (2), 195–231.

Ruggie, John Gerard (1997), "Globalization and the Embedded Liberalism Compromise: The End of an Era?," *MPIfG Working Paper* 97/1 (Köln: Max-Planck Institute for the Study of Societies). *MPIfG Lecture Series on Economic Globalization and National Democracy*. Internet Version: erhältlich unter http://www.mpi-fg-koeln.mpg.de/pub likation/working_papers/wp97-1_e/wp97-1_e.html.

Russig, Harald (1982), "Sozialversicherungs- und arbeitsrechtliche Rahmenbedingungen für die Ausgliederung älterer und/oder leistungsgeminderter Arbeitnehmer aus dem Betrieb," in Knuth Dohse, Ulrich Jürgens, and Harald Russig (eds.), *Ältere Arbeitnehmer zwischen unternehmensinteressen und Sozialpolitik* (Frankfurt am Main: Campus), 237–82.

Rüstow, Alexander (1932), "Freie Wirtschaft – starker Staat," in Franz Boese (ed.), *Deutschland und die Weltkrise* (München: Duncker & Humblot), 62–9.

Rüstow, Alexander (1945), *Das Versagen des Wirtschaftsliberalismus als religionsgeschichtliches Problem* (Istanbuler Schriften 12; Istanbul).

Rüstow, Alexander (1956), "Das Problem der Rentenreform," in Rüstow, *Das Problem der Rentenreform. Vortrag Aktionsgemeinschaft Soziale Marktwirtschaft. Ludwigshafen* (Ludwigshafen).

Rüstow, Alexander (1959 [1929]), "Diktatur inneralb der Grenzen der Demokratie," *Vierteljahreshefte für Zeitgeschichte*, 7, 85–111).

Rüstow, Alexander (1960), "Paläoliberalismus, Kollektivismus und Neoliberalismus in der Wirtschafts- und Sozialordnung," in Karl Forster (ed.), *Christentum und Liberalismus. Studien und Berichte der Katholischen Akademie in Bayern* (Heft 13; Munich: Zink), 149–78.

Rüstow, Alexander (1986 [1932]), "Interessenpolitik oder Staatspolitik?," in Wolfram Engels and Hartmut Froels (eds.), *Querschnitte* (Düsseldorf: Gesellschaft für Wirtschaftspublizistik), 66–71.

Sachverständigenrat zur Begutachtung der gesamtwirtschaftlichen Entwicklung (1980), *Unter Anpassungszwang* (Jahresgutachten, 1980/81; Stuttgart and Mainz: Verlag W. Kohlhammer).

Sachverständigenrat zur Begutachtung der gesamtwirtschaftlichen Entwicklung (1990), *Auf dem Wege zur wirtschaftlichen Einheit Deutschlands* (Jahresgutachten, 1990/91; Stuttgart: Metzeler-Poeschel).

Sachverständigenrat zur Begutachtung der gesamtwirtschaftlichen Entwicklung (1998), *Vor weitreichenden Entscheidungen* (Jahresgutachten, 1998/99; Stuttgart: Metzler-Poeschel).

Sachverständigenrat zur Begutachtung der gesamtwirtschaftlichen Entwicklung (various years), *Jahresgutachten* (Stuttgart: Metzler-Poeschel).

Sachße, Christoph and Tennstedt, Florian (1988), *Geschichte der Armenfürsorge in Deutschland. Bd.2, Fürsorge und Wohlfahrtspflege 1871 bis 1929* (Stuttgart: Kohlhammer).

Schäffer, Hans (1920), *Der Vorläufige Reichswirtschaftsrat. Kommentar der Verordnung vom 4. Mai 1920* (München: Schweitzer).

Scharpf, Fritz W. (1982), "Optionen der Arbeitsmarktpolitik in den achtziger Jahren," in Fritz W. Scharpf, Marlene Brockmann, Manfred Groser, Friedhart Hegner, and Günther Schmid (eds.), *Aktive Arbeitsmarktpolitik. Erfahrungen und neue Wege* (Frankfurt am Main: Campus), 12–28.

Scharpf, Fritz W. (1987), *Sozialdemokratische Krisenpolitik in Europa* (Frankfurt am Main: Campus).

Scharpf, Fritz W. (1991), *Crisis and Choice in European Social Democracy* (Ithaca, NY: Cornell University Press).

Scharpf, Fritz W. (1997), "Employment and the Welfare State: A Continental Dilemma," *MPIfG Working Paper* 97/7 (Köln: Max-Planck Institute for the Study of Societies).

Scharpf, Fritz W. (2011), "Monetary Union, Fiscal Crisis, and the Preemption of Democracy," *MPIfG Discussion Paper* 11/11 (Köln: Max-Planck Institute for the Study of Societies).

Scharpf, Fritz W. (2017), "Vom asymmetrischen Euro-Regime in die Transfer-Union—und was die deutsche Politik dagegen tun könnte," *Leviathan*, 45 (3), 286–308.

Scharpf, Fritz W. (2018), "International Monetary Regimes and the German Model." *MPIfG Discussion Paper* 18(1) (Köln: Max-Planck Institute for the Study of Societies).

Schmid, Günther (1990), "Was tut das Arbeitsamt? Kooperative Arbeitsmarktpolitik im Wandel der Arbeitswelt," in Helmut König, Bodo von Greiff, and Helmut Schauer (eds.), *Sozialphilosophie der industriellen Arbeit* (Opladen: Westdeutscher Verlag), 388–413.

Schmid, Günther and Wiebe, Nicola (1999), "Die Politik der Gleichstellung im Wandel. Von der passiven zur interaktiven Arbeitsmarktpolitik," in Max Kaase and Günther Schmid (eds.), *Eine lernende Demokratie. 50 Jahre Bundesrepublik Deutschland* (Berlin: Sigma), 357–96.

Schmid, Rolf (1930), "Das AVI-Abkommen als Mittel verbandsmäßiger Exportförderung." Dissertation, University of Cologne.

Schmidt, Manfred G. (1990a), "Staatsfinanzen," in Klaus von Beyme and Manfred G. Schmidt (eds.), *Politik in der Bundesrepublik Deutschland* (Opladen: Westdeutscher Verlag), 36–73.

Schmidt, Manfred G. (1990b), "Die Politik des mittleren Weges. Besonderheiten der Staatstätigkeit in der Bundesrepublik Deutschland," *Aus Politik und Zeitgeschichte*, B 9–10/90, 23–31.

Schmitter, Philippe C. (1979), "Still the Century of Corporatism?," in Philippe C. Schmitter and Gerhard Lehmbruch (eds.), *Trends towards Corporatist Intermediation* (London: Sage), 7–52.

Schmitter, Philippe C. and Lehmbruch, Gerhard (eds.) (1979), *Trends Toward Corporatist Intermediation* (London: Sage).

Schneider, Ben Ross (2013), *Hierarchical Capitalism in Latin America: Business, Labor, and the Challenges of Equal Development* (New York: Cambridge University Press).

Schneider, Michael (1982), *Die christlichen Gewerkschaften 1894–1933* (Bonn: Verlag Neue Gesellschaft).

Schönhoven, Klaus (1980a), *Expansion und Konzentration: Studien zur Entwicklung der Freien Gewerkschaften im Wilhelminischen Deutschland 1890 bis 1914* (Stuttgart: Klett-Cotta).

Schönhoven, Klaus (1980b), "Selbsthilfe als Form von Solidarität. Das gewerkschaftliche Unterstützungswesen im Deutschen Kaiserreich bis 1914," *Archiv für Sozialgeschichte*, 20, 147–93.

Schönhoven, Klaus (1985), "Localism – Craft Union – Industrial Union: Organizational Patterns in German Trade Unionism," in Wolfgang J. Mommsen and Hans-Gerhard Husung (ed.), *The Development of Trade Unionism in Great Britain and Germany, 1880–1914* (London: Allen & Unwin), 219–35.

Schröder, Martin (2013), *Integrating Varieties of Capitalism and Welfare State Research: A Unified Typology of Capitalisms* (New York: Palgrave Macmillan).

Schulz, Günther (1991), "Wohnungspolitik und soziale Sicherung nach 1945: das Ende der Arbeiterwohnungsfrage," in Klaus Tenfelde (ed.), *Arbeiter im 20. Jahrhundert* (Stuttgart: Klett-Cotta), 483–506.

Schumacher, Gijs (2011), *"Modernize or Die"? Social Democrats, Welfare State Retrenchment and the Choice between Office and Policy* (Amsterdam: Amsterdam University Press).

Schwander, Hanna and Manow, Philip (2017a), "'Modernize *and* Die'? German Social Democracy and the Electoral Consequences of the Agenda 2010," *Socio-Economic Review*, 15 (1), 117–34.

Schwander, Hanna and Manow, Philip (2017b), "It's Not the Economy, Stupid! Explaining the Electoral Success of the German Right-Wing Populist AfD," *CIS Working Paper* 94 (Center for Comparative and International Studies, University of Zurich).

Seidel, Ehrentraud (1990), "Die gesicherten Risiken," in Verband deutscher Rentenversicherungsträger (ed.), *Handbuch der gesetzlichen Rentenversicherung* (Neuwied: Luchterhand), 563–99.

Shalev, Michael (2007), "Limits and Alternatives to Multiple Regression in Comparative Research," in Lars Mjoeset and Tommy H. Clausen (eds.), *Capitalisms Compared* (Amsterdam: Elsevier), 261–308.

Siaroff, Alan (1999), "Corporatism in 24 Industrial Democracies: Meaning and Measurement," *European Journal of Political Research*, 36 (2), 175–205.

Sinn, Gerlinde and Sinn, Hans-Werner (1991), *Kaltstart. Volkswirtschaftliche Aspekte der deutschen Vereinigung* (Tübingen: J. C. B. Mohr/Paul Siebeck).

Smith, Helmut Walser (1995), *German Nationalism and Religious Conflict: Culture, Ideology, Politics, 1870–1914* (Princeton, NJ: Princeton University Press).

Soskice, David (1990a), "Reinterpreting Corporatism and Explaining Unemployment: Co-ordinated and Non-co-ordinated Market Economies," in Renato Brunetta and C. Dell'Aringa (eds.), *Labour Relations and Economic Performance: International Economic Association Conference* (London: Macmillan), 170–211.

Soskice, David (1990b), "Wage Determination: The Changing Role of Institutions in Advanced Industrialized Countries," *Oxford Review of Economic Policy*, 6 (4), 36–61.

Steinmetz, George (1991), "Workers and the Welfare State in Germany," *International Labor and Working-Class History*, 40, 18–46.

Steinmetz, George (1993), *Regulating the Social: The Welfare State and Local Politics in Imperial Germany* (Princeton, NJ: Princeton University Press).

Stolleis, Michael (1979), "Die Sozialversicherung Bismarcks. Politisch-institutionelle Bedingungen ihrer Entstehung," in Hans F. Zacher (ed.), *Bedingungen für die Entstehung und Entwicklung von Sozialversicherung* (Berlin: Duncker & Humblot), 387–420.

Strath, Bo (1994), "Modes of Governance in the Shipbuilding Industry in Germany, Sweden, and Japan," in P. C. Schmitter, W. Streeck, and J. R. Hollingsworth (eds.), *Governing Capitalist Economies: Performance and Control of Economic Sectors* (New York: Oxford University Press), 72–96.

Streeck, Wolfgang (1981), *Gewerkschaftliche Organisationsprobleme in der sozialstaatlichen Demokratie* (Königstein/Ts.: Athenäum).

Streeck, Wolfgang (1995), "German Capitalism: Does It Exist? Can It Survive?," *MPIfG Discussion Paper* 95/5 (Köln: Max-Planck Institute for the Study of Societies).

Streeck, Wolfgang (1997), "Beneficial Constraints: On the Economic Limits of Rational Voluntarism," in J. Rogers Hollingsworth and Robert Boyer (eds.), *Contemporary Capitalism: The Embeddedness of Institutions* (Cambridge: Cambridge University Press), 197–219.

Streeck, Wolfgang (2009), *Re-Forming Capitalism: Institutional Change in the German Political Economy* (Oxford: Oxford University Press).

Streeck, Wolfgang and Schäfer, Armin (eds.) (2013), *Politics in the Age of Austerity* (Chichester: Wiley & Sons).

Streeck, Wolfgang and Yamamura, Kozo (eds.) (2005), *The Origins of Nonliberal Capitalism: Germany and Japan in Comparison* (Ithaca, NY: Cornell University Press).

Streit, Manfred (1998), "Die deutsche Währungsunion," in Deutsche Bundesbank (ed.), *Fünfzig Jahre Deutsche Mark. Notenbank und Währung seit 1948* (München: C. H. Beck), 675–719.

Sturm, Roland (1998), "Die Wende im Stolperschritt – eine finanzpolitische Bilanz," in Göttrik Wewer (ed.), *Bilanz der Ära Kohl: christlich-liberale Politik in Deutschland 1982–1998* (Opladen: Leske + Budrich), 183–200.

Swenson, Peter (1997), "Arranged alliance: business interests in the New Deal," *Politics & Society,* 25, 66–116.

Swenson, Peter (1999), "Varieties of Capitalist Interests and Illusions of Labor Power: Employers in the Making of the Swedish and American Welfare States." Presentation at the Conference on Distribution and Democracy, Department of Political Science, Yale University.Swenson, Peter (2002), *Capitalists against Markets: The Making of Labor Markets and Welfare States in the United States and Sweden* (Oxford: Oxford University Press).

Tanner, Klaus (1987), "Antiliberale Harmonie. Zum politischen Grundkonsens in Theologie und Rechtswissenschaft der zwanziger Jahre," in Horst Renz and Friedrich Wilhelm Graf (eds.), *Umstrittene Moderne. Die Zukunft der Neuzeit im Urteil der Epoche Ernst Troeltschs* (Troeltsch-Studien, Bd. 4.; Gütersloh: Mohn), 193–208.

Tenfelde, Klaus (1985), "Conflict and Organization in the Early History of the German Trade Union Movement," in Wolfgang J. Mommsen and Hans-Gerhard Husung (eds.), *The Development of Trade Unionism in Great Britain and Germany, 1880–1914* (London: Allen & Unwin), 201–18.

Tennstedt, Florian (1976), "Sozialgeschichte der Sozialversicherung," in Maria Blohmke, Christian von Ferber, Karl Peter Kisker, and Hans Schaefer (eds.), *Handbuch der Sozialmedizin in 3 Bänden, Band 3: Sozialmedizin in der Praxis* (Stuttgart: Enke), 385–491.

Tennstedt, Florian (1977), *Soziale Selbstverwaltung* (Bd. 2. Geschichte der Selbstverwaltung in der Krankenversicherung; Bonn: Verlag der Ortskrankenkassen).

Tennstedt, Florian (1983), *Vom Proleten zum Industriearbeiter. Arbeiterbewegung und Sozialpolitik in Deutschland 1800 bis 1914* (Köln: Bund Verlag).

Tennstedt, Florian (1993), "Sozialpolitik und innere Reichsgründung. Politische Rahmenkonstellationen in Europa als Ausgangspunkt für Deutschlands Aufbruch zum

Sozialstaat," in Günter Lottes (ed.), *Soziale Sicherheit in Europa. Renten- und Sozialversicherungssysteme im Vergleich* (Heidelberg: Physica), 57–71.

Tennstedt, Florian (1994), "Sozialreform als Mission. Anmerkungen zum politischen Handeln Theodor Lohmanns," in Jürgen Kocka, Hans-Jürgen Puhle, and Klaus Tenfelde (eds.), *Von der Arbeiterbewegung zum modernen Sozialstaat. Festschrift für Gerhard A. Ritter zum 65. Geburtstag* (München: Saur), 538–59.

Tennstedt, Florian and Winter, Heidi (1995), *Einleitung. Quellensammlung zur Geschichte der Deutschen Sozialpolitik 1867 bis 1914. II. Abteilung: Von der kaiserlichen Sozialbotschaft bis zu den Februarerlassen Wilhelms II. (1881–1890). Band 2, 1. Teil: Von der zweiten Unfallversicherungs-Vorlage bis zum Unfallversicherungsgesetz vom 6. Juli 1884. XIX–XLIV* (Stuttgart: Fischer).

Thelen, Kathleen (1991), *Union of Parts: Labor Politics in Postwar Germany* (Ithaca, NY and London: Cornell University Press).

Thelen, Kathleen (2000), "Why German Employers Cannot Bring Themselves to Dismantle the German Model," in Torben Iversen, Jonas Pontusson, and David Soskice (eds.), *Unions, Employers and Central Banks: Macroeconomic Coordination and Institutional Change in Social Market Economies* (Cambridge: Cambridge University Press), 138–69.

Thelen, Kathleen (2004), *How Institutions Evolve: The Political Economy of Skills in Germany, Britain, the United States, and Japan* (New York: Cambridge University Press).

Thelen, Kathleen (2014), *Varieties of Liberalization and the New Politics of Social Solidarity* (New York: Cambridge University Press).

Tooze, Adam (2006), *The Wages of Destruction: The Making and Breaking of the Nazi Economy* (London: Allen Lane). Published in German as *Ökonomie der Zerstörung. Die Geschichte der Wirtschaft im Nationalsozialismus* (München: Siedler, 2008).

Tooze, Adam (2018), *Crashed: How a Decade of Financial Crises Changed the World* (London: Allen Lane).

Traxler, Franz and Kittel, Bernhard (2000), "The Bargaining System and Performance: A Comparison of 18 OECD Countries," *Comparative Political Studies*, 33 (9), 1154–90.

Tribe, Keith (1995), *Strategies of Economic Order: German Economic Discourse, 1750–1950* (New York: Cambridge University Press).

Trifiletti, Rossana (1999), "Southern European Welfare Regimes and the Worsening Position of Women," *Journal of European Social Policy*, 9 (1), 49–64.

Trischler, Helmuth (1994), "Gewerkschaftliche Sozialreform und burgerliche Sammlungspolitik. Die Volksversicherung im Wilhelminischen Deutschland," in Jürgen Kocka (ed.), *Von der Arbeiterbewegung zum modernen Sozialstaat: Festschrift für Gerhard A. Ritter zum 65. Geburtstag* (Berlin: de Gruyter), 618–33.

Tübben, Willi (1930), "Die nationale und internationale Verbandspolitik der Schwerindustrie vor und nach dem Kriege." Dissertation, University of Würzburg.

Turner, Henry Ashby (1985), *German Big Business and the Rise of Hitler* (New York: Oxford University Press).

Unger, Brigitte (ed.) (2015), *The German Model: Seen by its Neighbors* (Wien: SE Publishing).

Vail, Mark I. (2010), *Recasting Welfare Capitalism: Economic Adjustment in Contemporary France and Germany* (Philadelphia, PA: Temple University Press).

Verband Deutscher Rentenversicherungsträger [VDR] (1997), *Rentenversicherung in Zeitreihen* (Frankfurt am Main: VDR).

vom Bruch, Rüdiger (1985), "Bürgerliche Sozialreform im deutschen Kaiserreich," in Rüdiger vom Bruch (ed.), *Weder Kommunismus noch Kapitalismus. Bürgerliche Sozialreform in Deutschland vom Vormärz bis zur Ära Adenauer* (München: Beck), 61–179.

Walters, Alan (1992), "Walters Critique," in Peter K. Newman, Murray Milgate, and John Eatwell (eds.), *The New Palgrave Dictionary of Money and Finance* (Basingstoke: Palgrave Macmillan).

Watson, Sara (2015), *The Left Divided: The Development and Transformation of Advanced Welfare States* (Oxford: Oxford University Press).

Webber, Douglas (1989), "Zur Geschichte der Gesundheitsreformen in Deutschland – II. Teil: Norbert Blüms Gesundheitsreform und die Lobby," *Leviathan*, 17, 262–300.

Weber, Max (1988 [1918]), "Parlament und Regierung im neugeordneten Deutschland," in *Gesammelte Politische Schriften* (Tübingen: Mohr Siebeck), 306–443.

Weisbrod, Bernd (1978), *Schwerindustrie in der Weimarer Republik. Interessenpolitik zwischen Stabilisierung und Krise* (Wuppertal: Peter Hammer).

Wend, Henry (2001), *Recovery and Restoration: U.S. Foreign Policy and the Politics of Reconstruction in the West German Ship Construction Industry, 1945–1955* (Westport, CT: Praeger).

Widdig, Bernd (1994), "Cultural Dimensions of Inflation in Weimar Germany," *German Politics and Society*, 32, 10–27.

Wigger, Angela (2017), "Debunking the Myth of the Ordoliberal Influence on Post-war European Integration", in: Josef Hien and Christian Joerges (eds.) *Ordoliberalism, Law and the Rule of Economics* (Oxford: Hart Publishing), 161–77.

Winkler, Heinrich August (ed.) (1974), *Organisierter Kapitalismus. Voraussetzungen und Anfänge* (Göttingen: Vandenhoeck & Ruprecht).

Winkler, Heinrich August (1985), *Von der Revolution zur Stabilisierung. Arbeiter und Arbeiterbewegung in der Weimarer Republik 1918 bis 1924* (Bonn: Dietz).

Winkler, Heinrich August (1991), *Zwischen Marx und Monopolen. Der deutsche Mittelstand vom Kaiserreich zur Bundesrepublik Deutschland* (Frankfurt am Main: Fischer).

Wolf, Martin (2014), *The Shifts and the Shocks: What We've Learned—and Have Still to Learn—from the Financial Crisis* (New York: Penguin).

Wrede, Josef M. (1933), "Die internationale Verbandspolitik der nordwesteuropäischen Eisenindustrie in ihrer Bedeutung für die deutsche Eisenindustrie." Manuscript, University of Wurzburg.

Wren, Anne (ed.) (2013), *The Political Economy of the Service Transition* (Oxford: Oxford University Press).

Wren, Anne, Fodor, Máté, and Theodoropoulou, Sotiria (2013), "The Trilemma Revisited: Institutions, Inequality, and Employment Creation in an Era of ICT-Intensive Service Expansion," in Anne Wren (ed.), *The Political Economy of the Service Transition* (Oxford: Oxford University Press), 108–46.

Zimmermann, Clemens (1991), *Von der Wohnungsfrage zur Wohnungspolitik. Die Reformbewegung in Deutschland 1845–1914* (Göttingen: Vandenhoeck & Ruprecht).

# Index